Comparative Governments and Politics

Comparative GOVERNMENTS and POLITICS

(Including Case Studies of Britain, Brazil, Nigeria and China)

By

Chanchal Kumar

Assistant Professor, Department of Political Science,
Janki Devi Memorial College, University of Delhi, Delhi

New Century Publications
New Delhi, India

NEW CENTURY PUBLICATIONS
4852 / 24, 1st Floor,
Ansari Road, Daryaganj,
New Delhi – 110 002 (India)

Tel.: 011-4101 7798; 4358 7398; 98112 66355
E-mail: info@newcenturypublications.com

www.newcenturypublications.com

Editorial office:
4800 / 24, Bharat Ram Road,
Ansari Road, Daryaganj,
New Delhi – 110 002

Edition: 2025

ISBN: **978-81-7708-407-8**

First Published: July 2015

Published by New Century Publications and printed at Salasar Imaging Systems, New Delhi.

Designs: Patch Creative Unit, New Delhi.

PRINTED IN INDIA

About the Book

Comparative governments and politics is one of the most exciting and dynamic fields in political science. A comparative study of governments facilitates objective and rational judgement about political systems. Comparative politics seeks to study and understand different political systems analytically, systematically and relatively. It looks for patterns, regularities and systemic changes within and among them.

Comparative politics concerns itself with a great variety of issues. These include the comparative study of institutions, interest groups, political culture/values and public policies in different countries. Comparative politics also studies the processes by which countries become developed, modern and democratic.

This book is designed to provide insights into comparative governments and politics and related approaches for the study of the subject. More specifically, the book focuses on examining politics in a historical framework while engaging with various themes of comparative analysis in developed and developing countries.

About the Author

Dr. Chanchal Kumar is presently Assistant Professor in the Department of Political Science, Janki Devi Memorial College, University of Delhi, Delhi. She did her B.A. (Hons.) and M.A. in Political Science from University of Delhi and obtained Ph.D. degree from Ch. Charan Singh University, Meerut. She has published a number of research papers in academic journals of repute. She specializes in international politics and human rights. She is a life member of various professional bodies including Indian Political Science Association and Asia Pacific Panorama Society.

Contents

Preface

Comparative politics has a long and very distinguished history dating back to the very origins of systematic political studies in ancient Greece and Rome. Comparative politics is about 2,500 years old—may be older. One could argue that the study of comparative politics goes all the way back to humankind's first recorded history. Even the most ancient of the people, organized as clans, tribes, or extended families, compared their situations with those of other people with whom they came in contact.

Comparative politics is one of the most exciting and dynamic fields in political science. Comparative politics seeks to study and understand these political systems analytically, systematically, and comparatively. It looks for patterns, regularities and systemic changes within and among them.

Comparative politics concerns itself with a great variety of issues. These include the comparative study of institutions (political parties or legislatures) in different political systems, interest groups and their relations to the state or government, political culture or political values in different countries and public policies (health, education and social welfare) in different countries. Comparative politics also studies the processes by which countries become developed, modern, and democratic; how civil society (intermediary groups between the citizens and the state) emerges in different countries; and the effects of economic growth and social change on the developing nations.

There is ever increasing tendency among those concerned with politics to keenly observe and systematically examine and probe the working of every political institution and organization. Each problem is subjected to various processes and needs—both qualitative and quantitative measurements—and undergoes rigorous scrutiny before it is finally adopted or discarded by the society.

The importance of comparative politics has increased immensely in contemporary times because of the new opportunities provided by the existence of more than 193 nations managed by a variety of political structures as well as due to development of several new concepts, tools and approaches for the conduct of comparative study of politics.

This book is designed to provide insights into comparative governments and politics and related approaches for the study of the subject. More specifically, the book focuses on examining politics in a historical framework while engaging with various themes of comparative analysis in developed and developing countries.

New Delhi
June 2015

Chanchal Kumar

1

Comparative Governments and Politics: An Introduction

1.1 Introduction

Comparative politics is one of the most exciting and dynamic fields in political science. Its area of inquiry, its "living laboratory", is all of the world's political systems. Comparative politics seeks to study and understand these political systems analytically, systematically, and comparatively; it looks for patterns, regularities, and systemic changes within and among them. Comparative politics concerns itself with a great variety of issues. These include the comparative study of institutions (political parties or legislatures) in different political systems, interest groups and their relations to the state or government, political culture or political values in different countries and public policies (health, education, social welfare) in different countries. Comparative politics also studies the processes by which countries become developed, modern, and democratic; how civil society (intermediary groups between the citizen and the state) emerges in different countries; and the effects of economic growth and social change on the developing nations.

1.2 Evolution of Comparative Governments and Politics

Comparative politics has a long and very distinguished history dating back to the very origins of systematic political studies in ancient Greece and Rome. Comparative politics is about 2,500 years old—and may be older. One could argue that the study of comparative politics goes all the way back to humankind's first recorded history. Even the most ancient of peoples, organized as clans, tribes, or extended families, compared their situations with those of other people with whom they came in contact. The Bible is perhaps one of the first written statements of comparative politics. Particularly in the Old Testament, the prophets are constantly comparing the people of Israel with other people: Egyptians, Persians, etc.

The earliest systematic comparisons of a more modern, secular sort—with almost all the ingredients of today's comparative politics—were carried out by the ancient Greeks. The two foremost political scientists in ancient Greece were Plato and Aristotle. Plato's 'Republic' and Aristotle's 'Politics' are really the beginning of political science as we know it today—and among the great books of all time. In these two books, the authors cover almost all the key issues of politics: the nature of power and leadership, the different forms of government, public policy, and so on. For our purposes, what is important about Aristotle and Plato is their analysis of comparative politics.

Aristotle—more a "scientist"—collected approximately 158 constitutions of his time, mainly from the Greek city-states and from other areas as well. He studied these constitutions extensively. For him, the constitution was the mode of life which included not only the political institutions of a community but the distribution of wealth, the religious myths and the education and leisure of its citizens. His approach was also systematic mainly for two reasons: *first*, he observed facts in the light of a general framework; *second*, he used the law of limitation, the law of diffusion, and law of similar causes in order to explain similarities and dissimilarities. Aristotle is said to have given the first scientific classification of governments. He evolved two bases for his classification—the number of persons who ruled and the end of the state. By virtue of the application of these two bases, Aristotle came to the state of presenting his six-fold classification of government i.e., whether it is in the hands of one, few or many persons and whether it is the normal or perverted form. Both he and Plato arrived at a system or scheme for classifying the then known world's political systems.

In the Roman period, Cicero and Polybius also utilized the comparative method for better understanding of the working of political systems. During the Renaissance, Machiavelli adopted the same method as used earlier by Aristotle. He studied the politics and diplomacy of the various states. He was the first to make an effort to study political behaviour in terms of power. A modified form of this classification of systems is still used today. Montesquieu, the 18th century French philosopher, is the next great comparativists.

Table 1.1: Classical Social Theory, 1776-1923

Country	Author	Some Major Works
Britain	Adam Smith (1723-1790) David Ricardo (1772-1823) John Stuart Mill (1806-1873)	The Wealth of Nations (1996) On the Principles of Political Economy and Taxation (1817) The Principles of Political Economy (1848); Considerations on Representative Government (1861)
France	Auguste Comte (1798-1857) Alexis de Tocqueville (1805-1917) Herbert Spencer (1820-1903) Emile Durkheim (1858-1917)	Course in Positive Philosophy (1830-1842) Democracy in America (1835) The Old Regime and the French Revolution (1856) The Principles of Sociology (1876-1896) The Division of Labour in Society (1893); Rules of the Sociology Method (1895)
Germany	Karl Marx (1818-1883) Max Weber (1864-1920)	The Communist Manifesto (1848) The Eighteenth Brumaire of Louis Bonaparte (1852); The Protestant Ethic and the Spirit of Capitalism (1905); Economy and Society (1914); General Economic History (1923)
Italy	Vilfredo Pareto (1848-1923) Gaetano Mosca (1858-1941) Robert Michels (1876-1936)	The Mind and Society: A Treatise on General Sociology (1915-1919) The Ruling Class (1923) Political Parties: A Sociological Study of the Oligarchical Tendencies of Modern Democracy (1915)

Source: Gerardo L. Munck, Richard Snyder, "*Passion, Craft, and Method in Comparative Politics*", The Johns Hopkins University Press, USA.

Unlike Hobbes and Locke who focused on one country, but

assumed it had universal validity, Montesquieu was a true comparativist. In his book, "*The Spirit of the Laws*", Montesquieu attempted to move beyond the constitutional procedures of a country to examine its true culture and "spirit". His greatest contribution to the field was his model for the separation of powers that influenced the U.S. system.

Throughout the eighteenth and nineteenth centuries, comparison was 'in the air'. It was used by Auguste Comte, Lamarck, Darwin, Walter Bagehot and many others. J.S. Mill in his *Representative Government and System of Logic* further developed the comparative method. He used inverse deductive method in such a way that empirical verification became necessary. The classic theorists of social science viz. Karl Marx, Max Weber, Emile Durkheim, Vilfredo Pareto, Gaetano Mosca, and Roberto Michels established the field's research agenda, mode of analysis, and contrasting theoretical visions. The eighteenth and nineteenth centuries abounded in theories that claimed to be 'explanatory' or 'problem solving'.

The evolution of comparative politics is seen as punctuated by two revolutions: the behavioural revolution, during the immediate post-World War II years until the mid-1960s, and the second scientific revolution, which started around the end of the Cold War and is still on going. On both occasions, the impetus for change came from developments in the field of American politics and was justified in the name of science. However, the ideas advanced by these two revolutions differed. The behavioural revolution drew heavily on sociology; in contrast, the second scientific revolution imported many ideas from economics and also put a heavier emphasis on methodology. Though scholars of comparative politics have produced a vast amount of knowledge about politics, divisions within the field continue to hamper the progress. Emphasis is placed on the need to recognize the depth of the roots of comparative politics in a humanistic tradition and the vital importance of its scientific aspirations.

In the recent era, Samuel H. Beer, M. Hass, Bernard and Roy C. Macridis used the comparative methods in a more refined way. Their aim was to present a more useful and realistic study of various political institutions. According to G. K. Roberts, these writers "were concerned with the various strategies of comparison: area studies, the configurative approach, institutional and functional comparisons, a problem-based orientation, and with various methodological problems: conceptualization, the establishment of agreed categories for comparison, validity as a problem, cross-cultural difficulties and the availability of data". Several seminal theorists of contemporary political science—Harry Eckstein, David Apter, Robert Dahl, Seymour Lipset, Karl Deutsch, Gabriel Almond, and Sidney Verba—drew on this heritage to rebuild and reinvigorate the field of comparative politics.

1.3 What is Comparative Government?

The word government implies the administrative system of that country which includes mainly the formal organs like the constitution, administrative set up, legislature, executive and the judiciary. The decisions are taken in it and the same are executed. In the government, emphasis is laid on the study of the formal organs of the political system and the institutional study of the institutions of that country, whereas, the study of the politics of a country is concerned mainly with that specific behaviour of the individuals or institutions which is concerned with decision-making and its execution. Governments are organizations of individuals who are legally empowered to make binding decisions on behalf of a particular community. Governments thus have authoritative and coercive powers. Governments do many things. They wage war or encourage peace, cultivate or restrict international trade, open their borders to the exchange of ideas and art or close them, tax their populations heavily or lightly and through different means, allocate resources for education, health and welfare, or leave such matters to others.

A comparative study of governments not only facilitates objective and rational judgement about political systems, but at the same time dispels the 'dangerously misleading form of ethnocentrism' that one's own country is superior to any other. The study of governments is an important part of the study of politics. The structure and behaviour of government constitute an exciting and challenging area of concern for students of political science. Modern governments are emerging more and more as vital instrumentalities of multifaceted development, especially in the developing nations of Asia, Africa and Latin America, and also as an active force in the forming of economic, social and environmental conditions.

Comparative study means the comparative study of political institutions, governmental organisations and their functions in a country, changing from time to time. It implies the comparative study of the political institutions and governments of the different countries. According to Roberts, comparative government is mainly the study of the states, their institutions and governments. Jean Blondel also defines comparative government as the study of the patterns of the national governments in the contemporary world. Thus, comparative government is mainly the study of the state organisation of its formal institutions and their functions. In it, those social and economic influences are not studied which force the government to take decisions and execute them, as they are beyond the formal institutions.

Though, in comparative government, the state, government and their various institutions are studied mainly, yet, in the modern era, the organisations like political parties and pressure groups which influence the political procedure and provide order, are also extensively studied under it. The organisations express the sentiments of the people and influence the government for changing basic policies. G.K. Robert is of the opinion that comparative government includes the study of the political parties and pressure groups.

Ronald Chilcote writes, "comparative government usually refers to the study of countries or nation-states in Europe, and the focus of the study is on the institutions and functions of those countries, with attention of their executive, legislatures, and judiciaries as well as supplementary organisations as political parties and pressure groups. Jean Blondel is however, of the view that comparative governments can become comparative politics when both the vertical and horizontal aspects of comparison are taken into account.

1.4 What is Comparative Politics?

Comparative politics, in slightly more formal in terms, in the sense, that it involves both a method of study and a subject of study. As a method of study, comparative politics is—not surprisingly—premised on comparison. As a subject of study, comparative politics focuses on understanding and explaining political phenomena that take place within a state, society, country, or political system.

Comparative politics, as a field of study, provides us with a ready array of conceptual and analytical tools that we can use to address and answer a wide range of questions about the social world. Comparative politics provides a systematic, coherent and practical way to understand and make better sense of the things that happen in the world around us. In a broader sense, comparative politics is relevant to almost anyone, even those not interested in "studying foreign countries". A "comparative politics approach" can be applied to a huge variety of problems, from the mundane to the sublime, in a wide variety of areas.

Comparative politics may be defined as the systematic, comparative study of the world's political systems. It seeks to explain both similarities and differences among political systems and to develop comparisons between them. In exploring these issues, comparative politics seeks to be as rigorous, analytic, and systematic as possible. It develops hypotheses (for example, why some countries are more democratic or developed than others), seeks to be rigorous in its use of evidence (using scientific public opinion surveys, for example, in place of purely personal impressions), and tries to fashion rigorous propositions that can be tested by other scholars in other countries or research settings.

In the field of comparative politics, the term 'politics' has three connotations—political activity, political process and political power. Political activity consists of the efforts by which conditions of conflicts are created and resolved in a way pertaining to the interests of the people, as far as possible, who play their part in the 'struggle for power'. If politics means the authoritative allocation of values, some measures of conflicts is bound to arise between values as desired by the people and the values as held by the men in power. Arising conflicts, demands for their solution and the efforts in this regards constitute political activity. Political process comes after political activity and it is wider and covers all those who are included in the decision-making process.

According to Finer, "set of procedures whereby the private associations within the state seek to influence the government or to participate in policy formation by the government or to become the government is the political process". Political power is a key concept in the study of politics. Carl J. Friedrich describes it as 'a certain kind of human relationship'. Tawney regards it as the capacity of an individual, or a group of individuals, to modify the conduct of other individuals or groups in the manner which he desires. However, "political power is the capacity of affecting the behaviour of another person by the threat of some form of sanction. Greater the sanction, or the more numerous the sanctions, the greater will be the political power".

The characteristics of politics can be defined by two main things: the fact that "all the questions involve the making of a common decision for a group of people", and "the use of power by one person or a group of people to the affect the behaviour of another person or group of people". Politics is important in the making of a common decision for a group of people in that "a single decision will affect all members of the group". Politics as an exercise of power is perhaps even more important than its use in making common decisions. "Power is the ability of one person to cause another person to do what the first wishes, by whatever means". According to Shively, power may be exercised in three different ways:

1. **Persuasion:** "when we convince someone that that is what he or she really wishes to do";
2. **Coercion:** "when we force a person to do something he or she did not want to do"; or
3. **Construction of Incentives:** "when we make the alternative so unattractive that only one reasonable option remains".

Politics as an exercise of power is very effective in many different regards. History has proved that you do not always have to be the strongest—physically—to be an effective leader of power (i.e. Hitler). Comparative politics is an approach within political science that attempts to make reasonable statements about the functioning of political systems and political behaviour through theoretical hypotheses and empirical observation by giving explanations for found regularities and variation, within and among the political systems. Comparative politics is particularly interested in exploring patterns, processes, and regularities among political systems. It looks for tendencies, for changes in patterns; and it tries to develop general propositions or hypotheses that describe and explain these trends.

Comparative politics is a field of political science that engages in the systematic study of political outcomes through the comparison of different cases.
Comparativists are scholars who generally focus on domestic politics at the national level outside the United States.

Comparative politics is studied by looking at two or more different countries and comparing and contrasting different aspects about them. Things such as the economy, social behaviour, political ideas, and the type of government, are all areas that can be compared. Comparative politics seeks to do such comparisons rigorously and systematically, without personal, partisan, or ideological axes to grind, so the conclusive data is not interfered with.

There are many ways to study comparative politics. A first hand experience of each country that we are comparing would be best, although it isn't necessary. First we can look at the ideology of the country. This would give us a firm concept of how a country functions and it would allow us to see many of its values, since the ideology shows the country's belief system. Another stop in studying comparative politics would be to look at the various social cleavages within the country. If there are many differences between social classes, a country is much more likely to have problems, versus one with little or no difference between classes. In studying comparative politics, it is very important to keep an open mind and not assume anything. One must conclusively look at all known facts about a country before being able to compare it with another country successfully.

1.4.1 Definitions of Comparative Politics

- "Comparative politics is the study of the forms of political organizations, their properties, correlating variations and modes of change" (M.G. Smith).
- "Comparative politics involves the systematic study and comparison of the world's political systems. It seeks to explain differences between as well as similarities among countries. In contrast to journalistic reporting on a single country, comparative politics is particularly interested in exploring patterns, processes, and regularities among political systems" (Wiarda).
- "Comparative politics involves both a subject of study—foreign countries—and a method of study—comparison" (Wilson).
- "As the study of patterns of national governments in the contemporary world" (Jean Blondel).
- "What is comparative politics? It is two things, *first* a

world, *second* a discipline. As a 'world', comparative politics encompasses political behaviour and institutions in all parts of the earth. The 'discipline' of comparative politics is a field of study that desperately tries to keep up with, to encompass, to understand, to explain, and perhaps to influence the fascinating and often riotous world of comparative politics" (Lane).

- "Comparative politics is concerned with significant regularities, similarities and differences in the working of political institutions and political behaviour" (M. Curtis).
- "Comparative politics is identification and interpretation of factors in the whole social order which appear to affect whatever political functions and their institutions which have been identified and listed for comparison" (Braibante).
- "Comparative politics involves no more and no less than a comparative study of politics—a search for similarities and differences between and among political phenomena, including political institutions (such as legislatures, political parties, or political interest groups), political behaviour (such as voting, demonstrating, or reading political pamphlets), or political ideas (such as liberalism, conservatism, or Marxism). Everything that politics studies, comparative politics studies; the latter just undertakes the study with an explicit comparative methodology in mind" (Mahler).
- "Politics is the struggle in any group for power that will give a person or people the ability to make decisions for the larger groups. Comparative politics is a sub-field that compares this struggle across countries" (O'Neil).

1.5 Nature of Comparative Governments and Politics

Comparative politics involved the study of the political systems of the developed societies, in contemporary times it laid great stress on the study of the political systems of developing societies as well—study of the political systems of Asia, Africa and Europe. Modern political scientists, like

Almond, Coleman, Sidney Verba, David Easton, Powell, and Edward Shills, have given considerable importance to the study of politics of the developing societies. Comparative politics now seeks to analyse the actual behaviour of individuals, groups, structures, sub-systems and systems in relation to the environment in which the behaviour manifests. It seeks to analyse their behaviour in the environment.

Comparative politics accepts the desirability and need for adopting inter-disciplinary focus. It accepts the need to study politics in an inter-disciplinary focus i.e. the study of political process with the help of knowledge of psychology, sociology, anthropology, economics and other social sciences. Political behaviour is a part of the other aspects of human behaviour. As such, it can be systematically analysed only with reference to other social sciences. The study of political structure can be studied in relation to the social structures and this again makes it imperative for the students of comparative politics to adopt an interdisciplinary focus.

Although its heritage can be traced back to the ancient Greeks, the birth of modern comparative politics as a distinct field in political science in the United States is usually dated to the late 19th century. American scholars initially took a narrow view of the world; comparative politics was seen as the study of "foreign" political systems, and most studies focused on Western Europe, Soviet Union and Japan. The study of U.S. politics, meanwhile, was regarded as a separate field.

After World War II, attitudes changed. U.S. foreign policy interests broadened, and with the emergence of the Cold War, academics and policymakers became more interested in the countries lining up with the Soviet Union, and those Latin American, Asian and African countries that were potential allies and enemies in the confrontation between the two superpowers. The end of the colonial era also saw an explosion in the number of sovereign states, from just over 70 in 1945 to more than 193 in 2011. As well as a new interest in emerging states, there was also a change in the approach taken by comparative political scientists, whose work was often criticized for being too parochial, too descriptive, too lacking in theory, and not particularly comparative. As part of the behavioural movement, comparativists became interested in studying processes as well as institutions, in explaining as well as describing and in taking a more scientific approach towards the development of theory and methods.

There was also more transfer of ideas between the study of American and comparative politics, and a broader view of the world was encouraged by the break-up of the Soviet Union, the end of the Cold War, the emergence of the European Union, and the growing stability, wealth and influence of countries such as Brazil, China, India, Mexico, and South Africa.

During the last decade, an intellectual revolution has been taking place in the study of comparative governments. These developments are not confined to the field of comparative governments, nor are they peculiar to the discipline of political science. The study of foreign political systems has been greatly influenced by an earlier revolution in the study of American politics; and this in turn was the consequence of penetration of American political studies by sociological, anthropological and psychological methods and theories. Now the study of comparative polities holds out the promise of repaying its debt to those of man's experience with political institutions and processes, thus making its contribution to common search for more adequate theories of politics.

Another significant feature is the emergence of comparative analysis of public policy or political economy, which has attributed a new dimension to comparative politics since 1970s. A persistence or continuity from the past has been witnessed to the extent that it pinpoints on 'outcome' or output side. The contrast is a conversion from grand comparative theory of "political development" and problems of "modernization" to a much less wide space of focus, namely the State and its prime role in development. The change is from meta-analysis to meso-analysis, which concentrates or highlights upon the connection between definition of problems, setting of agendas, decision-making and implementation processes. It has provided comparative politics a more specific problem solving and policy orientation. Comparative politics continues to maintain its multi-disciplinary status, but has traversed away from sociological approach and towards the proximity of economics. It also heralds a re-arrival to more normative meditations rather than a prolonged emphasis upon purely scientific methods. It has also re-established a link between academic political science and practitioners of public administration.

A society is enabling to explain the relationship between the production of goods and services along the possible routes provided there are no constraint of resources. It examines the appropriate 'public' space of the state *vis-à-vis* the private area and the variety of policies leading to development. Consequently, public policy is descriptive, analytic as well as suggestive in its approach. Politics is now conceptualized as "public choice" among a number of alternative policies, and its goal is to integrate knowledge into an over-reaching discipline capable of analysing public choice and decision-making and thereby contributing to the democratization of society. Political economy, more specifically, is concerned with the effects of political choices on the production and exchange of goods and services; it is an analysis of the consequences of political choices that political leaders make, involving the polity's scarce resources.

The approach is evaluated in understanding and interpreting the choices as paths of development in developing societies. The leaders through select public policies, simply suffice with, motivate or help in radical social and economic change. Therefore, within a political economy, 'political development' is redefined as the increasing capacity to meet and induce changing and expanding demands and generate resources to be able to do so. While political economy theorizes, public policy is the method by which these can be materialized. The end results of all this has meant that the focus is on smaller comparisons or, on what is possible. Middle range comparison today is more modest, focusing on a single region or comparable set of regions. In conclusion, the field of comparative politics has fragmented and no single definition of comparative politics exists. This has its merits; it means that it allows focus on what is significant and useful and not necessarily what is global and all-encompassing as earlier.

Contemporary comparative politics studies gave more stress on analytical research. It is no longer confined to descriptive studies. It seeks to analyse, empirically and analytically, the actual activities of the governments and their structures and functions. Comparative politics involves a value-free empirical study of the various processes of politics in different environments. Only those values are admitted whose validity can be scientifically demonstrated. It concentrated upon the study of what is and not what should be. It has rejected the normative prescriptive approach of the traditional political science. Its aim is to develop an empirical and objective theory of politics capable of explaining and comparing all phenomena of politics.

Comparative politics involves both a comparative study of the political structures and functions of national political systems of various states and also a comparative study of the political institutions at work within a single state. The former is called horizontal comparative studies and the latter is called vertical comparative studies. Comparative politics passed through different phases of change contributed by scholars at times in the post-War period. Comparison is an analytical method—perhaps, the best available one—for advancing valid and cumulative knowledge about politics. At least since Aristotle, it has been argued that only by identifying and labelling the generic relations of power and then examining how they produce variable or invariable effects in otherwise different societies, can scholars claim that their discipline is scientific. Admittedly, controlled experimentation would be even better, but unlike the physical sciences—students of politics are not normally given the opportunity of introducing a treatment and holding everything else constant. We have to take the world as it is, observe its myriad similarities and differences and, then infer patterns of causality from simultaneous or time-lagged occurrences.

Comparison has always had a practical objective, namely, to produce useful descriptive information about how politics is conducted in countries other than one's own. Makers of public policy and investors of private funds, for example, need specialized bits of information in order to make reasonable choices when dealing with 'exotic' actors and organizations. They could not care less about the 'scientific basis' of the information, provided it is accurate and reliable. Predicting behaviour and, thereby, lowering the risk involved in transactions with foreigners is what they are interested in, and fancy theories may be no better at this than simple projections from past experience or calculation of statistical probabilities. Why a given country decides to expropriate foreign property may be much less significant for these consumers than whether polities with certain kinds of leaders, party systems, ethnic or class conflicts, etc. are more likely to do so and, therefore, can be predicted to engage in this kind of behaviour.

While there is no intrinsic reason why these two sides of the sub-discipline should contradict each other in principle, they often do in practice. Accurate and reliable information for description usually comes in the form of expressions and perceptions generated by the actors themselves; cumulative and valid data for analysis depends on analogies and concepts rooted in generic categories and themselves embedded in specific theories. The closer they are to each other, the narrower will be the potential for comparison in time and space—until comparative politics becomes nothing more than a description of "other people's politics", and every case has its unique explanation.

1. The first stage which converged its attention on the input aspect pinned its faith upon political sociology; it

propounded that the primary properties and components of political system were to be interpreted in the light of data about structural systems and procedures prevalent in society. Hence, it expounded the theory that political conflict dimensions were structured according to cleavage dimensions in the social fabric. Political scientists like Samuel Huntington adopted this reductionist attitude and demanded for the autonomy of politics with respect to social and economic conditions.

2. The second stage in comparative politics directed its objective at achieving an institutional analytical study of the variation of the multitude of political systems and their constituent parts such as parties and party systems, rightfully. Their primary focus was pointed on fundamentally essential differences between different kinds of democracy, authoritarian regime and modernizing politics. The transition was from democracy to 'order' through stable institutions.
3. Lastly, the increasing interest in the output aspect of politics within the domain of political science too, influenced the study of comparative politics. The question which obviously arises in the context is that what is the utility of studying different political systems if it was not the case that politics matter for policies? This was also possible due to the rediscovery of the centrality of the state both on the right and the left of the spectrum. Thus, the third stage involved a mixing of comparative politics with public policy and political economy, aiming to grasp the task of different political systems (policy inputs) and actual gains (policy outcomes). This led to comparative public policy.

Those who lay stress on the input aspect, typically refer to the significance of social cleavages—the key problem being the extent to which environment determines the polity. The cleavage approach, delimiting politics to cleavage dimensions in the social structure, seems as exaggerated as institutionalism or the hypothesis that there is no relationship whatsoever between social and economic factors and the political system. But how does one strike a balance between social and economic determinism and political indeterminism or the new institutionalism? How can one realize the crucial concepts to sort out impeccably, major system differences and similarities in the comparative analysis of the political system in various countries? Because the attempt to isolate traditional, developing and modern politics unsucceeded as a consequence of the value oriented nature of these approaches, the distinction between democratic and authoritarian regimes becomes the fundamental one.

Although, there is agreement as to the implication and applicability of the term 'democracy', there is difference of opinion about the properties or indicators that recognize a democratic regime. Two diametrically opposite types of democratic models have been identified: the Westminster type democracy versus the consensus or consociational type democracy. On the other hand, there exist a far more numerous categories of non-democratic structures. In the present times, we find over 160 polities called Third World, nevertheless there is no consensus about the taxonomy of Third World politics.

Comparative politics at the descriptive level continue to dedicate most of its effort to formally sovereign national states. That is the level at which such information is normally consumed by policy-makers, the media and the public at large. But at the analytical level, it will have to break through that boundary and recognize those units with the same formal status, e.g. all members of the United Nations or of some regional organization, may have radically different capabilities for taking and implementing collective decisions—and that virtually no national state can afford to presume that it is politically sovereign, economically self-sufficient and culturally distinct. In other words, comparativists have to give more thought to what constitutes a relevant and equivalent case once they have chosen a problem or puzzle to analyse and to do so before they select the number and identity of the units they will compare.

Contemporary comparative politics has tended to focus on variables. The antiquated version tried to explain the behaviour of whole cases—often one of them at a time. The usual approach has been to choose a problem, select some variables from an opposite theory to explain it, decide upon a universe of relevant cases, fasten upon some subset of them to control for other potentially relevant variables, and go searching for "significant" associations. Not only were the units chosen, presumed to reproduce the underlying causal relations independently of each other, but each variable was supposed to make an independent and equivalent contribution to explaining the outcome.

1.6 Scope of Comparative Governments and Politics

Traditionally, the scope of comparative politics was limited and parochial. It was confined to the study of constitutions and political institutions in respect of their features, powers and positions. It was parochial in the sense that it involved a study of only European constitutions, and amongst the European constitutions. Today, comparative politics has secured a very wide scope which includes the analysis and comparison of the political processes, political activities, political functions, political structures of all political systems, developed as well as developing of the European as well as Asian, African and Latin American countries. It includes all that comes within the purview of political activity and political processes. It seeks to study all mechanisms of politics with a view to build a science of politics, capable of explaining and comparing all political activities, processes, and systems.

With regard to the scope and objectives of comparative politics, though Pierson and Skocpol claim that comparativists are addressing big and substantive questions about politics, others express doubts about this. For example, Robert Dahl states that, "very few people study power today" and that "perhaps we have not only failed to progress in the study of power, we have actually gone into reverse". Juan Linz and

Samuel Huntington highlight the lack of attention to political leadership and political elites. Others raise questions about the policy relevance of comparative politics research. Thus, Giovanni Sartori argues that comparative politics places great emphasis on the theory-research nexus yet largely disregards the theory-praxis nexus or, as Adam Przeworski puts it, in less complex language, "we do not speak about politics to people outside academia".

Comparative politics is one of the three main disciplines of political science, alongside political theory and international relations. It deals with internal political structures (institutions like parliaments and executives), individual and collective actors (voters, parties, social movements, interest groups) and processes (policy-making, communication and socialization processes, and political cultures). The main goal of this empirical discipline is to describe, explain, and predict similarities and differences across political systems, be it countries, regions, cities, or supra-national political systems (such as empires in the European Union). This can be done through the intensive analysis of few cases or with large-scale extensive analysis of many cases, and can be either synchronic or diachronic. Comparative politics uses both quantitative and qualitative data. Increasingly, the analysis of domestic politics is challenged by the growing geographical scope and interdependence between regions and countries through globalization, bringing comparative politics and international relations closer.

Comparative study is to outline the features of political institutions, processes, and actions. In its early years, comparative politics did little more than describe, and it has only been with more recent generations of researchers that there has been more interest in explanation—meaningful explanation is impossible unless we first tie down the facts about politics and government. Comparative politics today is a much broader and more eclectic field of study than ever before, where many new concepts and ideas are being allowed to shake up old assumptions, but in which Cold War thinking still has more influence on scholarship than it deserves. Particularly in the United States, the field is being slow to catch up with the changing realities of politics around the world, including the declining role of the state, the rise of new economic powers, the impact of new technology and globalization, and the impact of failed and failing states. It may be time for another revolution in thinking.

Comparative study can be characterized as the study of patterns of systematic interactions between and among individuals and groups in a community or society. This study does not involve random interactions, but rather focuses upon those interactions that involve power or authority. Comparative politics involves no more and no less than a comparative study of politics—a search for similarities and differences between and among political phenomena, including political institutions (such as voting, demonstrating, or reading political pamphlets), or political ideas (such as liberalism, conservatism, or Marxism). Everything that politics studies, comparative politics studies undertakes the study with an explicitly comparative methodology in mind.

Comparative politics involves the systematic study and comparison of the world's political systems. It is particularly interested in exploring patterns, processes, and regularities among political systems. It looks for trends, for changes in patterns, and it tries to develop general propositions or hypotheses that describe and explain these trends. Comparative politics covers a broad range of topics. The field has no single focus. Different scholars have different preferences. There are several different kinds of studies. Among the types of studies that students of comparative politics actually do are the following:

- Studies of one country or a particular institution (political parties, militaries, parliaments, interest groups), political process (decision-making), or public policy (e.g., labour or welfare policy) in that country. When we focus on a single country or institution, it is necessary to put the study into a larger comparative framework. That means we should tell why the subject is important and where it fits in a larger context.

- Studies of two or more countries provide for genuine comparative studies (usually harder and more expensive in terms of research and travel costs).
- Regional or area studies may include studies of Africa, Latin America, the Middle East, East Asia, Southeast Asia, South Asia, Europe, or other sub-regions. Such studies are useful because they involve groups of countries that may have several things in common, e.g. similar history, cultures, language, religion, colonial backgrounds, and so on. Regional or area studies allow you to hold common features constant, while examining or testing for certain other features.
- Studies across regions are often expensive and difficult to carry out. Such studies might involve comparisons of the role of the military in Africa and the Middle East, or the quite different paths of development of the East Asian countries and Latin America.
- Global comparisons, with improved statistical data collected by the World Bank, the UN, and other agencies, are now possible to do on a specific basis.
- Thematic studies focus on themes as well as countries and regions. For example, themes such as dependency theory, corporatism, role of the state, process of military professionalization. Thematic studies are often complex and usually carried out by more senior scholars.

The scope of comparative politics—derived from a widely accepted definition of the field as the study of politics and political power around the world—entails a substantive and empirical dimension. The substantive dimension pertains to the subject matter and research questions addressed by comparativists, whereas the empirical dimension pertains to the spatial and temporal range of comparative analysis.

Students of comparative politics have focused on a diverse array of subject matters and research questions centrally related to politics.

Comparative research has also addressed many other key issues. A substantial amount of research focuses on political order and regimes, addressing questions about states, wars, revolutions, ethnicity, regimes, and democratization and thus exploring the processes that render the institutionalized decision-making of democracies possible, or impossible, in the first place. Other research focuses on actors, such as social movements, interest groups, and citizens, going beyond the voters and politicians that are essential to democratic politics; on substantive outcomes, such as economic development, the welfare state, the developmental state, capitalism and neo-liberalism, that are linked closely with the well-being of most of the world's population; and on processes, such as globalization and supranational integration, that have a growing impact on politics and even challenge the assumption that the nation-state is the dominant site of political power.

Comparative politics includes all that comes within the scope of political activity and process; it is to 'drown' the governments "among the whole universe of partial governments which exist in any community". It is needed that the study of government (as an element of the state) should be made vis-à-vis the governments so as to influence the government of the country and also be influenced by it in some way or another.

As Blondel says, "government is the machinery by which values are allocated, if necessary by using compulsion: what is, therefore, important is to examine the three stages of the operation by which these values are allocated. Firstly, we must see the way in which the values come to be formulated and government is made aware of them.

Secondly, we must see how the machinery of government 'digests' and transforms these values into decisions applicable to the whole community. Thirdly, we must see how these decisions come to be implemented down the level of governmental command. The whole operation of government thus takes the form of a two-way operation, or, perhaps more appropriately, of a machine which receives signals and transforms these signals into others".

The scope of comparative politics includes the study of all structures—formal and informal, governmental and extra governmental—which directly or indirectly are involved in the struggle for power taking place in all states. Along with these, bureaucracy, interest groups, pressure groups, elites, political parties and other associations of human beings form part of the scope of comparative politics.

The study of comparative politics is useful because it gives us a broader perspective of political phenomena and political behaviour, and this broader perspective can contribute a great deal to both our understanding and our appreciation of the phenomena we are studying. We compare to escape from our ethnocentrism, our assumptions that everyone behaves the same way we do; we seek to broaden our field of perspective. We compare to discover broader rules of behaviour than we might find in more narrow studies. For example, the simplicity and brevity of the Constitution of the United States is even more impressive when it is examined alongside much longer constitutions of other nations. We can better understand the significance of presidential government when we know about alternatives to presidential government. We can learn something about those factors contributing to political stability by studying a country that is regarded as being politically stable.

Comparative politics is concerned with the comparative study and analysis of political systems. It aims to overcome the shortcomings of approaches focused purely on case studies of individual countries and of those that build purely abstract theoretical models of decision-making. Comparing the similarities and differences between political phenomena across countries allows social scientists to judge if and how the experience of some states is similar to that of others and to assess whether theoretical models of how people make decisions are able to claim universal validity. The primary focus of both theoretical and empirical work in comparative politics is on the comparison of institutional practices between states. It examines how institutions vary between states and the effect that different institutional practices have on the outcomes of the political process in different societies.

The contemporary politics is a movement rather than a sub-field or sub-discipline. Comparative politics in recent years has been greatly influenced by behaviourism. The motives behind the modern search for conceptual frameworks, the more rigorous approach to the search data, and the emphasis on careful precision and statistical accuracy are beneficial. The behavioural approach "is an attempt to improve our understanding of politics and criteria of proof that are accceptable according to the canons, conventions and assumptions of modern empirical science".

Comparative politics therefore asserts an ambitious scope of inquiry. No political phenomenon is foreign to it; no level of analysis is irrelevant, and no time period beyond its reach. Civil war in Afghanistan; voting decisions in Britain; ethnic conflict in Quebec, Bosnia, and Burundi; policy interactions among the bureaucracies of the European Union in Brussels, government agencies in Rome, regional offices in Basilicata, and local powers in Potenza; the religious bases of political action in Iran, Israel, and the United States; the formation of democracies in Eastern Europe are an array of contemporary issues that stand before the field. Questions about the origins of capitalism; the formation of European states; the rise of fascism and collapse of interwar democracies; and the transition to independence after colonial rule are some of the themes of past eras that still command attention.

To sum up, comparative politics has firmly established itself as a significant, vibrant, and definitive tradition and field of inquiry in the discipline of political science. The main goal of comparative politics is to study different political systems in order to better understand the different ways in which people are governed, and to make comparisons that will give us the reference points that we need to help us better understand politics and government. Comparative politics, in its contemporary form, involves a comparative study of not only the institutional and mechanistic arrangements but also an empirical and scientific analysis of no-institutionalized and non-political determinants of political behaviour such as the patterns of culture or the socio-economic arrangements within which the political system operates.

The empirical study of political processes, structures and functions forms a major part of comparative political studies. It seeks to build up a scientific and valid theory of politics capable of explaining all phenomena of politics. Comparative politics is not limited to the comparison of national political systems but includes other units such as sub-national and supra-national regions, international organizations, single political actors, processes and policies. Comparative politics includes as a subject matter, all features of political systems and, recently, has turned its attention increasingly towards the interaction between them, approaching international relations.

References

Alfred Stephen (2001), *Arguing Comparative Politics*, OUP, US.

Charles Hauss (2006), *Comparative Politics: Domestic Responses to Global Challenges*, Thomson Wadsworth Higher Education, US.

Gabriel A. Almond, G. Bingham Powell, Jr., Kaare Strom and Russell J. Dalton (2009), *Comparative Politics Today*, Pearson Education, India.

Howard J., Wiarda and Esther M. Skelley (2007), *Comparative Politics: Approaches and Issues*, Rowman and Littlefield Publishers Inc., US.

Jeffrey Kopstein and Mark Irving Lichbach (2005), *Comparative Politics: Interests, Identities, and Institutions in a Changing Scenario,* Cambridge University Press, US.

John McCormick (2010), *Comparative Politics in Transition*, Woodsworth, US.

Mark Irving Lichbach and Alan S. Zuckerman (2002), *Comparative Politics: Rationality, Culture and Structure*, Cambridge University Press, UK.

Todd Landman (2008), *Issues and Methods in Comparative Politics: An Introduction,* Routledge, US.

2

Need for Comparative Analysis

2.1 Introduction

Across all space and time, man has questioned things. Which system of government works best? Will our country prosper if we try and change our ideals as a nation? Many generalizations have since been made in reference to the various political systems that exist. Because of the fact, that man has a questioning nature—he compares. According to the Oxford English Dictionary, to compare is to "estimate, measure, or note the similarity or dissimilarity between things". The essence of science is inquiry. Inquiry involves comparisons that may be between groups, societies, organizations, or across national boundaries. It involves clear definition and the specification and use of measurable variables. In other words, evidence is gathered and used in order to advance an argument, to explain or predict political phenomena, since comparison is the basis of scientific knowledge. Man is not able to know which political system could best work for his country, lest he compares with other systems. Thus, he compares to not only find differences in the systems, but also similarities.

Comparative politics is an approach within political science that attempts to make reasonable statements about the functioning of political systems and political behaviour through theoretical hypotheses and empirical observation by giving explanations for found regularities and variations, within and among political systems. Comparative politics is particularly interested in exploring patterns, processes, and regularities among political systems. It looks for tendencies, for changes in patterns; and tries to develop general propositions or hypotheses that describe and explain these trends. Comparative politics has emerged from the necessity of having to know more about one's own political system by looking more closely at other political systems. When one compares, an understanding of political reality may be achieved by comparing the political institutions and practices of two or more countries. Thus, one is able to gain much knowledge about the countries at hand. Other reasons we compare are to increase our political knowledge by systematically ordering information, and to order events on the basis of their characteristics.

2.2 Importance of Comparison

Comparative politics is studied by looking at two or more different countries and comparing and contrasting different aspects about them. Things such as the economy, social behaviour, political ideas, and the type of government, are all areas that can be compared. Comparative politics seeks to do such comparisons rigorously and systematically, without personal, partisan, or ideological axes to grind, so that the conclusive data is not interfered with.

Comparison is one of the most fundamental of all human activities, lying at the heart of almost every choice we make in our lives. Comparison is something that we all do almost daily—consciously or unconsciously. In order to better understand human behaviour, we need to look at different cases, examples and situations in order to draw general conclusions about what drives people to act the way they do. Political scientists can study government and political processes in isolation, but they can never fully understand them, and can never be sure that they have considered all the explanatory options, without establishing whether the objects of their study are usual or unusual.

Comparative politics is vastly important in our modern society. There is a great need for comparisons to be made between various governments to find things that should be changed in one's own government to help it further succeed, and so one can have a greater knowledge of other countries. Looking at various ideologies, one is able to see many things and make many generalizations about a country. Without the study of comparative politics, governments would never have the opportunity to gain ideas from other governments. With contributions of political scientists such as Shively, Roskin, and Conrad, students are able to grasp some of the most important facts of various countries and begin to compare them, and thus have a greater appreciation and understanding for the world in which they live. Comparative politics is an extremely important field of study.

There are many ways to study comparative politics. A first-hand experience of each country that one is comparing would be best, although it is not necessary. First one can look at the ideology of the country. This would give a firm concept of how the country functions and it would allow one to see many of its values, since the ideology shows the country's belief system. Another stop in studying comparative politics would be to look at the various social cleavages within the country. If there are many differences between social classes, a country is much more likely to have problems, versus the one with little or no difference between classes. In studying comparative politics, it is very important to keep an open mind and not assume anything. One must conclusively look at all known facts about a country before being able to compare it to another country successfully.

The characteristics of politics can be defined by two main things: the fact that "all the questions involve the making of a common decision for a group of people", and "the use of power by one person or a group of people which affects the behaviour of another person or group of people". Comparative politics is important in the making of a common decision for a group of people in the sense that "a single decision will affect all members of the group". Politics as an exercise of power is perhaps even more important than its use in making common decisions. "Power is the ability of one person to cause another person to do what the first wishes, by whatever means". According to Shively, power may be exercised in three different ways: *persuasion:* "when we convince someone that that is what he or she really wishes to do", *coercion:* "when we force a person to do something he or she did not want to do", or by construction of *incentives:* "when we make the alternative so unattractive that only one reasonable option remains". Politics as an exercise of power is very effective in many different regards. History has proved that you do not always have to be the strongest physically, to be an effective leader of power (e.g. *Hitler*).

Often it is difficult to explain why one country has one set of beliefs and the other country, another set. It is perhaps most difficult to explain this in regards to democracy. The linearity thesis was designed to help explain why this sometimes occurs. The thesis states that democracy is more likely to flourish in affluent establishments versus influent ones. This thesis shows that there is a linear relationship between economic status and democracy. Countries that are exceptions to this thesis are Saudi Arabia and India. Another important research in regards to comparative politics is the threshold. It states that economic development can only take a country to a certain level in regards to moving to democracy. Thus, moving towards democracy then depends on other circumstances such as leadership, elites, etc.

Tocqueville has opined that that comparison is fundamental to all human thoughts. It is the methodological core of the humanistic and scientific method as well. It is the only way we can fully understand our own political system. Comparing the past and present of our nation and comparing our experience with that of other nations deepen our understanding of our own institutions. Examining politics in other societies permits us to see a wider range of political alternatives and illuminates the virtues and shortcomings of our own political life. By taking us beyond our familiar arrangements and assumptions, comparative analysis helps expand our awareness of the possibilities of politics. Comparison is the methodological core of the scientific study of politics.

Comparative analysis helps us develop explanations and test theories of the ways in which political processes work and in which political changes occur. The logic and the intention of the comparative methods used by political scientists are similar to those used in more exact science. Political scientists cannot normally design experiments to control and manipulate political arrangements and observe the consequences, especially when dealing with large-scale events that drastically affect many people. For example, researchers cannot and would not want to start a social revolution to see its effects. Nor would they want to initiate military escalation to see if it leads to war. It is possible, however, to use the comparative method to describe and explain the different combinations of political events and institutions found in different societies. More than two thousand years ago, *Aristotle* in his "Politics" contrasted the economies and social structures of many Greek city-states in an effort to determine how the social and economic environment affected political institutions and policies.

A contemporary political scientist, Robert Dahl, in his studies of democracy, compares the economic characteristics, cultures, and historical experiences of many contemporary nations in an effort to discover the combinations of conditions and characteristics that are associated with that form of government. Other theorists, in their attempt to explain different systems, have compared constitutional regimes with tyrannies, two-party democracies with multiparty democracies, parliamentary with presidential regimes, and stable governments with unstable ones.

Giovanni Sartori offered a very simple answer, namely, we compare to control. By control, Sartori means to say—albeit in a very loose way—that we use comparisons as a way to check (verify or falsify) whether our claims or assertions about certain phenomena are valid by controlling for, or holding constant, certain variables. Take the statements, "poverty causes corruption" or conversely, "corruption causes poverty"; "authoritarianism is more conducive to high levels of economic growth than democracy"; and "social revolutions are caused by relative deprivation". How do we know, Sartori asked, whether any of these statements is true, false, or something else? "We know", Sartori answered, "by looking around, that is, by comparative checking".

It is important to understand that, in most comparative analysis, actual control variables are not used. This issue may not be very clear right now and, for our purposes, is not critical. The main point is this: different types of comparisons allow a researcher to treat a wide variety of similarities or differences as if they are control variables. In so doing, the researcher can safely eliminate a whole range of potentially significant factors and, instead, concentrate on those variables he deems most important. Comparing to control is an undeniably important purpose of comparative analysis.

Yet many comparativists, especially those with a strong predisposition toward qualitative and historical analysis, are not always, or even mostly, involved in "testing" hypotheses through their comparisons. Ragin suggested, therefore, that some researchers are often most interested in using comparative analysis to get a better grasp of these individual "stories," rather than primarily using them as a way to verify or falsify specific arguments. In other words, for these researchers, an in depth understanding is the goal of comparative analysis. Comparing to understand, to put it in slightly different terms, means that researchers use comparison to see what other cases can tell them about the specific case or country in which they have the most interest.

The comparative method is a distinctive mode of comparative analysis. According to Ragin, it entails two main predispositions. *First*, it involves a bias toward (although certainly not an exclusive focus on) qualitative analysis, which means that comparativists tend to look at cases as a whole and to compare whole cases with each other. Thus, the tendency for comparativists is to talk of comparing Germany to Japan or United States to Canada. This may not seem to be an important point, but it has significant implications, one of which is that comparativists tend to eschew—or at least, put less priority on—quantitative analysis, also known as statistical or variable -centred analysis. In the social sciences, especially over the past few years, this orientation away from quantitative and toward qualitative analysis definitely sets comparativists apart from other social scientists. Even within comparative politics, however, this is beginning to change. The *second* predisposition among comparativists is to value interpretation and context. This means, in part, that comparativists begin with the assumption that "history matters".

Although understanding the predisposition of comparativists is important, this still does not tell us what it means to compare—a question that may seem easy to answer, but in fact is not. Just pointing out or describing differences and similarities between any two countries, for example, is not by any account the be-all and end-all of comparative analysis. Indeed, if you stay strictly at the level of superficial description—for example, China has a Confucian heritage, whereas the United States does not; both France and Russia experienced social revolutions—you will never genuinely engage in comparative analysis, no matter how accurate your observations may be.

Comparative (case-oriented) analysis, by contrast, is especially—perhaps uniquely—suited for dealing with the peculiar complexity of social phenomena. Why? Quite simply because comparative analysis, to repeat a point made above, can and often does deal with cases as a whole—meaning that a full range of factors can be considered at once within particular historical contexts (which themselves vary overtime). This is especially apparent with regard to "deviant" or anomalous cases. Comparative analysis can help explain why, for example, some relatively poor countries—such as India, Mauritania, and Costa Rica—is democratic, when statistically based studies would predict just the opposite.

To account for such anomalous cases (as many comparativists might argue), we need to look very closely at the particular configuration of social, cultural, and political forces in these individual countries and understand how, from a historical perspective, these configurations emerged and developed. Comparative analysis (especially when carried out in a qualitative as opposed to quantitative manner) allows the researcher to better understand or explain the relationship between and among factors. Quantitative or statistical research, by contrast, does a very good job in showing that relationships exist (for example, that capitalist development is related to democratization) but does not generally do a good job at telling us what the nature or underlying dynamic of this relationship is. To use a metaphor from aviation, we might say that quantitative analysis shows a strong correlation between engine failure and plane crashes, but it typically does not tell us the exact reasons (or the chain of causal events leading to the crash—since not all engine problems, even very similar ones, lead to the same outcome, and vice versa).

Comparativists have different views about the challenges facing their field and about the best way of realizing its potential, the most fundamental disagreement relating to the best level of analysis: some study a single country using comparative techniques: others study a small number of states using a limited number of variables: some are area specialists (studying states in just one part of the world, like Europe or Asia): some are institutional or process specialists (studying legislatures or voting, for example) and some are thematic specialists studying a particular problem or phenomenon affecting a select group of states, such as welfare in wealthy countries, the causes of civil war, or the reasons behind the collapse of weak or failing states.

2.3 Objectives of Comparison

The field of comparative politics has much to contribute to

this important area of research both in substantive and methodological terms. The comparison of countries centres on four main objectives: (i) contextual description, (ii) classification, (iii) hypothesis testing, and (iv) prediction.

1. Contextual description allows political scientists to learn about the historical events, important actors, and cultural aspects, among other elements in countries with which they have little or no prior knowledge. Typically, such contextual description does not seek to make larger inferences beyond the confines of the study's immediate focus.
2. Classification seeks to simplify the world of politics by providing the researcher with "data containers" into which empirical evidence is organized. Indeed, from Aristotle to Samuel Finer, political observers and political scientists have sought to classify regimes, regime transitions, modes of political behaviour, classes of people, events, among other factors, in an effort to clarify and simplify the world of politics.
3. Hypothesis testing helps eliminate rival explanations about particular events, actors, and structures in an effort to help build more general theories. Since comparativists cannot manufacture their own counterfactuals, comparing across a range of countries or time periods provides a "quasi-experimental" situation of control test rival hypotheses.
4. Finally, the generalizations that result from comparing countries help predict likely outcomes in other countries not included in the original comparison, or outcomes in the future, given the presence of certain antecedent factors.

These four functions of comparative politics are not mutually exclusive, and in most instances, they are cumulative—such classification requires description, hypothesis testing requires description and classification, and prediction needs all three. This cumulative nature of these four functions is evident in many popular comparative studies. For example, in 'Problems of Democratic Transition and Consolidation', Linz and Stepan describe different periods of democratic transition and consolidation, provide a classification of regime types that precede the moment of transition, test rival hypotheses about the key factors that affect the period of consolidation, and offer tentative predictions about problems that are likely to confront other countries going through similar process of democratization. These functions are directly related to different methods of comparison, which allow scholars to make larger inferences about the political world they observe.

To sum up, comparative politics is vastly important in our modern society. There is a great need for comparisons to be made between various governments to find things that should be changed in one's own government to help it further succeed, and so one can have a greater knowledge of other countries. Looking at various ideologies, one is able to see many things and make many generalizations about a country. Without the study of comparative politics, governments would never have the opportunity to gain ideas from other governments. With opinions of political scientists such as Shively, Roskin, and Conrad, one is able to grasp some of the most important facts of various countries and begin to compare them, and thus have a greater appreciation and understanding for the world in which they live. Comparative politics is an extremely important field of study.

References

Charles Hauss (2006), "*Comparative Politics: Domestic Responses to Global Challenges*", Thomson Wadsworth Higher Education, US.

Gabriel A. Almond, G. Bingham Powell, Jr., Kaare Strom and Russell J. Dalton (2009), "*Comparative Politics Today*", Pearson Education, India.

J. Howard, Esther Wiarda and M. Skelley (2007), "*Comparative Politics: Approaches and Issues*", Rowman and Littlefield Publishers Inc., US.

Jeffrey Kopstein and Mark Irving Lichbach (2005), "*Comparative Politics: Interests, Identities, and Institutions in a Changing World*", Cambridge University Press, US.

3

Going Beyond Eurocentrism

3.1 Introduction

Eurocentric discourse projects a linear historical trajectory leading from classical Greece (constructed as "pure", "Western" and "democratic") to imperial Rome and then to the metropolitan capitals of Europe and the US. It renders history as a sequence of empires: Pax Romana, Pax Hispanica, Pax Britannica. Pax Americana. In all cases, Europe, alone and unaided, is seen as the "motor" for progressive historical change: it invents class society, feudalism, capitalism and the industrial revolution. Eurocentrism attributes to the "West", an inherent progress towards democratic institutions (Torquemada, Mussolini, and Hitler must be seen as aberrations within this logic of historical amnesia and selective legitimation). Eurocentrism elides non-European democratic traditions, while obscuring the manipulations embedded in Western formal democracy and masking the West's part in subverting democracies abroad.

Eurocentrism as a concept first came into existence in approximately 1963, during the decolonization period of the latter 1900s. The word was developed to describe the outlook of the world from a strictly European perspective and with European experiences in mind. The word implies an exclusion of other non-European societies. With Eurocentrism, individuals tend to see the world from a western or specifically European mindset. In many cases, Eurocentric also means "Anglo-American". Eurocentrism minimizes the West's oppressive practices by regarding them as contingent, accidental and exceptional. Colonialism, slave-trading, and imperialism are not seen as fundamental catalysts of the West's disproportionate power.

3.2 What is Eurocentrism?

The word "Eurocentric" is often seen in a negative light due to its implications. The word is associated with distaste for and superiority over other cultures, and also implies criticisms of the cultures and lifestyles of other non-European societies.

The term Eurocentrism was coined relatively late, during the decolonisation period following World War II, based on an earlier adjective Europe-centric which came into use in the early 20th century. The term appears in precisely this form in the writings of the right-wing German writer Karl Haushofer during the 1920s. For instance, in Haushofer's '*Geo-Politics of the Pacific Space*', Haushofer contrasts this pacific space in terms of global politics to the 'European' and 'Europe-centric'. The term Eurocentrism appears in the 1970s, through the Marxist writings of Samir Amin as part of a global, core-periphery or dependency model of capitalist development. Eurocentrism appeared only by 1988, in the titles of Amin books as the definition of an ideology.

Early Eurocentrism can be traced to the European Renaissance, during which the revival of learning based on classical sources, were focused on the ancient Greek and Roman civilizations, due to their being a significant source of contemporary European civilization. The effects of these assumptions of European superiority increased during the period of European imperialism, which started slowly in the 15th century, accelerated by the Scientific Revolution, the Commercial Revolution and the rise of colonial empires in the "Great Divergence" of the Early Modern period, and reached its zenith in the 18th to 19th century with the Industrial Revolution and a Second European colonization wave.

Eurocentrism as a historical phenomenon is not to be understood without reference to the structures of power that Euro America produced over the last five centuries, which in turn, produced Eurocentrism, globalized its effects, and universalized its historical claims. Those structures of power include the economic (capitalism, capitalist property relations, markets and modes of production, imperialism, etc.), the political (a system of nation-states, and the nation-form, most importantly, new organizations to handle problems presented by such a reordering of the world, new legal forms, etc.), the social (production of classes, genders, races, ethnicities, religious forms as well as the push towards individual-based social forms), and the cultural (including new conceptions of space and time, new ideas of the good life, and a new developmentalist conception of the life-world). The list is woefully inadequate, and the categorizations themselves are admittedly problematic; but it suffices to indicate the intractability of the problem of Eurocentrism.

The progressively mechanised character of European culture was contrasted with traditional hunting, farming and herding societies in many of the areas of the world being newly conquered and colonised by Europeans, such as the Americas, most of Africa, and later the Pacific and Australia. Many European writers of this time construed the history of Europe as paradigmatic for the rest of the world. Other cultures were identified as having reached a stage through which Europe itself had already passed—primitive hunter-gatherer; farming; early civilisation; feudalism; and modern liberal-capitalism. Only Europe was considered to have achieved the last stage.

For some writers, such as Karl Marx, the centrality of Europe to an understanding of world history did not imply any innate European superiority, but he nevertheless assumed that Europe provided a model for the world as a whole. Others looked forward to the expansion of modernity throughout the world through trade, imperialism or both. The colonising period involved the widespread settlement of parts of the Americas and Australasia with European people, and the establishment of outposts and colonial administrations in parts of Asia and Africa. As a result, the majority population of the Americas, Australia and New Zealand typically trace their ancestry to Europe. A Eurocentric history is taught in such countries, despite geographic isolation from Europe, with many European cultural traditions.

The longitude meridians of world maps based on the prime meridian, placing Greenwich, London in the centre, has been in use since 1851. Various other prime meridians were in use during the Age of Exploration. The current prime meridian has the advantage that it places the International Date Line in the Pacific, inconveniencing the smallest number of people. Eurocentrism refers to a discursive tendency to interpret the histories and cultures of non-European societies from a European (or Western) perspective. Common features of Eurocentric thought include:

- Ignoring or undervaluing non-European societies as inferior to Western; and
- Ignoring or undervaluing what Asians or Africans do within their own society or seeing the histories of non-European societies simply in European terms, or as part of "the expansion of Europe" and its civilizing influence.

3.3 Beyond Eurocentrism

Aristotle (384-322 B.C.E.) regarded Africa and Asia as monolithic and influenced by their hot climates, contrasting with temperate or cold Europe. He saw their governments as despotic and peoples as servile and lacking in spirit. On the other hand, he regarded Asians as intelligent and was impressed with Egypt because leisure among the priestly caste had allowed them to found the mathematical arts. Medieval Europe's main impression of North Africa and Asia was distrust, then fear of, and hostility to, Islam. And in 1242, the Mongols came very close to Vienna and could have captured it but for news reaching them of their Khan's death. Yet the thirteenth century also produced Marco Polo, who travelled through much of Asia and left a detailed account of life in China, which is remarkably positive and even romanticized.

The missionaries of the Catholic Society of Jesus (Jesuits) worked in many parts of Asia and Africa. In that, they preached a religion that was strongest in their own (European) countries, they were Eurocentric. However, their policy was to try to understand the people they were converting and to adapt to local conditions, practices, and rites as far as they could. Moreover, they were pioneers in scholarship about several Asian countries, especially China. Jesuit missionaries sent back to Europe a flood of information from various parts of Asia, including, from 1703 to 1776, the "Lettresedifiantes et curieuses" (Edifying and curious letters), about one-third of which dealt with China.

The West is a name for a subject which gathers itself in discourse but is also an object constituted discursively; it is, evidently, a name always associating itself with those regions, communities, and people that appear politically or economically superior to other regions, communities, and people. Basically, it is just like the name "Japan",...it claims that it is capable of sustaining, if not actually transcend in European history is no longer seen as embodying anything like a "universal human history". No major Western thinker, for instance, has publicly shared Francis Fukuyama's "*vulgarized Hegelian historicism*" that saw in the fall of the Berlin wall a common end for the history of all human beings. The contrast with the past seems sharp when one remembers the cautious but warm note of approval with which Kant once detected in the French Revolution a "*moral disposition in the human race*" or Hegel saw the imprimatur of the "world spirit" in the momentousness of that event.

The phenomenon of "political modernity"—namely, the rule by modern institutions of the state, bureaucracy, and capitalist enterprise—is impossible to think of anywhere in the world without invoking certain categories and concepts, the genealogies of which go deep into the intellectual and even theological traditions of Europe. Concepts such as citizenship, the state, civil society, public sphere, human rights, equality before the law, the individual, distinctions between public and private, the idea of the subject, democracy, popular sovereignty, social justice, scientific rationality, and so on, all bear the burden of European thought and history. One simply cannot think of political modernity without these and other related concepts that found a climactic form in the course of the European Enlightenment and the nineteenth century.

These concepts entail an unavoidable—and in a sense indispensable—universal and secular vision of the humans. The European colonizers of the nineteenth century preached both aspects of this Enlightenment—humanism for the colonized and at the same time denial of the same in practice. But the vision has been powerful in its effects. It has historically provided a strong foundation on which to erect—both in Europe and outside—critiques of socially unjust practices. Marxist and liberal thought are legatees of this intellectual heritage. This heritage is now global.

'*After the Third World*' signals both the end of an era and way of thinking and the birth of new challenges, dreams and real possibilities; both observations, however, can be hotly contested. On the one hand, what has really ended? Assuming that the historical horizon that has finally come to a close is that of anti-colonial nationalist struggles in the Third World, how about the other, perhaps less intractable, aspects of the spirit of Bandung and Third Worldism? For instance, how about the tremendous international solidarity that this spirit elicited among exploited people? How about its passionate call for justice, or its eloquent demand for a new international economic order? And is the centrality of the politics on which that spirit was based also a thing of the past? Are all of these features ineluctably left behind by the steamroller of modern capitalist history?

The post-colonial assumption is that, the world today is the world of inequality where much of the difference falls across the broad division between people of the west and those of the non-west. Hence, post-colonial theories come in as intervention mechanisms from the non-western scholars. Post-colonialism argues that, "the right of all people on this earth to the same material and cultural well-being".

The pioneers of post-colonialism (examples of scholars and their works in brackets are: Edward Said (Orientalism and Culture and Imperialism); Ngugiwa Thing'o (Weep not Child, The River Between, Decolonizing the Mind-urging African writers to write in their native languages rather than European languages in order to renounce colonialties); Kwame Nkuruma (Unites States of Africa), Julius Nyerere (The Challenge to the South), Chinua Achebe (Things Fall Apart); Ali Mazrui (Re-traditionalizing Africa and Africa's IR); Frantz Fanon (Black Skin, White Musks); Homi Bhabha (Problems of treating post-colonial countries as homogenous block); Samir Amin (critiques of the Western Imperialism); Robert Young (linking a genealogy of post-colonialism to the contemporary activism of the new social movements in non-West); Spivak (Can the Subaltern Speak?); Judith Butler (Gender Troubles); Valentine Mudimbe (Reinvesting Africa); Ozay Mehmet (Westernizing the Third World: Eurocentrism of Economic Development) concerned themselves with the political, social and cultural effects of colonization on the colonized.

According to Franz Fanon (1952), post-colonialism is a way of thinking about knowledge production, and how certain kinds of knowledge about other people can act as a prop to economic or military or physical domination.

Post-colonial scholars regard the way in which the west paved its passage to the orient and the rest of the world as based on mystified truths.

In particular, Edward Said' critique of Western representations of the non-western culture in his 1978 book, Orientalism, is an influential text for post-colonial studies and has produced a range of theories on the subject. Said provides useful conceptual tool for understanding western political discourses of 'self' and 'others'.

Moreover, Edward Said's, "Culture and Imperialism" represents discourse analysis and post-colonial theory as tools for rethinking forms of knowledge and the social identities of post-colonial systems. An important feature of post-colonial thought is its claim that modernism and modernity are both part of the colonial project of domination. Thus, the ambition of post-colonial scholarship is to undo the legacies of all forms of European or Western imperialism and colonialism in order to transform the international order and associated notions of community, society, and morality. Nevertheless, debates about post-colonialism are yet to be resolved. Major issues raised by Said and other post-colonial scholars against the Western descriptions of non-Euro-American and others, suggest that colonialism as a discourse is based on the ability of Westerners to examine other societies in order to produce knowledge and use it as a form of power deployed against the very subjects of inquiry. As should be readily apparent, the issues of post-colonialism are uncomfortably relevant to contemporary Western scholars.

As a work of adversary scholarship, beyond Eurocentrism critiques, the universalization of Eurocentric norms, the idea that any race, in Aime Cesaire's words, "holds a monopoly on beauty, intelligence, and strength". Our critique of Eurocentrism is addressed not to Europeans as individuals but rather to dominant Europe's historically oppressive relation to its internal and external "others". We are in no way suggesting, obviously, that non-European people are somehow "better" than Europeans, or that Third World and minoritarian cultures are inherently superior. There is no inborn tendency among Europeans to commit genocide, as some "ice people" theorists would suggest—such theories are merely colonialist demonization—nor are indigenous or Third World people innately noble and generous. Nor do we believe in the inverted European narcissism that posits Europe as the source of all social evils in the world.

Such an approach remains Eurocentric ("Europe exhibiting its own unacceptability in front of an anti-ethnocentric mirror", in Derrida's words) and also exempts Third world patriarchal elites from all responsibility. Such "victimology" reduces non-European life to a pathological response to Western penetration. It merely turns colonialist claims upside down. Rather than saying that "we" (that is, the West) have brought "them" civilization, it claims instead that everywhere "we" have brought diabolical evil, and everywhere "their" enfeebled societies have succumbed to "our" insidious influence. The vision remains Promethean, but here Prometheus has brought not fire but the Holocaust, reproducing what Barbara Christian calls the "West's outlandish claim to have invented everything, including Evil".

3.4 Peter Gran's View on Beyond Eurocentrism

Peter Gran is a historian at Temple University who received his Ph.D. at the University of Chicago in 1974 with the dissertation title as "Indigenous Roots of Modern Egyptian Culture". Some of his representative publications include, 'Beyond Eurocentrism' (1996) and 'The Islamic Roots of Capitalism: Egypt, 1760-1840' (1979). Peter Gran's overt goal in Beyond Eurocentrism is to stress a revisionist historical narrative within the field of World History itself. Stating that World history has been mainly dominated by Western elites (William McNeill, Wallerstein), he provides an alternative world-historical narrative which, with the help of social science, seeks to "express history through the lives of the majority" since the world historians' elitism "De historicizes the mass population". In that respect, Peter Gran places the emphasis on the necessity to go beyond the Eurocentric worldview of history and turn to a more inclusive comparative analysis.

A new way of engaging world history is put forward in Gran's 'Beyond Eurocentrism', not only in debunking Eurocentric narratives of history, but in providing a sort of world map on which different roads help us better define the poly-centricity of the frameworks and units of analysis. The most interesting feature of the books is the mapping out of four different roads, "The Russian Road", which has developed in Asia (Iraq), "The Italian Road" in Mexico and in India, the

"The Tribal-Ethnic road" exemplified in Albania and Belgian Congo and "the Bourgeois Democracy" in Great Britain and in the United States.

The similarities of the areas analyzed throughout the book include political economy, the organization of culture and the State-sponsored scholarship through four different hegemonic logics. The similarities, Gran argues, are intended to disrupt the Eurocentric paradigm that ascribe credit to Europe's homogeneity and bourgeois democracy as one of its essential characteristics. For instance, due to the industrial discrepancy between the North and the South, Gran suggests that "Italy is defectively European" and that Russia is "half European, half Asiatic". In the North-South dichotomy, Peter Gran has heavily relied on Antonio Gramsci's philosophy and insights on the State's hegemony in its attempt to homogenize its subjects and cover up class conflicts.

The specificity of the "Russian Road" and its ramification into Iraq is characterized by a political "oscillation between liberalism and authoritarianism", mostly because of the underdevelopment of a civil society and the fact that the vast majority of the population see themselves as "peasants not citizens", thus hindering their ability to make an entrance into the hegemonic system and challenge it from within. In Iraq for example, the positivist liberal historians, because of their alliance with the State, undermined the history of the Ottoman Empire, which they considered as a "morass of anarchism". In reaction to that bourgeois/elite historiography, romantic historians waved Pan-Islamist sentiments, the same they did for Pan-Slavism in Russia. Despite the many similarities in the "Russian Road", including the development of political economy in its three phases—a first liberal phase, the corporatists phase and a new liberal era—Peter Gran, has, however, argued for some differences between the two countries. These include, but not limited to an "essentially unchallenged political system" in Russia where Iraq was characterized by a "state crisis".

Another European road that ramified itself in Asia and Latin America is the "Italian Road". In Italy, Mexico, and in India, scholars disguised class conflicts by emphasizing the notion of "regional differences". The "umbrella like dominant political party" and its satellite minor parties turned into a Left and/or Right corporatism, fascist Right in Mussolini's Italy and the Left's state socialism in Nehru's India and Cardenas's Mexico. Along this road, the organization of culture is based on regionalism about which a southern metaphysical tradition and a liberal positivist tradition were vying for credit. In Italy for example, "positivism and Marxism emphasized change and progress whereas Romanticism favoured tradition and continuity".

A similar critique of Eurocentrism is put forward with the "Tribal-Ethnic Road". In Albania, against western elite scholars' contention that Europe is altogether democratic and secular, due to the multiplicity of ethnic groups, culture in Albania is "per formative" because of the absence of a traditional "high culture", strong enough to periodically challenge positivism. In addition, cultural affiliation was split between the Northerners' attempt of alliance to the Roman alphabet to link them with Western Europe and the South's reliance on the Arabic one which "would link them to the Islamic world". The ramification of the "Tribal-Ethnic Road" in Belgian Congo disrupts the "scholarship dichotomizing of Europe and Africa". What is questionable in Peter Gran's analysis of colonial administration in Congo, however, is his argument on "the built-in confrontation between secular and religious authority", when the administration tended to protect tradition and the Church undermining it through "modernization, education and development". Secular and religious authorities collaborated in the process of imperialism and colonization in Africa.

The last road in Gran's narrative is the "Bourgeois democracies" in Great Britain and in the United States. Because of the haziness of the notion democracy, one cannot argue for the uniformity of its application in the different roads. Much of what is behind the bourgeois democracy is the idea of "the chosen people", Manifest Destiny in the United States and the notion of "Englishness/Britishness" in England. The specificity of this road, contrary to the other ones, lies in the fact that "the metaphysical tradition serves to reinforce positivism more than to challenge it", and the ambivalence of the state in officially giving credit to historical consciousness but "promoting a historicism in the culture as a while". Interesting enough is the discrimination of the four different hegemonic logics, based on caste on the "Russian Road", regionalism on the "Italian Road", gender on the "Tribal-Ethnic Road", and race on the "Bourgeois Democracy". In the latter road, Gran argues, one finds "scientific racism" whereas in the "Russia Road", cultural racism is more prominent.

One of the strength of Peter Gran's, 'Beyond Eurocentrism' is its reliance on the insights of some philosophers such as Benedetto Croce, Antonio Gramsci, Michel Foucault, to name a few. For example, Antonio Gramsci helps the historian better grasp the role of intellectuals in hegemony and the "massification" of the socially downtrodden populations whereas Michel Foucault helps him understand the intangibility of power diffused in state apparatus. In addition, Peter Gran disrupts the often taken for granted Europe's homogeneity, emphasizing the striking similarities between Europe and the rest of the world, albeit through different hegemonic logics.

Beyond Eurocentrism, however, falls short in attaining its objective in "representing similarities without making all human beings into economic man". On the issue of woman self-immolation in India, Gran writes, "to make *sati* typify gender oppression about women is illogical; to explain it in terms of religion is equally illogical, by so doing one ignores the economic components which have nothing to do with gender or religion". This assertion is questionable, especially in the field of Subaltern Studies and its historiography in India. Subaltern Studies' overt goal, though debatable, aims at disrupting the history of the market (Marx, Wallerstein) which downplays the religious, cultural and political movements of the masses, and makes the history of the masses, a historical and/or out of capital. In other words, because Peter Gran relies too much of capitalism, he is inside out Eurocentrism.

3.5 The End of the West

Europe since 1914 has become provincialized. Only the natural sciences are able to call forth a quick international echo. The West is a name for a subject which gathers itself in discourse but is also an object constituted discursively; it is, evidently, a name always associating itself with those regions, communities, and people that appear politically or economically superior to other regions, communities, and people. Basically, it is just like the name "Japan",...it claims that it is capable of sustaining, if not actually transcending European history is no longer seen as embodying anything like a "universal human history". No major Western thinker, for instance, has publicly shared Francis Fukuyama's "vulgarized Hegelian historicism" that saw in the fall of the Berlin wall, a common end for the history of all human beings. The contrast with the past seems sharp when one remembers the cautious but warm note of approval with which Kant once detected in the French Revolution, a "moral disposition in the human race" or Hegel saw the imprimatur of the "world spirit" in the momentousness of that event.

The phenomenon of political modernity—namely, the rule by modern institutions of the state, bureaucracy, and capitalist enterprise—is impossible to think of anywhere in the world without invoking certain categories and concepts, the genealogies of which go deep into the intellectual and even theological traditions of Europe. Concepts such as citizenship, the state, civil society, public sphere, human rights, equality before the law, the individual, distinctions between public and private, the idea of the subject, democracy, popular sovereignty, social justice, scientific rationality, and so on, all bear the burden of European thought and history. One simply cannot think of political modernity without these and other related concepts that found a climactic form in the course of the European Enlightenment and the nineteenth century.

These concepts entail an unavoidable—and in a sense indispensable—universal and secular vision of the human. The European colonizer of the nineteenth century both preached this Enlightenment humanism at the colonized and at the same time denied it in practice. But the vision has been powerful in its effects. It has historically provided a strong foundation on which to erect—both in Europe and outside—critiques of socially unjust practices. Marxist and liberal thought are legatees of this intellectual heritage.

This heritage is now global. A long series of illustrious members of this social group—from Raja Rammohun Roy, sometimes called "the father of modern India", to Manabendranath Roy, who argued with Lenin in the Comintern—warmly embraced the themes of rationalism, science, equality, and human rights that the European Enlightenment promulgated. Modern social critiques of caste, oppressions of women, the lack of rights for labouring and subaltern classes in India, and so on—and, in fact, the very critique of colonialism itself—are un-thinkable except as a legacy, partially, of how Enlightenment Europe was appropriated in the subcontinent. The Indian Constitution tellingly begins by repeating certain universal enlightenment themes celebrated, say, in the American Constitution. And it is salutary to remember that the writings of the most trenchant critic of the institution of "untouchability" in British India refer us back to some originally European ideas about liberty and human equality.

Post-colonial scholarship is committed, almost by definition, to engaging the universals—such as the abstract figure of the human or that of reason—that were forged in eighteenth century Europe and that underlie the human sciences. This engagement marks, for instance, the writing of the Tunisian philosopher and historian Hichem Djait, who accuses imperialist Europe of "denying its own vision of man". Fanon's struggle to hold on to the Enlightenment idea of the human—even when he knew that European imperialism had reduced that idea to the figure of the settler-colonial white man—is now itself a part of the global heritage of all post-colonial thinkers. The struggle ensues because there is no easy way of dispensing with these universals in the condition of political modernity. Without them, there would be no social science that addresses issues of modern social justice.

In the social sciences, these are invariably thinkers one encounters within the tradition that has come to call itself "European" or "Western". We are aware that an entity called "the European intellectual tradition" stretching back to the ancient Greeks is a fabrication of relatively recent European history. Martin Bernal, Samir Amin, and others have justly criticized the claim of European thinkers that such an unbroken tradition ever existed or that it could even properly be called "European".

The point, however, is that, fabrication or not, this is the genealogy of thought in which social scientists find themselves inserted. Faced with the task of analysing developments or social practices in modern India, few if any, Indian social scientists or social scientists of India would argue seriously with, say, the thirteenth century logician Gangesa or with the grammarian and linguistic philosopher Bartrihari (fifth to sixth centuries), or with the tenth or eleventh century aesthetician Abhinava Gupta. Sad though it is, one result of European colonial rule in South Asia is that the intellectual traditions once unbroken and alive in Sanskrit or Persian or Arabic is now only matters of historical research for most—perhaps all—modern social scientists in the region. They treat these traditions as truly dead, as history.

Yet, the very history of politicization of the population or the coming of political modernity, in countries outside of the Western capitalist democracies of the world produces a deep irony in the history of the political. This history challenges us to rethink two conceptual gifts of nineteenth century Europe, concepts integral to the idea of modernity. One is historicism—the idea that to understand anything it has to be seen both as a unity and in its historical development—and the other is the very idea of being political. What historically enables a project such as that of "provincializing Europe" is the experience of political modernity in a country like India. European thought has a contradictory relationship to such an instance of political modernity. It is both indispensable and inadequate in helping us to think through the various life practices that constitute both the political and the historical.

3.6 Power Shifts

America is in decline and Europe is in a deep political and economic malaise. China is rising and emerging regional economic powers are challenging the West. The beginning of Europe's formation, challenges us to think of Europe and its relation to today's emerging economies in both economic and geopolitical (East-West) cyclical terms. 'As late as 1700, the combined GDP of India and China was twice as large as Europe's'. The West wasn't always on top. However, following the transformative Renaissance and Enlightenment periods, that fact dramatically changed. 'By 1913, Europe's share of global GDP was more than twice that of India and China put together. (It was twice that of the United States)'.

There are moments in international politics when shifts in power seem particularly acute. One occurred in 1990, with the sudden demise of the Soviet Union. Another may now be upon us, this time ushered in by American overextension and the 'rise of the rest', which together have shifted the global balance of influence. Some analysts envision a 'post-American world', or use the term 'non-polarity' to describe a world in which the United States' unipolar moment has passed and no alternative power centres exist. Others focus on the emergence of specific powers or regions, particularly China and India. That China and India occupy a more powerful position in global political debates than in the past, is an observable phenomenon; that Brazil, Russia, the Gulf states and South Africa have a certain set of powers within regional contexts, and can at times affect policies globally as well, is equally so. But the basis of that power, outside the economic sphere, is not well understood.

The emerging powers have also increasingly been using their influence to challenge the legitimacy of the post-Second World War order, calling instead for more pluralist or multipolar conceptions. China, for instance, has long been a 'sovereignty hawk', generally opposing the notion that interventions for humanitarian purposes are legitimate. Its model of authoritarian capitalism has also increasingly become an ideological export, challenging the United States' liberal model. India, despite having aligned itself with Washington on many fronts (most recently on issues of nuclear technology), and having significantly deepened bilateral economic ties with the United States.

It has frequently criticised an economic system that it sees as crowding out a development agenda; has generally opposed the humanitarian-intervention agenda; and has openly called for a return to a more equitable and just political order. South Africa has used its weight within the Africa group to amplify its diplomacy in multilateral institutions such as the UN, playing both a critical role in General Assembly negotiations and a blocking role (principally in the UN Security Council). Brazil has been able to assert itself primarily in the trade and energy realm, but its multilateral diplomacy within the UN and other security arrangements lags substantially behind the other emerging powers.

The United States has often acted as a stabiliser of the balance of power in regions of strategic importance. Just as the United Kingdom has historically done on the European continent, the United States has worked to make sure that no single state could come to dominate its region. Traditionally, the United States intervened with substantial military force or went to war when American officials believed that the relevant regional actors were unable to maintain a balance, thus enabling a potentially dominant state the opportunity to make a bid for hegemony. In Europe, the United States relied on multilateral institutions for this purpose, with the oft-quoted logic of NATO being to 'keep the US in, the Soviets out, and the Germans down'. In the Middle East and Asia, meanwhile, the United States has tended to use bilateralism to ensure territorial boundaries and regime security, creating 'hub and spokes' systems with America at their centre. But while methods have differed across regions, the ultimate goal has not.

Some observers have forecast a multipolar world, with regional heavyweights, like Russia, China, India, Brazil or Turkey, grouping their smaller neighbours and building power blocs that can potentially create a global equilibrium between themselves. The United States is a Pacific country; it cannot be excluded from East Asia, nor China or India from the Middle East and other resource-rich regions. Issues like energy or the environment or proliferation cannot be regionalised. They require global approaches. Niall Ferguson has coined the term *'apolar world'*, in which an overstretched United States gradually recedes from its hegemonic role around the globe but is replaced by nobody. China, in this view, is too focused on maintaining stability as it modernises its society to take on broad international commitments; Europe is hobbled by its long-term demographic decline. In the absence of a global rule-keeper, religious strife, local internecine conflicts and non-state rogue actors, like al-Qaeda, will rend the world.

To sum up, although Eurocentrism has been common through the ages, it has not been constant, nor has it affected the way Europeans have viewed all non-European societies equally. Moreover, Europeans have not always been in full agreement with each other over the merits or failings of particular non-European societies. In some writers and periods, we find a tendency to romanticize Asia and Africa. In general, Eurocentrism has been more pronounced during periods of greatest European assertiveness or self-confidence, the most outstanding example being the age of imperialism and colonialism in the nineteenth and early twentieth centuries.

References

Matt Buttsworth (2011), "*Beyond Eurocentrism-Rethinking the Commercial, Scientific, and Industrial Revolution*", Matt Buttsworth, Australia.

Rajani Kannepalli Kanth (2009), "*The Challenge of Eurocentrism: Global Perspectives, Policy, and Prospects*", Palgrave Macmillan, New York.

Samir Amin (2009), "*Eurocentrism*", Monthly Review Press, New York.

4

Capitalism and Globalization

4.1 Capitalism Defined

Capitalism is a system of economic and social relations characterised by the dependence of the bulk of the population on the sale of their labour power for subsistence. Although wage labour and private ownership of the means of production have existed sporadically and in various forms over the millennia, capitalism is of relatively recent origin, making its first appearance in the English countryside some four to five hundred years ago. Capitalism has generated a tremendous increase in the productive capacity of the capitalist economies of North America, Western Europe, Japan, Australia and New Zealand.

Yet, this tremendous growth in the forces of production has been accompanied by vast inequalities in the distribution of the fruits of that production. The disparity in income and wealth between the industrialized nations at the centre of the world capitalist system and the underdeveloped areas on the periphery has been increasing continuously since the early days of colonial plunder. Moreover, within each capitalist nation, tremendous fortunes co-exist with indescribable poverty in spite of the growth of the modern "welfare state". And while inequalities in income and wealth reveal the primary dimension of inequality in a capitalist society, they also give rise to further inequalities—in power, political influence, occupation status, and privilege which exist alongside and reinforce the inequalities in income and wealth.

Capitalist relations of production are characterized by the complete separation of the producers (wage workers) from the means of production. Capitalists as a class have a monopoly on the means of production while workers have only their labour-power, which they are to subsist with. The capitalist directly organizes the labour process, so that workers labour under the supervision of capitalists or their managers. In respect to control of the work process and ownership of the means of production, capitalism resembles slavery and differs from feudalism and petty commodity production. The objective of the capitalists is to expand their initial capital by combining labour and means of production and selling the resultant commodities, which are their property, for a profit. Hence, capitalist production is for exchange, not for use. Capitalists are free to hire and fire workers as needed. Capitalist relations of production thus differ from slavery and feudalism in that the relationship between the workers and the owner of the means of production is purely contractual, with no direct coercion involved.

According to Winston Churchill, "The inherent vice of capitalism is the unequal sharing of blessings; the inherent virtue of socialism is the equal sharing of miseries".

Capitalism is based on self-interest and self-esteem; it holds integrity and trustworthiness as cardinal virtues and makes them pay off in the marketplace, thus demanding that men survive by means of virtue, not vices. It is this superlatively moral system that the welfare statists propose to improve upon by means of preventative law, snooping bureaucrats, and the chronic goad of fear (Alan Greenspan, "The Assault on Integrity").

According to Jawaharlal Nehru, "The forces in a capitalist society, if left unchecked, tend to make the rich richer and the poor poorer".

Karl Marx, "The need of a constantly expanding market for its products chases the bourgeoisie over the whole surface of the globe. It must nestle everywhere, settle everywhere, and establish connexions everywhere".

William Greiderin his book, *The Soul of Capitalism* describes, "The brilliant creative core of capitalism is the story the entrepreneurs and capital investors tell themselves about the future. How they intend to alter it, what they expect to gain in return, where they will raise the capital to accomplish their vision. Many of their stories turn out to be flawed or mistaken, of course, but the capacity to envision a set of future events and then act to fulfil them is a central source of capitalism's strength and its dominance of society".

David Korten opined, "capitalism is not about free competitive choices among people who are reasonably equal in their buying and selling of economic power, it is about concentrating capital, concentrating economic power in very few hands using that power to trash everyone who gets in their way".

4.2 Characteristic Features of Capitalism

Capitalism is the existence of two classes—a class of capitalists who among themselves have a class monopoly over the means of production, and a class of property less wage-workers who sell their capacity to work, or labour power, to capitalists in exchange for a wage or salary. The vast majority of people own very little or no property, aside from personal property such as their clothes, cars, homes, and household items. More precisely, most people own very little income-earning property and they therefore can obtain the income they need to maintain themselves and their families only by selling their labour power on a labour market to the highest bidder. Hence, under capitalism labour power is a commodity, subject to the fluctuations of "supply and demand" in the market for labour. The capitalist mode of production therefore pre-supposes both the existence of commodity production in general and the transformation of labour power itself into a commodity in particular.

Capitalism is a socio-economic system in which private ownership means profit to the owner. The owner controls the means of production, so the profit belongs to the private business owner. In capitalism, the free market determines the production, distribution and price of goods and services. A free market is unregulated supply and demand with little government interference in matters of trade. Capitalism has owners completely controlling all resources through purchase or hire. Labourers have a free choice of workplace but this is limited because they have to choose from existing capitalists' workplaces. Capitalists own tools and raw materials. Work methods are completely under the capitalists' control. Capitalism created groups that give guidance and others that have control. Technical experts give guidance and control is delegated to managers and directors.

Labourers were tied to their owner's assigned workplace under slavery and land duty. Capitalism gave a free, but limited, choice of workplace. Under land duty, labourers often owned them, similar to primitive societies. Guidance and control of methods has moved through opposites. Management of work methods was completely under the owners' control under slavery and capitalism. In slavery and capitalist societies, the agents provided guidance and control was sometimes delegated. Under primitive societies and to a significant extent under land duty, work methods management was in labourers' control. In primitive and land duty societies, labourers had control and provided self and collective guidance. Labourers pooled resources in primitive and land duty societies.

The economic system is based on private enterprise and private ownership, under which a major proportion at least of economic activity is carried out by profit seeking organizations and individuals. It involves the use of markets and self-regulation rather than centralized planning to allocate resources, with the regulation of supply and demand through the price mechanism in a free market. As a theory, it assumes the free movement of capital, labour and trade and is to be contrasted with communism, under which major economic decisions have to be taken collectively, with rigid state control over the economy and trade—the command economy. Capitalism has undergone many modifications, not least with the development of major international corporations, with the expanding role of the state and the increasing sophistication of financial systems and speed of transaction. Marxists and others have argued that capitalism has been the dominant motive behind imperialism, leading to international rivalry and war, the thesis advanced by Lenin (1870-1924) in *Imperialism the Highest Stage of Capitalism* (1916).

The theory is that the declining rate of profit at home has forced major capitalist countries and their entrepreneurs and investors to expand overseas, and that this has outlasted decolonization, with the less developed countries (LDCs) in a dependency relationship on the industrialized world. Karl Marx (1818-1883) in his critique envisaged capitalism as a specific stage in global economic development. However, the demise of the USSR and Communist regimes in Eastern Europe, the opening of the economy of Communist China to market forces and globalization, have affirmed not only the longevity of capitalism, but also its claim to be a world system.

In capitalism, mode of production is that capitalists and not workers control the process of production itself. As part of the wage bargain, workers relinquish control over their labour during the stipulated working day and have no say in the disposition of the things the workers produce—the product. Hence, the workers are deprived of control over both their work activities and the work product. The decisions about what to produce, how to organize the production process, and what technology to use and so forth, are made by capitalists.

As the forces of production develop over time, capitalists tend to organize the production process along increasingly hierarchical lines, creating many different levels of employment, from production and clerical workers on the bottom to "middle management" to high level managers and executives. Capitalists organize production hierarchically in order to maintain their control over the production process and to further the productivity of their workers. Thus, the social relations of production take hierarchical forms under capitalism.

The lack of freedom and equality that characterizes the capitalist mode of production becomes much clearer once we leave the sphere where commodities are exchanged and investigate directly the organization of production in capitalist factories, offices, farms, and mines. In any capitalist firm, the organization of production is authoritarian in that the basic decisions are made by capitalists and executed by workers. The right to participate in decision-making defines, in the political sphere, what we mean by a democracy. This basic, democratic right is relinquished by workers when they sell the disposition of their labour power to capitalists for a stipulated time period.

Capitalists want to get as much work as possible out of workers, to turn their potential to work, or labour power, into maximum labour actually done. Capitalists expend a great deal of energy trying to increase the productivity of workers, using the threat of firing them, the incentives of promotions, bonuses and so on. Workers, on the other hand, are active human beings who want to minimize the unpleasantness of the time they must spend working, and they certainly do not want to work so hard as to increase the work demanded of them; so they spend much energy trying to circumvent the aims of the capitalists. The conflict between workers and capitalists is thus one that involves not only bargaining over wage rates but also the organization of production itself.

In capitalism, exploitation takes place automatically within the economic system; that is, the extraction of coercion—open or latent—of feudalism or slavery. The generation of surplus value is secured without conscious control by means of the market. Due to this, the capitalist economy has a momentum or dynamic of its own which is again basically outside the control of any agent or class. Together, these indicate that under capitalism, the 'economy' becomes separated from politics and the 'private' sphere from the 'public'. The notion of a distinct political sphere is, therefore, peculiar to capitalism. The very individualism of capitalism, the fact that all subjects are formally free and equal to pursue their own ends, requires a separate structure, the state, to represent their 'common interest'. Capitalist system demands freedom and equality before the law for exploitation to take place.

Every society has some method of organising its material life. It must produce the goods and services that are deemed useful and/or desirable by the society and then must distribute them for consumption. Societies have accomplished the management of material life in vastly different ways, which are sometimes referred to as social formations. The feudalism of Western Europe in the middle ages, the centralisation of production and distribution decisions in the Soviet Union, and the capitalisms of modern Japan, Western Europe, and the United States are all examples of different social formations. One of the ways in which social formations such as feudalism, capitalism, or Soviet-style socialism differ is in the control and use of the social surplus.

There is a social surplus whenever a society is able to produce more than what is needed to sustain material life at the established standard of living. The pyramids of ancient Egypt, the public buildings and vast armies and navies of the Roman Empire, and the ornate cathedrals of medieval Europe are all evidence of a social surplus. Modern capitalism is a market-based social formation because the market is the primary organising principle, yet we can find plenty of examples of command and some examples of tradition even here. For example, you may select an occupation based on family traditions. Most farmers also have farmers for parents. And there are certainly elements of command in modern capitalism. Government commandeers, through taxation, the resources to provide for defence, a system of courts, education, and much of our infrastructure (such as roads and harbours). In extreme cases, such as major wars, government may commandeer labour directly through the military draft.

4.3 Stages of Development of Capitalism

The capitalist systems are based on the *laissez faire* ideology of economy and society. It holds private property as the sacred right of the individual. Free trade, free contract, free economy, free market and competition are the hallmark of this ideology. It believes that market economy ideally optimises economic welfare as well as development. The market economy strives for development without any central direction whatsoever. Individuals striving to maximise their economic welfare respond to a system of prices which is in itself the result of the interaction of the forces of demand and supply.

The capitalist state, thus, gives priority to the interests, rights and liberties of the individual and believes that all social progress depends upon the unhampered initiative of the individual. It regards the state as human institution, created by man for certain specific purposes like maintenance of law and order, peace and security of life and property. The guiding principle is maximum possible individual freedom and minimum state action. This freedom can be secured by leaving individual alone and allowing him/her to pursue his/her good in own way so long as it does not interfere with the similar good of others. An important aspect of capitalist system is competition. Capitalist systems generally are liberal democracies, but is not always so. Some capitalist systems at times have been thorough authoritarian.

Baran and Sweezy emphasize the great watershed between competitive and monopoly capitalism, thereby suggesting two main periods. Fine and Harris argue for three stages: *laissez faire* capitalism; monopoly capitalism; and state-monopoly capitalism. In 'Class, Crisis and the State', E.O. Wright presents a schema of six stages: primitive accumulation; manufacture; machinofacture; monopoly capital; advanced monopoly capital; and state-directed monopoly capitalism. According to Uno and Sekine, Marxian political economy, or the theory of capitalism, divides into three levels of analysis. The theory of a purely capitalist society treats the law of value as the necessary inner logic of capitalism. Stage theory explores the structural manifestations of the law of value in the stages of mercantilism (1650-1775), liberalism (1775-1870), and imperialism (1870-1917). Historical analysis is guided by the other two levels of theory in carrying out a concrete analysis of capitalist history.

The development of capitalism falls into a number of

stages, characterized by different levels of maturity and each of them recognizable by fairly distinctive traits. But when we seek to trace these stages and to select one of them as marking the opening stage of capitalism, there is an immediate consideration about which it is of some importance that there should be no confusion. When we look at the history of capitalism, conceived in this way, it becomes clear that we must date its opening phase in England, not in the twelfth century nor even in the fourteenth century with its urban trade and guild handicrafts as others have done, but in the latter half of the sixteenth and early seventeenth century when capital began to penetrate production on a considerable scale, either in the form of a fairly matured relationship between capitalist and hired wage earners or in the less developed form of the subordination of domestic handicraftsmen, working in their own homes, to a capitalist on the so-called "putting-out system".

It is true that already prior to this, fairly numerous examples are to be found of a transitional situation where the craftsman had lost much of his independence, through debt or in face of the monopoly of wholesale traders, and already stood in relations of some dependence on a merchant, who was a man of capital. It is also true that in the fourteenth century or even earlier, there was a good deal of what one may call *kulak* types of enterprise—the well to do peasants in the village or the local trader or worker-owner in town handicrafts, employing hired labour. But these seem to have been too small in scale and insufficiently matured to be regarded as much more than adolescent capitalism, and scarcely justify one in dating capitalism as a new mode of production, sufficiently clear cut and extensive to constitute any serious challenge to an older one, as early as this.

By the early period of the sixteenth century then, there existed in England, the beginning of a proletariat—a stratum of dispossessed peasants who are a 'floating', mobile group, separated from their means of production, and thrown onto the market as 'free' wage labourers. At the turnoff of the sixteenth century, the decaying remnants of feudalism were poised between further disintegration and a movement into a more advanced productive form: capitalism. A factor of some importance in stimulating the latter's development is the rapid and vast expansion of overseas commerce which develops as a result of the startling geographical discoveries made in the last part of the fifteenth century. These include principally the discovery of America and the rounding of the Cape, which 'gave birth to commerce, to navigation, to industry, an impulse never before known, and thereby, to the revolutionary element in the tottering feudal society, a rapid development.

From the beginning of the Industrial Revolution to the end of the Napoleonic Wars, was one such period of long-term (upward) trend. It was followed until the middle or late 1840s, by a period of difficulties, though of rapid economic growth, and this in turn by the golden years of the mid-nineteenth century, the high point of capitalist, liberal, economics. Although as early as the fourteenth century, we find 'the beginnings of capitalist production' in Italy, and in the fifteenth century in England, but these are very restricted in scope. The towns are dominated by strong guild organisations which strictly limit the number of journeymen and apprentices whom a master may employ, and the guilds keep themselves separate from mercantile capital, 'the only form of free capital with which they came into contact'.

In the career of capitalism since this date, it is evident that there are two decisive moments. One of them resides in the seventeenth century: in the political and social transformations of that decisive period, including the struggle within the chartered corporations, which the researches of Unwin have brought to light, and the Parliamentary struggle against monopoly, reaching its apex in the Cromwellian revolution, the results of which were very far from being submerged, despite a certain measure of compromise and reaction at the Restoration.

The second consists of the industrial revolution of the late eighteenth and earlier half of the nineteenth century, which was primarily of economic significance; it had a less dramatic, but far from unimportant, reflection in the political sphere. In the history of capitalist development, we may distinguish *five* broad stages of expansionary activity. These stages, while they do not conform in a precise way to historical eras, are useful analytical tools for examining the internationalization of capital.

4.3.1 First Stage: Development of National Economies: The early development of capitalism required the expansion of the size of the capitalist economic unit. In this expansion, the state played a crucial role. Capitalism, or bourgeois society, captured the world progressively, transformed its various parts which were in very different phases of their own development at various times, and what is more, progressed and still, progresses at an uneven rate. This is true of the poor countries of the capitalist system, and of the so-called developed or industrialised countries of the West, and later Japan. The Industrial Revolution before 1848 was virtually confined to Britain, Belgium and a few patches in Western Europe and the European seaboard. The Industrial Revolution in Germany and most of the US occurred after 1848, in Scandinavia even later, in Russia from the 1890s and so on.

The key aspect of capitalist production is that the worker must be separated from the control of any productive factors other than his or her own labour and the production capital. The process of separating workers from their means of production, and thus forcing them into the labour market and into capitalist production relationships, was facilitated by the power of the state. The state was instrumental in the development of capitalism in England, for example, through promotion of the enclosure movement in the eighteenth century and through legislations forcing the poor to enter the work force in the nineteenth century. It played a similar role in other parts of Western Europe and in Japan (after the Meiji restoration in 1868), where the persistence of feudal institutions threatened to impede the growth of capitalism.

The profitable use of a developing labour force by the capitalist firm depends upon an expansion in the size of the unit of production. The division of labour that provides the basis for capitalist efficiency could not take place in a small craft shop of the pre-capitalist era. Thus, it was necessary for capitalist development that local restrictions on trade be broken down, that means of transportation and communication be developed, that a uniform system of law and order be established over a wide area—in short, it was necessary that national economic units be developed and strengthened.

4.3.2 Second Stage: Colonies and Spheres: The stage in capitalist development that followed the political and economic development of the nation was characterized by colonial expansion and the creation of spheres of influence. With certain exceptions, capitalism was only beginning to seize hold of the under-developed world from the middle of the nineteenth century onwards and to engage in intensive capitalist investment there. Very little of the world was actually colonised, occupied and ruled from abroad, the major exceptions being India. At all events, the moment when world capitalism was entirely successful, confident and secure, was comparatively brief, the mid-Victorian period, which may possibly be prolonged towards the end of the nineteenth century. In history, this period is preceded by [an age] of revolution from, say, 1776, the date of the American Revolt, to 1848, about 70 odd years.

As in the preceding stage, the economic integration of a larger geographic area was the key to the expansion process. However, while the need for market also played some role, the effort to develop sources of supply for important foodstuffs and raw materials became particularly important in the second stage. The role of the state remained as before: to break down local restrictions on economic activity; to create a labour force; to create means of transportation and communication; to ensure stability through the imposition of law and order. Britain, for example, united the regional economies of India and opened the whole subcontinent to penetration by British capital. Each colonial power established its own currency as the medium of exchange throughout its realm. The European colonial powers in Africa imposed monetary taxes on the indigenous people, forcing them to leave the traditional economy and enter the capitalist labour force to earn cash incomes to pay the taxes. Throughout the colonial world, railways directed towards import-export activity were given priority. Britain, France, Germany, and all of the colonial powers backed up their economic decisions in the most direct manner with armed force.

In organizing trade within its particular sphere, each nation reserved for its own capitalist class, special economic privileges with respect to both the subordinate areas in its control and other leading capitalist powers. Thus, for example, Portugal prohibited the development of manufacturing in Brazil, reserving the market for goods produced in the parent country, and England restricted the trade of its North American colonies with other European powers. It was a transition to the era of modern industrial capitalism, to bourgeois society; and what made it revolutionary was not only the attempt to break the fetters of earlier social and political orders which were believed to stand in its way, to construct an international system suited to the expansion of capitalism.

4.3.3 Third Stage: International Capitalist Integration: The giant and prolonged boom of the mid-nineteenth century was not based on a new technological breakthrough; by and large it utilised and acknowledged and developed the first Industrial Revolution, and coal as a source of energy, the steam-engine as motor-power, iron rather than steel as the basic raw material for capital goods such as machinery and so on. But this technology was now used on a far greater scale internationally both in the countries which were now entering industrialisation, and also to create what is now-a-days called an infrastructure in colonial and semi-colonial under-developed areas, railways, port installations—all that sort of thing. These allowed them to be integrated, mainly as suppliers of primary products into the capitalist world economy.

Hence, the three major consequences of this boom: *first*, it replaced industrial world monopoly by Britain, by what you might call world industrial oligarchy by a handful of competing industrial powers among whom the USA and Germany were rapidly over-hauling Britain. So long as the technology and methods of the first Industrial Revolution exist, this did not diminish the industrial role of Britain, but eventually it would do so.

Second, in making possible through railways, steamships, etc., an economic trade in bulk goods from hitherto inaccessible areas, it created a number of potential mass exporters of primary products, generally specialising in one or two commodities—American and South Russian wheat, Argentinian and Australasian meat, South Asian tea, Latin American coffee etc.—each dependent on the developed industrial world for their outlets. When these became actual rather than just potential mass exporters, the result would be a major disruption of agriculture, both in the exporting and importing countries, and also the development of dependent, mono-culture export economies like the banana and coffee republics of Latin America.

Third, and in consequence of the first two developments, the boom enormously expanded imports and exports of both goods and capital. This world trading and payments system continued to hinge on Britain and in this respect the British economy continued to occupy a key position even after its industrial role began to diminish. However, the boom was particularly quick in getting underway because of two factors: a rather large reserve of hitherto under-utilised resources, notably the labour which had been uprooted but was available for fairly short-term employment and the discovery of vast supplies of precious metals, mostly gold, in California and Australia and also silver in the US.

4.3.4 Capitalism after 1900: Now capitalism seemed set for a long and untroubled future around 1900. Even British capitalism, which was by now lumbered with a lot of old fashioned plants and methods, and both slowing down and falling behind the Germans and Americans, enjoyed the profits of being both the largest empire and increasingly the world's financier, shipper, insurance-broker, and in general the advantages of a world system which rested on the pound sterling. And, in fact, of the three major areas of conflict within the capitalist system, the one which had seemed most dangerous before 1848 now appeared to become quite manageable. During the so-called *Great Depression*, mass trade union and labour movements developed in industrial countries, even to a substantial extent in the US, mostly socialist and indeed largely Marxist. But, in fact, though these Marxists mass movements continued to salute the flag of revolution every time their leaders opened their mouths in public, we know that they rapidly turned into harmless, social-democratic movements, though not, of course, in the illegal and marginal movements in the peripheral and under-developed countries such as Russia.

Between 1905 and 1914, a breaking point was reached in three areas. *One,* the traditional structures of pre-capitalist empires in the Islamic world and Asia collapsed under the pressure of western penetration and conquest: Tsarist Russia, in so far as it belonged to this group—Persia, Turkey and most significant of all in 1911, China. *Second*, social revolution of peasants and workers broke out in Tsarist Russia—the first major social revolution of the 20th century. And, *third,* in Mexico in 1910, there occurred the first anti-imperialist social revolution in which the workers played no significant part because they did not form a significant part of the population. These developments constituted the beginning of the 20th century age of revolutions. At the same time, the tensions of the state system led directly towards an era of international wars which had not existed since the 18th and early 19th centuries. After 1914, nothing would ever really be the same again. Then after 1917, one-sixth of the world's surface moved out of the capitalist economy and after the Second World War large regions of Europe and Asia joined this movement. Capitalism was not destroyed as a world system, but the First World War opened an era when all three main types of conflict became for a period, apparently dominant and unmanageable.

4.3.5 Capitalism in the New Great Boom: The capitalist states of the new great boom moved back to some variant or other of an admittedly very much more bureaucratised and, so to speak, state-administered bourgeois parliamentarianism. Capitalism out-produced socialism and even began to re-infiltrate and re-integrate socialist economy from outside by virtue of its technological superiority and greater wealth. What happened is rather that capitalism abandoned the old assumption of a self-regulating, competitive market economy and changed its structure accordingly.

In the first place, the state expanded its economic function in all developed countries, including the US, to the point where it deliberately planned the extent, including an enormous public sector, and in many countries, even a largely nationalized industry. In the second place, the developed economies abandoned the economies of cheap labour and market control of unemployment, thus incidentally making possible a vast extension of the market for consumer goods. In the third place, the concentration of capital created the phenomenon of the modern, super-giant, largely self-financing, independent-of-the-market, transnational corporations. The developed countries entered the era of state monopoly capitalism and welfare capitalism in as-much as welfare was implicitly in full employment as a major government policy.

The extension of capitalist production and particularly the factory system, undermined the role of the family as a major unit of both socialization and production. Small peasant farmers were driven off the land or competed out of business. Cottage industry was destroyed. Ownership of the means of production became heavily concentrated in the hands of landlords and capitalists. Workers relinquished control over their labour in return for wages or salaries. Increasingly, production was carried on by the large organizations in which a small management group directed the work activities of the entire labour force. The rise of the capitalist system was accompanied by urbanization, labour migration, the spread of democratic ideologies, and a host of other developments which created an environment—both social and intellectual—which would ultimately challenge the political order.

Capitalism is the dominant social formation in the world today, but its future remains uncertain. In particular, it is unclear how the relationship between states and markets will evolve. We live in an era when the state appears to be subordinate to the global market, but capitalism is not a self-sustaining economic order, and its ability to generate wealth depends on the capacity and willingness of states to manage the instability and inequality that capitalism generates at a global level.

4.4 Globalization of World Economies

The word 'globalization' can refer to a phenomenon, which will have long-lasting effects. It is a movement, a revolution in terms of bringing the world closer and closer. Whether the repercussions have been harmful rather than good, is a question that we have to ask ourselves. Globalization has a lot of effects, interference; some may call it the creation of a global village, which is good in their eyes. One of the cautions that the world must take is not to be governed by only a set of bodies or organisations, which seek only their interests in various regions around the world, but project an image of do-gooders, the protector of democracy and the free world.

4.4.1 Meaning of Globalization: The term globalization implies economic integration through cross-country flow of information, ideas, technologies, goods and services. Its seminal features are: removal of trade barriers to facilitate free flow of goods all over world; generating environment which is conducive to free flow of capital among nation-states;

facilitating the free flow of technology and providing opportunities for the free and unfettered movement of labour among various nations of the world. To put it in a nutshell, globalization leads to economic growth and integration which can happen through trade in goods and services, movement of capital and flow of finance through movement of people. But in reality, globalization is a multi-layered phenomenon. Across the border, unity ushered under the impact of globalisation has several dimensions—cultural, social, political and economic. That is why some economists termed it as a process of creation of global economy, whereas others talked of political and social globalization, a globalization of ideas that led to technological changes. Broadly speaking, it can be suggested that "though the word globalization is more often used in its economic sense of removing trade barriers and state controls on economic activities of people, it implies widely the unification of people, cultures, nations and continents through interaction in various fields".

Globalization is a process that creates intensive and extensive international connections, which in the process, change traditional relationships of time and space. Globalization is strongly marked with economic interests with businessmen searching for more profits all around the world without glancing at the damages that they can cause. The existence of national economy is determined by exchange values between internal and external agents. The end of the Cold War and the appearance of new elements in the global economy helped in the emergence of the globalization phenomenon. These elements are:

1. The widening of trade operation spheres.
2. The speed and facility of exchanges.
3. The progress of technology; means of communication (internet, TV, telephone, fax, etc.).
4. The progressive disappearance of state influence due to a rude competition.

On a purely technical ground, the world globalization means "the increasingly close international integration of markets both for goods and services and for capital". Globalization is a process in which "goods, money, people, technology, and ideas are moving across the national borders at an accelerated pace". It is "shorthand for a cluster of related phenomena" in economic, political and socio-cultural spheres which are making the "state borders and governments increasingly less meaningful as barriers" and creating an integrated global world market. The process of globalization as defined in terms of greater global integration is not new; as in history different phases of integration has come and gone and the latest being the colonial empires created by the European nations since seventeenth century and the dominance of finance and capital, promoted by Bretton Woods institutions like International Monetary Fund, World Bank and World Trade Organization, is entirely new phenomena that took shape in 1980s and early 1990s.

4.4.2 Processes Involved in Globalization: Globalization can be viewed as a process by which this web of global connections becomes increasingly *"thick"*, creating an extensive and intensive web of relationship between many people across vast distances. In the twenty-first century, people are not distantly connected by overland routes plied by traders, diplomats, and missionaries; they are directly participating in a vast and complex international network through travel, communication, business and education. Globalization is a system in which human beings are no longer part of isolated communities that are themselves linked through narrow channels of diplomatic relations or trade. Entire societies are now directly "plugged in" to global affairs.

Thus, globalization represents a change in human organization and interconnection, but these are a function of those technological changes that make it possible. Globalization presents a number of potential implications for comparative politics. Because of the thickening of connections between people across countries, globalization breaks down the distinction between international relations and domestic politics, making many aspects of domestic politics subject to global forces. The growth of neo-right ideas in the 1970s in Europe reversed the idea of welfare state and state-controlled economy which had been popular since the Great Depression of 1930-33. The post-Second World War world was an era of 'golden age' of capitalism without any major incident of depression. However, in the early 1970s, due to oil crisis of 1973 and other factors, world economy witnessed slow growth, strengthening the critics of the state controlled economy with a new lease of life.

Meanwhile, most of the post-colonial developing countries failed to achieve high levels of economic growth and were dependent on the Bretton Woods institutions or the Soviet Union for aids and donations. The new connection with the IMF and World Bank and with the help of US, a policy of structural adjustment programmes (SAP) was started for all those countries who wanted aids and loans from the institutions.

Globalization is commonly associated with a variety of cross-border flows: typically, flows of goods, investment, and information, but also holiday-makers, migrant workers, asylum seekers, environmental pollutants, infectious agents, and so forth. The term "*global village*", was coined by Marshall McLuhan in the 1960s to express his belief that electronic communication would unite the world. The advent of the internet over the past 10 years has paralleled the emergence of globalization as a concept. Globalization has made the world smaller and interdependent. Bringing the world closer together may throw up new opportunities for cultural and economic interaction, but it also exposes us to the negative aspects of life on a shrinking planet, whether it is the threat of global warming, the international traffic in women for sexual exploitation or the spread of AIDS throughout the world.

By and large, it is presumed that globalization has opened up several new opportunities for the developing nations through trade liberalisation, expansion of foreign direct investment (FDI) and providing wider avenues to the young educated citizens. But on a closer analysis, one can foresee several adverse effects on the autonomy, regards the decision-making of these nations. Some analysts have emphasized that globalization has marginalised the role of nation-state on the one hand, and have given a domineering role to several global financial institutions like the World Bank, International Monetary Fund, Asian Development Bank etc. on the other. It is often believed that globalization is largely an American creation mostly rooted in the Second World War period and is based on the myth of Pax Americana. Globalization has made serious inroads into the effective functioning of civil societies in different global regions. As a matter of fact, these NGOs have often played a participatory role and behaved as agents of change for their people from that of "national citizens to global citizens".

Globalization can be conceived as a process (or set of processes) which embodies a transformation in the spatial organization of social relations and transactions, expressed in transcontinental or interregional flows and networks of activity, interaction and power. It is characterized by four types of change.

First, it involves a stretching of social, political and economic activities across frontiers, regions and continents.

Second, it is marked by the intensification, or the growing magnitude of interconnectedness and flows of trade, investment, finance, migration, culture etc.

Third, it can be linked to a speeding up of global interactions and processes, as the development of world-wide systems of transport and communication increases the velocity of the diffusion of ideas, goods, information, capital and people.

Fourth, the growing extensity, intensity and velocity of global interactions can be associated with their deepening impact such that the effects of distant events can be highly significant elsewhere and specific local developments can have considerable global consequences. In this sense, the boundaries between domestic matters and global affairs become increasingly fluid.

4.4.3 Dimensions of Globalization: Globalization has certain identifiable characteristics, although there is no consensus in the field about any of them. In the first place, it involves a growing consciousness of the world as a single place. This is reflected in phrases such as 'the global village' and 'the global economy'. Few places are more than a day's travel away and communication across territorial borders is now almost instantaneous. New information and communications technology have improved access to overseas markets and streamlined both the production and distribution of goods and trade in foreign exchange. Human beings are becoming more and more dependent upon one another as problems such as global warming, international drugs trade, and terrorism can only be managed through greater cooperation at a supranational level. Some observers argue that globalization is erasing cultural differences. Sociologists, for example, like to talk about the *Coca-Colaisation* or *McDonaldisation* of global culture.

Some observers claim that the sovereign state's capacity for independent political action is weakened by globalization. This is especially true in the area of economic policy. The idea of a domestic economy hemmed in by well-defined borders and managed by the state is now obsolete. Today, domestic economic policy is subject to global market forces. The state has little effective influence or control over these forces. Any state that tries to exert its influence, risks disinvestment, capital flight and recession. In short, globalization involves a radical transformation of existing economic and political structures in international relations. It involves an aspiration to think and act globally and an acknowledgement that humanity cannot effectively be ordered along geographical lines. To talk about globalization then, is not only to embark on a description of the present, but involves a comprehension of the forces shaping the future. In this sense, it is a multifaceted, complex, and dynamic concept.

4.5 Globalization: The Latest Stage of Capitalism

Periodization of capitalism is an analytical tool that allows us to grasp changes in the system over time. Globalization represents an epochal shift, the fourth in the history of world capitalism. The *first,* mercantilism and primitive accumulation, was ushered in with the birth of capitalism out of its feudal cocoon in Europe and outward expansion. The *second,* competitive, or classical capitalism marked the industrial revolution, the rise of the bourgeoisie, and the forging of the nation-state. The *third* was the rise of corporate (monopoly) capitalism, the consolidation of a single world market and the nation-state system into which world capitalism became organized. The first epoch ran from the symbolic dates of 1492 through to 1789, the second to the late nineteenth century, and the third into the early 1970s. Globalization as the fourth (the current) epoch began with the world economic crisis of the 1970s and the profound restructuring of the system that has been taking place since. It features the rise of transnational capital and the supersession of the nation-state system as the organizing principle of capitalist development.

In this process, those cultural and political institutions that fettered capitalism are swept aside, paving the way for the total commodification or 'marketization' of social life world-wide. Economic globalization has been well researched. Capital has achieved a new found global mobility and is reorganizing production world-wide in accordance with the whole gamut of political and factor cost considerations. This involves the world-wide decentralization of production together with the centralization of command and control of the global economy in transnational capital. In the earlier epochs, each country developed national circuits of accumulation that were linked to each other through commodity exchange and capital flows in an integrated international market (a world economy). In the emerging global economy, the globalization of the production process itself breaks down and functionally integrates these national circuits into global circuits of accumulation.

Globalization, therefore, is unifying the world into a single mode of production and bringing about the organic integration of different countries and regions into a global economy and society. From the seventeenth century treaties of Westphalia into the 1960s, capitalism unfolded through a system of nation-states that generated concomitant national structures, institutions, and agents. Globalization has increasingly eroded these national boundaries, and made it structurally impossible for individual nations to sustain independent, or even autonomous economies, polities, and social structures. A key feature of the current epoch is the supersession of the nation-state as the organizing principle of capitalism, and with it, of the inter-state system as the institutional framework of capitalist development.

Globalization basically refers to the acceleration and intensification of mechanisms, processes, and activities that are allegedly promoting global interdependence and perhaps, ultimately, global political and economic integration. It is, therefore, a revolutionary concept, involving the de-territorialisation of social, political, economic, and cultural life. It would be a mistake, however, to view globalization deterministically. Just as there are powerful forces of integration at work through the shrinkage of distance on a global scale, so there are forces of disintegration as well.

4.6 Globalization and the Changing Role of the State

Contemporary globalization is associated with a transformation of state power, as the roles and functions of state are re-articulated, reconstituted and re-embedded at the intersection of globalizing and regionalizing networks and systems. The metaphors of the loss, diminution or erosion of state power can misrepresent this reconfiguration. For whilst, globalization is engendering, for instance, a reconfiguration of state-market relations in the economic domain, states and international public authorities are deeply implicated in this very process. Economic globalization by no means necessarily translates into a diminution of state power; rather, it is transforming the conditions under which state power is exercised.

Moreover, in other domains, such as the environment, states have adopted a more activist posture whilst in the political domain they have been central to the explosive growth and institutionalization of regional and global governance. These are not developments which can be explained convincingly through the language of the decline, erosion or loss of state power per se. For such metaphors presume that state power was much greater in previous epochs; and, on almost every conceivable measure, states, especially in the developed world, are far more powerful than their antecedents. But so too are the demands placed upon them. The apparent simultaneous weakening and expansion in the power of states under conditions of contemporary globalization is symptomatic of an underlying structural transformation. This is nowhere so evident as in respect of state sovereignty, and autonomy, which constitute the very ideological foundations of the modern state.

Globalization is by no means a homogenizing force. The impact of globalization is mediated significantly by a state's position in global, political, military and economic structures; the institutional pattern of domestic politics; and specific government as well as societal strategies for contesting, managing or ameliorating globalising imperatives. The ongoing transformation of the Westphalian regime of sovereignty and autonomy has differential consequences for different states. The current globalization movement, aided by Governments of many developed countries and led by private sector enterprises, reveals unprecedented levels of international trade and exchange, married to unparalleled technological innovations, fuelled by levels of consumer demand never previously known and carrying a potential for growth and prosperity transcending anything the world has ever recorded. However, the impact on human development and human security, as distinct from economic growth, has varied considerably depending upon how government institutions are structured, upon how they mobilize themselves and upon the nature of government policies developed in response to globalization.

For many developing countries, which lack strong governance institutions, and the technology and the skills base to harness globalization, the impact has thus far been primarily negative. While globalization has brought capital, technology and new market potential to some developing countries and to some groups within those countries, the benefits have been accompanied by financial uncertainty, economic crisis, weakened state structures, loss of government autonomy and a disturbing concentration of wealth, all of which have exacerbated poverty, inequality and social instability in the developing countries.

The most visible effects of globalization are in the economic sphere—the expansion of international trade and foreign direct investment (FDI) including the reduction of barriers and an opening of national economies to trade, capital flows and information exchange. This remarkable integration and expansion of the world economy, boosted by liberalization both at the international level and within national economies, is associated with substantial increases in capital flows, particularly FDI, spearheaded by multinational corporations, in the production of goods and services for the world market.

Globalization dynamically interacts with some national level trends and key institutions. For example, the State and its Government as the basic political unit create and enforce basic standards for individuals and business. Private business as the basic economic organization generates jobs and civil society provides people with the space in which to express their needs and interests. Globalization is largely private sector-driven. It represents a shift in the locus of decision-making not only from the nation state to transnational actors but also from national governments to the private sector. Economic liberalization includes financial sector deregulation, foreign exchange decontrol and freedom of trade, and goes hand-in-hand with globalization.

Globalization presents entrepreneurs and corporations with

unlimited opportunities to participate in economic activities in national, regional and global contexts. The opening up of economic opportunities allows the movement of foreign capital, technology and management, largely from transnational corporations to host country entrepreneurs and corporations. As national economies open up, mergers between businesses from different countries and outright purchases or investment in the equity of businesses in one country by owners from other countries are becoming more and more common. This involvement puts private sector organizations at centre stage, and also requires them to meet certain levels of performance in terms of the quality, standards and timeliness of their business activity. This competitive market pressure upon business leaders, executives and workers, especially in developing countries, urges high standards of organization, training and discipline if they are to run their operations successfully. In some countries, there is a lacking of full understanding and appreciation of these business, government, regulatory and financial agencies, labour organizations, media and training institutions.

Nation states vary enormously in scale, but both the smallest and as well as the largest, face a narrowing down of options, resulting in globalization. As the globalization process unfolds, a larger state may seem to be more resilient and less vulnerable to disruption. Early in the transition to globalization, a state has to analyse the consequences of increasing contact with the global economy. Building necessary physical infrastructure, legal framework and governance processes can attract foreign capital and technology. Government and political leaders, as well as technical and managerial executives, may have to reorient their processes of policy making in order to make them responsive to shifts in global forces. After initiating global integration, a government will be committed to making its policies and actions more compatible with globalisation's needs.

This commitment involves basically competing for greater market shares in the global economy, making alliances and partners with like-minded globally oriented standards for operation in respect of globalised expectations of economic, financial and social practices. Although states cede authority over some aspects of economic and financial governance, there are areas within which national governments retain substantial degrees of discretion. While pooling sovereignty to create institutions and processes to maintain a globalised environment, many governments maintain immigration controls to a significant degree for both economic and social reasons. Such controls can adversely affect some countries where governments may facilitate the export of labour for their development purposes.

Globalization impacts heavily on the state—its policies, institutions and functionaries. Major disruptions occur for many individuals and groups; and as the state is no longer the sole authority for protecting and promoting the interests of the poor and the disadvantaged, other social, economic and political institutions begin to take responsibility for dealing with some of those disruptions in the society. The impact of globalization on the individual state varies with the extent of economic integration that each state has so far achieved and the degree of its exposure to the process of globalization.

Generally, countries, such as OECD members, that are more integrated within the global economy have less difficulty in further internationalizing their domestic decision-making. They are relatively well prepared for adopting a global orientation, and global standards and practices, and for countries are committed to preserving and maintaining socio-political stability and legal frameworks that will facilitate global operations and activities. Developing countries transitioning to globalization may face short-term problems, like the significant loss of jobs as businesses move out and the lowering of income for some groups of workers as foreign products and services compete with higher-priced local products and services. Some transition countries, like Mexico, Brazil, Argentina, the republic of Korea, Singapore, Thailand and Malaysia, are becoming slowly integrated with global economic and other standards. They are gaining significant experience in internationalizing their domestic policy-making, in building capacities for dealing with the demands of globalization, in improving their physical infrastructure and in making significant efforts to build institutions and capacities to represent social sectors.

Although labour standards and social policy seem to be national matters, there is an increasing pressure to globalize these policies through harmonization of international standards. Similarly, in public spending preferences, monetary policy and taxation, national action can adversely affect the economies of other. There is an underlying tension and contradiction in the policies of most governments participating in the globalization process resulting from the question: how to embrace globalization without loss of sovereignty. Globalization as reflected in the forces of international competition and the mixture of opportunity and risk, affects a wide spectrum of the population. Global integration has specifically affected the conditions of labour, as it is not as mobile as capital. Globalization affects the wages and job prospects of unskilled labour, creating one potentially large, disadvantaged, alienated and powerless element in the society. The mobility of high-value labour reduces the power of the nation state to control or protect its human resources.

To sum up, globalization has different meanings for different people; some analysts prefer to use the more specific term "international economic integration" thereby focusing on the economic and financial aspects. On the other the hand, globalization has reached political, social and cultural dimensions. Modern states need to deal with all dimensions. Globalization involves complex interactive processes that internationalize domestic policy-making and subject foreign policies to growing domestic pressures. Nation states have learned to share some sovereignty with regional and global institutions and at the same time, have opened their economies to regional and global dimensions.

Today, "national competitiveness" needs to be seen in a wider context. While technological change and economic integration have pushed the "state" in the direction of greater conformity and adoption of global standards and behaviours, social and political forces within nation states have pulled in the direction of asserting the state's role and power in protecting the interests and livelihood of its less privileged citizens. Consequently, the extent and pace of globalization are much more evident in some areas, notably trade, finance and communication, than in others.

Capitalism was not simply production for the market, but the system in which all the means of production—the tools/machines, the raw materials, and the location—belonged to the capitalist, and the labourer had nothing to sell but his/her own labour power; labour power had itself become a commodity bought and sold in the market. Feudalism had needed the use of custom, law and force to extract the surplus from the producers, who possessed plots of land, or artisans' tools/equipment, but under capitalism it was no longer necessary to rely on such non-economic methods.

In conclusion, one must examine the whole spectrum of countries within the globalisation process: leader, quick adopters, slow adapters, reluctant participants and those that are still very much isolated form globalization forces. For countries that are significantly involved in the globalization process, national governments seem to have fewer options for policy and operations. These governments are challenged to redefine the role of the state. A common strategy at the beginning of the twenty first century is to recognize that businesses rather than nations compete.

In this framework, governments retain some influence in steering economic decisions, for example, in respect of policies that attract mobile capital; policies that ensure financial stability; policies that improve the physical and cultural environments; and policies that create a sense of civic fairness. Much more needs to be done to close the widening gap between the world's rich and poor so that affected groups—for example, textile workers in Bangladesh, industrial workers in Uruguay and farmers in Zimbabwe—continue to benefit and prosper form the globalization process. Trade must be supplemented with greater aid and investment in human capital, education, health care and needs to consider significant debt relief for the debtor nations in order that the debtor nations may invest more in their people and in their future.

References

A. Hoogvelt (2002), "*History of Capitalism Expansion*", in Globalization and Third World Politics, Palgrave, London.

David Schweichart (2011), "*After Capitalism*", Rowman and Littlefield Publishers, United Kingdom.

Immanuel Wallerstein (1994), "*In Leslie Sklair, Capitalism and Development*", Routlege, London.

Jagdish Bhagwati (2004), "*In Defence of Globalisation*", Oxford University Press, New Delhi.

Nicloa Yeates (2001), "*Globalisation and Social Policy*", Sage Publications, New Delhi.

V.I. Lenin (1982), "*Imperialism: The Highest Stage of Capitalism*", Progress Publishers, Moscow.

5

Socialism: Development, Experiences and Current Status

5.1 Origins and Meaning of Socialism

Socialist societies were formed in opposition to the political and economic systems of the capitalist world. It is questioned, however, whether they were able to form an autonomous bloc interacting with the capitalist system or whether they became a constituent part of the "capitalist world system". Analysis of this relationship has a new significance in the period of transformation because it informs our understanding of the constellation of interests while pursuing national or international policies. It also raises the question of the classes driving the transition process: were they newly formed groups within the socialist societies, or were the classes already in place? The collapse also raises questions on the extent to which new national capitals have been formed and remain, and the place the post-communist countries and their corporations have in the global political and economic order.

5.1.1 Russian Revolution: The October Revolution of 1917 gave rise to a model of social, political and economic organization in the form of Soviet Russia which was borrowed extensively by a wide range of self-styled '*communist countries*' ranging from China to Cuba. The Soviet order provided a challenge to capitalism: in October 1961, Nikita Khrushchev, head of the Communist World Party of the Soviet Union, claimed that in conditions of 'the crisis of world capitalism' the period of 'full-scale communist construction' had begun. By 1980, self-defined Marxist-Leninist states accounted for a third of the world's population and claimed 40 percent of its industrial production. In Russia, Mongolia,

China, Cuba, Yugoslavia, Albania, Vietnam, Laos and Kampuchea, the communists had fought their way to power and had defended it at a great cost: in the USSR alone, over 20 million people perished following the German invasion in the Second World War. Socialism appeared a solid, well-founded system, it was a beacon to many radicals in the industrialized countries and it gave hope to the oppressed in the Third World.

The word "socialism" was coined in 1832 by Pierre Leroux, editor of the Parisian journal, Le Globe. From then on, "socialism" took on many different meanings, as the varieties of socialism grew and expanded, from Western Europe to Russia, America, Asia, and Australia. Socialism is a political and economic approach that calls for state-owned businesses and state-controlled distribution of wealth brought about by democratic means. The doctrines of socialism also include demands for major industries, banking, utilities, and natural resources to be nationalized as well as for nationalization of social services such as health care.

'*Socialism*' is an ambiguous term. In its most general sense, it refers to an array of ideas and policies, the most important of which are equality, a positive role of government as a distributive agency (particularly in the provision of welfare) and the absence of political domination over the individual; public or social ownership is usually considered to be a necessary condition to achieve the socialist objective. Socialism, in a Marxist sense, is the first stage of Communist society. The latter is a classless society, based on social harmony, in which the state has withered away and people receive 'according to their need'. Socialism—defined as a centrally planned economy in which the government controls all means of production—was the tragic failure of the twentieth century. Born of a commitment to remedy the economic and moral defects of capitalism, it has far surpassed capitalism in both economic malfunction and moral cruelty.

Socialism is a socio-economic system in which property and the distribution of wealth are subject to control by the workers, either directly through popular collectives such as workers' councils, or indirectly exercised on behalf of the people by the state, and in which Egalitarianism or equality is an important goal. Thus, under socialism, the means of production are owned by the state, community or the workers. Socialism is a society distinguished by a state-owned, more or less centrally administered economy, controlled by a dominant communist party which seeks, on the basis of Marxism-Leninism and through the agency of the state, to mobilize the population to reach a classless society. Socialism is an important component of the socialist movement and tradition. As a political movement, it is contended that socialism occupies the space between the beginning of capitalism and its mature form.

The term "socialism" is variously attributed to Pierre Leroux (1798-1871) or to Marie Roch Louis Reybaud (1799-1879) or to Robert Owen (1771-1858) in the mid-19th Century. According to Frederick Engels (1820-1895), by 1847, the term "socialism" usually referring to the utopian philosophies of Robert Owen and Charles Fourier (1772-1837), was considered quite respectable on the continent of Europe, while "communism" was the opposite.

5.1.2 Powers of the State: Under socialism, the state has much more far-reaching powers than under capitalism. Factories, communications, farms, transport and publishing are owned and controlled by the state, as well as labour, police, education, military forces, trade and foreign relations. The state bureaucracies are large, powerful and pervasive, and this is why this form of social organisation is often called bureaucratic socialism. Socialism is a form of economic organisation which is set against markets and private property. It believes that priorities should be decided by 'rational' politicians, not by the 'irrational' market, and as such is dependent on economic planning. Such regimes, where there is no duality of economy and polity nor a widespread 'civil society' of non-state groups, tend to be anti-democratic and governed on a permanent basis by the sole legal party, inevitably the communist party.

Socialism could be considered a rule by the bureaucracy except for the important role of the communist party. The communist party in a given state is officially the political representative of the people, the means by which the '*dictatorship of the proletariat*' is implemented. In practice, the communist party is also organised bureaucratically, but in a way which penetrates the other state bureaucracies. In its role as political executive of the state, the communist party organisation serves to control, and if necessary shake up or purge, other bureaucracies in order to maintain the system of centralised political control and to advance the goals of the state and the party.

5.1.3 One-party Rule: The system embodied one-party rule, an economy based overwhelmingly on state ownership and, at least in theory, central state direction. In the official ideology, it was a socialist system, ensuring greater rationality than the capitalist alternative and providing a more equitable, stable, and prosperous future. Particularly from the 1970s, the terms 'real' or 'existing' socialism were used as a part of the effort by those in power to rule out discussion of alternative models of socialism.

Both the world system approach associated with Immanuel Wallerstein and the "state capitalist" interpretation of Alex Callinicos consider the socialist countries to be a part of the capitalist world economic system. The world system orientation attempts to combine a Marxist capitalist ownership paradigm of capitalism with a political-military state system. World system writers divide the world economy into three sectors: the hegemonic core (the dominant "Western" capitalist countries), the periphery (developing countries of the South) and the semi-periphery countries with industrial capacity and national capital but not part of the capitalist core. Socialist countries were part of the semi-periphery. There were no "socialist economies".

Wallerstein claims that the world capitalist economy

included the entire world, including those states, ideologically committed to socialism. Socialist systems, it is contended, were not socialist modes of production, but interacted with the capitalist world economy. The socialist state, which exhibited some features of socialism (e.g. employment security, comprehensive welfare provision), nevertheless became a major player in capitalist accumulation, which in turn provided a basis for reintegration into the world capitalist system. An analogy is made with socialist parties under capitalism: they are separate from, but part of, capitalist economies; with time, trade unions have become functionally integrated parts of modern capitalist societies.

With the establishment of community's control over the economy and integrated national planning, socialism seeks to unite man with his work, free him from the control of blind forces of the capitalist economy, and emancipate him from wage-slavery. In consequence, man is restored to the un-alienated, un-crippled individual. Besides, socialism through fairer and planned economic arrangements allows every man, freedom from material cares and anxieties, and thus enables him to explore the continent of mind. In a socialist society alone where material hardships and environmental limitations do not hinder spontaneity and freedom of human action, man's mental and spiritual development is possible. The socialists through the establishment of social ownership of the means of production seek to build up an egalitarian society. In socialist economy where there is no profit motive, resources will be directed into the channels which are socially useful.

Others refer to socialism, emphasizing that the system drew inspiration from socialist thinking and remained true to that in some features but endured an overbearing state in all spheres of life. This is the best of the available characterizations, including recognition of the system's ideological origins but also its distinctiveness from others within the Socialist tradition—most importantly, Western European social democracy. It also indicates that this is more than a system of political power.

Political and economic structures were part of one coherent whole, and the links between them helped to shape its strengths and weaknesses.

Socialism in state could be considered rule by bureaucracy except for the important role of the communist party. The communist party in a given state is officially the political representative of the people, the means by which the 'dictatorship of the proletariat' is implemented. In practice, the communist party is also organised bureaucratically, but in a way that penetrates the other state bureaucracies. In its role as political executive of the state, the communist party organisation serves to control, and if necessary shake up or purge, other bureaucracies in order to maintain the system of centralised political control and to advance the goals of the state and the party. Socialist regimes have been called permanent war economies, since even in the absence of external war they are politically organised like capitalist societies during wartime. The wartime suppression of dissent under capitalism is the usual policy in state socialist regimes. Likewise, the pervasive control of the economy by state bureaucracies under wartime capitalism, the use of police and the military to maintain internal control, and generally the dominance of state power are all normal characteristics of socialism.

5.1.4 Wars and Socialism: War has played a key role in the creation of socialism. The establishment of the Soviet Union was made possible by the collapse of the Czarist army in First World War. After the Bolsheviks took power, a number of governments supported a military attack on the fledgling Soviet regime. To defend the new regime, the Russian army was reconstituted and expanded along traditional hierarchical lines. Many Czarist military officers were restored to commands. Soon the Soviet military forces were organisationally indistinguishable from their opponents. This process helped to militarise the Soviet system. Many other state socialist regimes have been established following military struggles. This includes wars of liberation against colonial powers as in the case of China and Vietnam, and direct conquest by other state socialist military forces as in the case of most states in Eastern Europe.

Perhaps most important in the militarising of socialism has been the squeezing of socialism into a state mould. Essentially, when socialism encountered statism, statism prevailed. To survive in a state system, including hostile capitalist states, socialism adopted a state form, which meant bureaucratisation and militarisation. For this reason, the problem of challenging socialism and promoting democratic socialism came to be closely linked with the problem of challenging the state and promoting self-management.

Supporters of socialism used to think that the worldwide triumph of socialism, even in a statist form, would automatically lead to the abolition of war. That this is an illusion, is apparent from the wars and military confrontations between the governments and military forces of China and the Soviet Union, China and Vietnam, Vietnam and Kampuchea, and others. Until 1945, there was only one socialist state. Since 1945, almost all combat action by Soviet military forces has been against other socialist states, or against the Soviet people.

5.2 Types of Socialism

5.2.1 Democratic socialism advocates socialism as an economic principle (the means of production should be in the hands of ordinary working people), and democracy as a governing principle (political power should be in the hands of the people democratically through a co-operative commonwealth or republic). It attempts to bring about socialism through peaceful democratic means as opposed to violent insurrection, and represents the reformist tradition of socialism.

5.2.2 Social democracy refers to an ideology that is more centrist and supports a broadly capitalist system, with some social reforms (such as the welfare state), intended to make it more equitable and humane. Democratic socialism, by contrast, implies an ideology that is more left-wing and supportive of a fully socialist system, established either by gradually reforming capitalism from within, or by some form of revolutionary transformation.

5.2.3 Revolutionary socialism advocates the need for fundamental social change through revolution or insurrection (rather than gradual reforms) as a strategy to achieve a socialist society. The Third International, which was founded following the Russian Revolution of 1917, defined itself in terms of Revolutionary Socialism but also became widely identified with Communism. Trotskyism is the theory of Revolutionary Socialism as advocated by Leon Trotsky (1879-1940), declaring the need for an international proletarian revolution (rather than Stalin's "socialism in one country") and unwavering support for a true dictatorship of the proletariat based on democratic principles. Luxemburgism is another Revolutionary Socialist tradition, based on the writings of Rosa Luxemburg (1970-1919). It is similar to Trotskyism in its opposition to the Totalitarianism of Stalin, while simultaneously avoiding the reformist politics of modern social democracy.

5.2.4 Utopian socialism is a term used to define the first currents of modern socialist thought in the first quarter of the 19th Century. In general, it was used by later socialist thinkers to describe early socialist, or quasi-socialist intellectuals who created hypothetical visions of perfect egalitarian and communalist societies without actually concerning themselves with the manner in which these societies could be created or sustained. They rejected all political (and especially all revolutionary) action, and wished to attain their ends by peaceful means and small experiments, which more practical socialists, like Karl Marx, saw as necessarily doomed to failure. But the early theoretical work of people like Robert Owen (1771-1858), Charles Fourier (1772-1837) and Etienne Cabet (1788-1856) gave much of the impetus to later socialist movements.

5.2.5 Libertarian socialism aims to create a society without political, economic or social hierarchies, in which every person would have free and equal access to tools of information and production. This would be achieved through the abolition of authoritarian institutions and private property, so that direct control of the means of production and resources will be gained by the working class and society as a whole. Most Libertarian socialists advocate abolishing the state altogether, in much the same way as Utopian socialists and many varieties of anarchism (including social anarchism, anarcho-communism, anarcho-collectivism and anarcho-syndicalism).

5.2.6 Market socialism is a term used to define an economic system in which there is a market economy directed and guided by socialist planners, and where prices would be set through trial and error (making adjustments as shortages and surpluses occur) rather than relying on a free price mechanism. By contrast, a socialist market economy, such as that practiced in the People's Republic of China, where major industries are owned by state entities, but compete with each other within a pricing system set by the market and the state does not routinely intervene in the setting of prices.

5.2.7 Eco-Socialism (or green socialism or socialist ecology) is an ideology merging aspects of Marxism, socialism, green politics, ecology and the anti-globalization movement. They advocate the non-violent dismantling of capitalism and the State, focusing on collective ownership of the means of production, in order to mitigate the social exclusion, poverty and environmental degradation brought about by the capitalist system, globalization and imperialism.

5.3 Development of Socialism

5.3.1 Early Phase: 'Early socialism' is not simply the first cluster of socialist doctrines; it is a set of values and beliefs that has never wholly vanished, even if it being always in a different dress. 'Primitive' or 'community' socialism might better convey what is meant, if by primitive one understands 'basic'. Perhaps to call it 'pre-Marxian' is clearest, but even the two mean something that continued to underlie even the most dogmatic Marxian socialism, so that it could become post-Marxian or neo-Marxian wherever and whenever Marxism finally loses its excessive rigidity and pseudo-scientific aspirations to totality. Certain elements of socialist thought long predate the socialist ideology that emerged in the first half of the 19th Century. For example, Plato's, "The Republic" and Sir Thomas More's, "Utopia", dating from 1516, have been cited as including socialist or communist ideas.

5.3.2 Modern Phase: Modern socialism emerged in early 19th Century Britain and France, from a diverse array of doctrines and social experiments, largely as a reaction or protest against some of the excesses of 18th and 19th Century capitalism. Early 19th Century socialist thought was largely utopian in nature, followed by the more pragmatic and revolutionary socialist and communist movements in the later 19th Century. Socialism emerged in the nineteenth century as a reaction against the growth of industrial capitalism and was linked to the development of the working class, otherwise known as the proletariat. The proletariat suffered from exploitation by the middle class, otherwise known as the bourgeoisie. The ruling class both degraded and caused poverty for the working class. Early socialists sought radical change to industrial capitalism.

Fourier and Owen both subscribed to an early form known as utopian socialism. This is a variant of socialism that believes in the unlimited possibilities of human development in a perfect society. On the other hand, Marx and Engels saw the fall of capitalism through revolution as inevitable. Some socialists sought power not through revolution but through universal suffrage and continued reform. These socialists were known as reformist/revisionist socialists and sought the end of the state through evolutionary means rather than the revolutionary ones. This form of socialism was seen as more 'moderate' and believed in the 'inevitability of gradualism'. They sought change through parliamentary means and formed parties to promote socialist thinking.

Social critics in the late 18th Century and early 19th Century such as Robert Owen (1771-1858), Charles Fourier (1772-1837), Pierre-Joseph Proudhon (1809-1865), Louis Blanc (1811-1882) and Henri de Saint-Simon (1760-1825) criticized the excesses of poverty and inequality of the Industrial Revolution, and advocated reforms such as the egalitarian distribution of wealth and the transformation of society into small utopian communities in which private property was to be abolished.

5.3.3 Socialist Religious Movements: Some socialist religious movements, such as the Shakers in America, also date from this period, as does the Chartist movement for political and social reform in the United Kingdom (possibly the first mass working class movement in the world). It was Karl Marx, though, who first employed systematic analysis (sometimes known as "scientific socialism") in an ambitious attempt to expose Capitalism's contradictions and the specific mechanisms by which it exploits and alienates. His ambitious work "*Das Kapital*", the first volume of which was published in 1867 with two more edited and published after his death by Friedrich Engels (1820-1895), is modelled to some extent on Adam Smith's, "*Wealth of Nations*", one of the cornerstones of capitalist theory. In it, he transforms Smith's labour theory of value into his own characteristic "*law of value*" (that the exchange value of a commodity is actually independent of the amount of labour required to appropriate its useful qualities), and reveals how commodity fetishism obscures the reality of the capitalist society.

Marx and Engels, who together had founded the Social Democratic Workers' Party of Germany in 1869, were also responsible for setting up the Second International (or Socialist International) in 1889, as the ideas of socialism gained new adherents, especially in Central Europe, and just before his death in 1895, Engels boasted of a "single great international army of socialists".

Marxism after Marx's death in 1883 underwent qualitative changes at the hands of its followers who belonged to various schools of thought. There were true socialists who defended the central Marxian concepts like materialistic interpretation of history, the doctrine of class struggle, the inevitability of the violent revolution to establish the dictatorship of the proletariat. These socialist came to be known as revolutionary socialists in view of their commitment to the idea of revolution as a means of social and political change.

On the other hand, there were socialists who accepted Marx as their source of inspiration, but at the same time, introduced certain new ideas and interpretations in the Marxian theory so much so that Marxism lost its revolutionary character. In view of their dual loyalties to the liberal ideas of justice, liberty and non-violent social change and Marxian ideas of social and economic equality, the evolutionary socialists believed that although socialism was a superior doctrine to capitalism, the change-over to socialism should be gradual and non-violent. In other words, while the revolutionary socialists believed in the inevitability of the violent revolution as a pre-condition for setting up a dictatorship of the proletariat, democratic/liberal/evolutionary socialists put their faith in a peaceful, gradual and constitutional change aimed at the establishment of a socialist state.

The differences in the approach of these two schools of thought have been nicely summed up by Ebenstein. If the whole economic system, he writes, be compared to a basket of eggs, communism (true Marxian Socialism) burns the basket and scrambles all eggs at once—never to be unscrambled again. Democratic or evolutionary socialism keeps the basket, and cooks only small orders of scrambled eggs at one time, because it believes in Aristotle's wise counsel that the guest will judge better of a feast than the cook.

5.3.4 Charles Fourier and Robert Owen: The year 1848 is considered to be the dividing line that marks off one phase of socialism from the other. Charles Fourier (1772-1837), Robert Owen (1771-1858) etc., were the principal exponents of utopian socialism. They were not interested in political action for ushering in socialist society, nor did they appeal to class fidelity of the multitude. These early socialists scorned the politicians and politics. Through persuasion and example they wanted to convert the people to the pressing need for a new social order. Owen, for example, through demonstration of humane and just relations in his own mills, sought to inspire the people in a socialist vision. Believing that human character depended on environment, Owen wanted to replace the competitive system by a co-operative one, where justice and harmony would prevail. Significantly enough, "that a pre-Marx socialist is not necessarily a utopian, in the sense of having an understanding of the organic filaments of society, and of its associative core, is shown by Saint-Simon (1760-1825)".

5.3.5 Marx and Engels: In 1848, Marx and Engels through the publication of "Communist Manifesto" imparted a new insight to socialist theory, and sought to redefine socialism in tune with realities.

Socialist and communist theories grew out of the events and social conditions of the late 18th century and early 19th century. This was the period when the Industrial Revolution swept across Western Europe. The Industrial Revolution brought about the rapid expansion of industries through mass production. The industrialization of Western Europe, however, led to deleterious consequences as companies competed ferociously without regulation and exploited the growing class of industrial workers. As a result, the living conditions of industrial workers deteriorated substantially by the middle of the 19th century as poverty, squalor, and degradation grew.

As a political ideology, socialism rose to prominence during the 20th century Bolshevik, Leninist and later Marxist-Leninist revolutions where single-party control over the state, and by extension, over the political and economic spheres of society was justified as a means to safeguard the revolution against counter-revolutionary insurrection and foreign invasion. The Stalinist theory of socialism in one country further legitimized state-directed activity in an effort to rapidly mobilize the Soviet Union's resources to industrialize its internal economy.

The scientific theories of Marx and Engels, as well as the expectations they generated, gave rise to the formation of communist parties and to the intensification of social mobilization aimed at speeding the historical process and bringing capitalism to an end. Some mobilizations were successful in achieving and consolidating state power. Communist parties in power claimed to construct a socialist mode of production within the limits imposed by their particular historical, geopolitical, natural, and other "real" circumstances. Of significance in this regard was the success of the Russian Revolution of October 1917.

This was the first socialist revolution to succeed, and for the influence of its experimentation in construing socialism all over the world, a critical case for the assessment of the supposed advantages of socialism over capitalism. After some three years of civil war and chaos from the beginning of the Revolution, the Bolshevik party under the leadership of Lenin consolidated power and instituted a new type of socio-economic and political regime that was to highly influence world politics for some seven decades. By 1922, the distinctive features of this regime were already in place. Under the allegation that the state embodies the collective, the socialist principle of collective ownership took the form of state ownership over the most important means of production including natural resources, large-scale industry, transport, and banking. For the "rational allocation of resources", a central planning commission was established, by the state, and staffed with state personnel. The "*dictatorship of the proletariat*", a controversial concept for Marxists appearing in Marx's writings as an inevitable political feature of the transition process to the upper stage of communism, justified the legal suppression of all political parties other than the communist—as a "temporary" measure of unspecified duration.

5.3.6 Socialism and Russian Economy: Russian Revolution was followed by civil war and terror, then by the mobilization of the population to build an industrial society which led to economic growth, a full-employment economy and relatively low income differentials in the context of comprehensive state control. The state itself assumed a forceful directing role. Coercion was a consequence; it is contended, of the continuation of internal war, of the traditional lack of control over Russian rulers and of the external threat.

Socialism arose as an answer to Russian conditions and provided a form of industrialism which was an alternative to capitalism and concurrently a counter culture to it. Its distinctive features included public/state ownership rather than private, an ideological emphasis on equality rather than freedom, an economy organized on a plan, control and direction from the centre rather than through a market, and a collectivist and public form of personal integration rather than an individualist one. It is maintained that Marxism-Leninism gave rise to an *'ethic of communism'* similar in character to Weber's protestant ethic of capitalism. Socialism, as it evolved between the two World Wars, was a coherent alternative to the capitalist form of industrialization. In Almond's terms, Soviet socialism was a successful strategy of modernization.

For more than sixty years after the Russian Revolution, enough evidence could be found in the development of the Soviet Union and subsequent state socialist experiences to confirm to a considerable degree, the expectations of early socialist thinkers on the advantages of collective over private ownership, and of planned allocation over the market, for the development of the productive forces of society. While during the 1930s, western capitalist economies were struggling with the worst of their economic recessions, the economy of the Soviet Union grew at "unprecedented" rates, estimated at between 9 and 15 percent from 1928 to 1938. Soviet planners put particular emphasis on the development of heavy industry, which allowed the construction of powerful war machinery. In turn, the Soviet Union emerged victorious from WWII defeating a former industrial great power like Germany. Economic growth in the Soviet Union and the then new socialist states in Europe also compared favourably with developed capitalist economies for some thirty years in the post WWII period:

"Over the period 1950-80, the average annual rate of growth of the national income of the European Socialist countries was 7 percent, compared with 4 percent attained by the capitalist world, and the respective growth rates in industrial output were 8 percent and 5 percent. These countries' share in the world's industrial output increased from less than 10 percent in 1938 to about 30 percent in 1970, and in 1978 it was about 31 percent (but according to some Socialist estimates, it was 37 percent)".

Especially during this period, the structure of the international system was marked by the worldwide economic, military, and ideological rivalry between socialism and capitalism, symbolized by the Soviet Union and the United States as the leading forces in each camp. A symbol of both the success of socialist regimes in the development of science and technology and of the rough military parity of the two camps was the Soviet launching of the first two satellites into space in 1957. In comparison of the two systems during this span of time, socialist states often scored higher than capitalist states in terms of distributive equality, full employment, and welfare indicators such as health and education. In part as a direct consequence of the Soviet victory in War and in part because the Soviet way of development favourably impressed revolutionary governments around the world, socialism expanded considerably from the mid-1940s to 1980, reaching a hold across all geographical and cultural regions of the world. At the height of socialism in the mid-1970s, some twenty six state governments in the world claimed to be building a socialist regime. Scholars generally acknowledge that in fourteen of them a socialist regime was consolidated.

Socialism is contrasted with forms of socialism that advocate direct self-management, adhocracy and direct cooperative ownership of the means of production, such as libertarian socialism, anarchist socialism, anarchist communism, syndicalism, free-market socialism, De Leonism, internationalism and economic democracy. These forms of socialism are opposed to hierarchical technocratic socialism, scientific management and state-directed economic planning.

Socialism, which may be described as the doctrine that all the affairs of men should be managed by the government, regardless of individual choice—Marx, its founder, concluded that the only way to abolish the class monopolies was to centralize and consolidate all industrial and commercial interests, all productive and distributive agencies, in one vast monopoly in the hands of the State. The government must become a banker, manufacturer, farmer, carrier, and merchant, and in these capacities must suffer no competition. Land, tools, and all instruments of production must be wrested from individual hands, and made the property of the collectivists. To the individual can belong only the products to be consumed, not the means of producing them. A man may own his clothes and his food, but not the sewing machine which makes his shirts or the spade which digs his potatoes. Product and capital are essentially different things; the former belongs to individuals, the latter to the society. Society must seize the capital which belongs to it, by the ballot if it can, by revolution if it must.

Once in possession of it, it must administer it on the majority principle, though its organ, the State, utilize it in production and distribution, fix all prices by the amount of labour involved, and employ all the people in its workshops, farms, stores, etc. The nation must be transformed into a vast bureaucracy, and every individual into a state official. Everything must be done at the cost principle, the people having no motive to make a profit out of themselves. Individuals not being allowed to own capital, no one can employ another, or even himself. Every man will be a wage receiver, and the State the only wage payer. He who will not work for the state must starve, or, more likely, go to prison. All freedom of trade must disappear. Competition must be utterly wiped out. All industrial and commercial activity must be cantered in one vast, enormous, all-inclusive monopoly. The remedy for monopolies is monopoly.

Such was the economic programme of State socialism as adopted from Karl Marx. In the country the parties that uphold it are known as the Socialistic Labour Party, which pretends to follow Karl Marx; the Nationalists, who follow Karl Marx, filtered through Edward Bellamy; and the Christian Socialists, who follow Karl Marx, filtered through Jesus Christ.

State socialists may claim or disclaim, their system, if adopted, is doomed to end in a State religion, to the expense of which all must contribute and at the altar of which all must kneel; a State school of medicine, by whose practitioners the sick must invariably be treated; a State system of hygiene, prescribing what all must and must not eat, drink, wear, and do; a State code of morals, which will not content itself with punishing crime, but will prohibit what the majority decide to be vice; a State system of instruction, which will do away with all private schools, academies, and colleges; a State nursery, in which all children must be brought up in common at the public expense; and, finally, a State family, with an attempt at stirpiculture, or scientific breeding, in which no man and woman will be allowed to have children if the State prohibits them and no man and woman can refuse to have children if the State orders them. Thus, will authority achieve its acme and monopoly be carried to its highest power.

In Russia, workers exercised control neither over industry nor over the State. The last remnant of workers' control over production, the "Troika", was abolished in 1929. In its place, stepped the manager whose orders were to be unconditionally binding on his subordinate administrative staff and on all workers. Trade unions were stripped of all functions, and particularly their right to negotiate wages. An internal passport system was introduced into the country, and in 1930 all industrial enterprises were forbidden to employ workers who had left their former jobs without permission. Forced or slave labour was introduced on a massive scale as Stalin's terror campaign against the working class gathered momentum in the 1930s. As the Russian authorities cynically put it, "With the entry of the USSR into the period of socialism, the possibilities of using coercive measures by corrective labour have immeasurably increased".

In Russia, the state owned the means of production, but who owns the state? Certainly not the workers! The Russian state was intended, by those Marxists who made the revolution in 1917, to be a union of Soviets, or workers' councils, in which delegates were elected from the work place. All efforts to start any independent workers' initiatives, let alone workers' councils, were suppressed and rewarded with extreme forms of repression. As Kirov, Stalin's henchman accurately prophesied, "We shall be pitiless to those lacking in firmness in the factory and the villages and who fail to carry out the plan". Thousands of managers were imprisoned for not repressing their workers enough. So it takes little imagination to realise the fate of workers who went so far as to demand some measure of workers' power. Hundreds of slave labourers were shot down in 1953 for striking in protest at the failure of the authorities to carry out their promises that there would be an amnesty. The viciousness of this response is typical, and has been repeated many times before and since.

5.4 Cross-country Experiences of Socialism

The Yugoslav experience with socialism can be summed up as one long intellectual, economic, and political odyssey in search of the right combination of plan and market. Yugoslavia followed the Soviet model of socialism for only five years. Since 1950, its economic institutions differed from other state socialist experiences mainly in that the state conferred self-management rights to firms. Yugoslavian enterprises had the direct power of decision over matters that in other socialist states were directly decided by planners, such as the appointment of management positions, wages of employees, the level of employment, and the proper use of net profits. For the limited scope of planning in Yugoslavia in comparison to other socialist states, it is often said that enterprises in the country basically obeyed the laws of supply and demand, as enterprises in market economies do. And in fact the Yugoslav economy had problems common to market rather than planned economies, notably high rates of inflation and unemployment.

However, problems of planned rather than market economies such as shortages of materials and consumer goods were not alien to it. Private ownership always existed in socialist Yugoslavia, and—like in other socialist economies where it existed—it was subjected to limits unthinkable under capitalism. Up to the end of self-management in the most pro-market Yugoslavian republic in 1989, even after recurring programs of "structural adjustment" that involved relaxation in restrictions of the private sector, any company employing more than fifteen workers could not be owned privately. Foreign investors were exempted from this limitation, but their investments had to be made in the form of joint ventures with local companies in which the local companies had to hold the majority of assets.

Legal limits to private ownership such as these have long since been left behind in China and Vietnam. Since 1987, there are no more employment restrictions in the Chinese private sector and since 1988 none in the Vietnamese. Since 1986 in China and 1988 in Vietnam, wholly-owned foreign enterprises are permitted. In both countries foreign investors are *de facto* allowed to directly manage the hire, layoff, and wages of local employees, even if *de jure* restrictions to the foreign invested labour market still apply. In both countries, also, there is a legal basis for the protection of private ownership and for the functioning of a market economy. These two countries represent the second approach to market socialism.

Following the Soviet model, state socialism was instituted in China in 1949, in North Vietnam in 1945, and in 1976 it was extended to the South. In both countries, the state sector was dominant in ownership and resource allocation when the market-oriented reforms began in 1978 in China and in 1986 in Vietnam. In both the countries, economic reforms started, following the period of economic slowdown and were presented as a way to speed up economic growth. Since the process of economic reforms in both countries shows marked similarities, and since in China it began first, it is often referred to as the "Chinese path".

In both China and Vietnam, the market-oriented reforms began in the agricultural sector on a limited regional basis, and based on the experience obtained, they were extended to other sectors and regions. In both the countries, the market reforms were foreign oriented, in the sense that it sought the integration of the national to the world economy by attracting foreign investments and by promoting production for export.

In both countries, the economic reforms "bypassed" the essentials of the one party political system. In contrast to their paucity in terms of legislation and stated official policy, the reforms in both countries have paved the way for rapid growth of private enterprises and capitalist markets. In both the countries since the early 1990s, the market-oriented sector has outstripped the state sector in its share of the overall economic output.

In Poland, communism was compromised from the very beginning by its association with the erstwhile USSR, the strong opposition of the traditional intelligentsia and the Catholic Church; consequently, the communists were unable to 'penetrate society'. The position of the communist rulers was exacerbated by problems of economic management which led to a political legitimacy crisis. Whereas in Poland, communism was instigated from outside, under the influence of the Red Army, in China the communists had fought a protracted civil war in which they made a national as well as a social revolution. They secured a base among the peasants and established a popular political identity.

The leadership of Mao anticipated the degeneration of communist political leadership and provided a leftist critique of Soviet communism culminating in the great Cultural Revolution. Policy in China also had the goal of achieving modernity.

Revolution was characterized not only by the rhetoric of idealism and equalitarianism but also by corruption and during the Great leap forward, by famine. In both Poland and China, nationalism provided a focus of identity, but in different ways; in the former it was an alternative to communism which was associated with a traditionally imperialist Russia, whereas in the latter, a national liberation movement was concurrently a communist revolutionary movement. In Cuba, Castro led a national liberation movement which, in a Marxist sense, was originally bourgeois in orientation. This was gradually transformed into a Marxist-Leninist one. The Communist Party had not been at the fore of political activity, whereas the charismatic leadership of Castro and the army had played important roles. External forces, particularity hostility to the United States government precipitated Cuba into the communist bloc.

Countries like the USSR, Poland, the German Democratic Republic (GDR or East Germany), Czechoslovakia, Hungary, Bulgaria and Romania had somewhat particular experiences with the state socialism. The USSR was the dominating power, where state socialism also lasted the longest. Differences among the smaller countries were also noteworthy. Poland, with a strong Catholic Church and emergent independent labour unions, came closest to having a civil society. Hungary was the most reform-oriented country, where change came to a large degree from the ranks of the ruling political elite. Czechoslovakia's political and economic state at the onset of World War II was most comparable to that of her western neighbours. Romania's rulership most closely resembled a Stalinist system in the late phase of socialism.

Finally, the GDR was plagued by the neighbourhood of a second German state that guaranteed GDR citizens full citizenship rights. Further, West German radio and television stations reached into almost every East German living room. Yet, despite these historic differences, all of these countries shared the basic design of socialism. Their political systems were dominated by dictatorship of the proletariat, represented by the Communist party. The party monopolized the Soviet and the administration as well as the judiciary in a (sometimes lightly modified) one-party system. The economy was centrally planned and law did play a specific, but subordinate role.

5.5 Communism and Socialism in the 1990s

Communism has virtually disappeared 120 years after Karl Marx declared the imminent collapse of capitalism and is only loosely practiced in a few countries such as China, Cuba and North Korea. However, China has been slowly moving away from communism and Marxism-Leninism since the 1980s, when the Communist Party declared these doctrines did not contain all the answers to political, economic, and social problems. Furthermore, North Korea has suffered from extreme poverty and has relied on aid from non-communist countries. Hence, its days as a communist nation may be numbered. Even Cuba considered economic reforms in the 1990s to stave off its economic problems stemming from the demise of the Soviet-bloc that provided aid and was a major trading partner.

Various forms of socialism or social democracy were adopted by Western European countries such as France, Germany and Italy, which provided citizens with an array of social services. Advocates of socialism have striven to separate themselves as far as possible from communism and the communist regimes that established themselves under the name of socialism. Some have even parted ways with the principles of Marx and Engels, considering them idealistic and untenable. Instead, they focus more on practical and realizable ways of improving social and economic conditions and bringing about equality through democratic processes.

In August 1991, the last desperate attempt was made to salvage the old Soviet Union. Gorbachev, the great reformer and architect of both Glasnost and Perestroika, was deposed as President of the USSR and replaced by an eight man junta in an almost bloodless coup. Yet, within sixty hours this coup had crumbled in the face of the opposition led by Boris Yeltsin, backed by all the major Western powers. Yeltsin's triumph not only hastened the disintegration of the USSR but also confirmed US as the final victor in the Cold War that had for forty years served as the matrix of world politics.

Even 'democratic socialists' in the West, such as those on the left of the Labour Party in Britain, who rejected the 'totalitarian' methods of the Lenin and the Bolsheviks, and who sought a parliamentary road to socialism, still took from the Russian model, nationalization and centralized planning of the commanding heights of the economy as their touchstone of socialism. The question as to what extent the USSR was socialist, and as such was moving towards a communist society, was an issue that has dominated and defined socialist and communist thinking for more than three generations.

It is hardly surprising then that the fall of the USSR has thrown the left and beyond into a serious crisis. While the USSR existed in opposition—however false—to free market capitalism, and while social democracy in the West continued to advance, it was possible to assume that history was on the side of socialism.

The ideals of socialism and communism were those of progress. With the collapse of the USSR such assumptions have been turned on their head. With the victory of '*free market capitalism*' socialism is now presented as anachronistic, the notion of centralized planning of huge nationalized industries is confined to an age of dinosaurs, along with organized working class struggle. Now it is the market and liberal democracy that claim to be the future, socialism and communism are deemed dead and gone.

References

Bernard Crick (1998), "*Socialism*", World View Publications, Delhi.

Bhiku Parekh (ed.) (1976), "*The Concept of Socialism*", Ambika Publications, New Delhi.

D. Deol (1976), "*Liberalism and Marxism: An Introduction to the Study of Contemporary Politics*" Sterling Publishers Pvt. Ltd., New Delhi.

Joseph A. Schumpeter (2011), "*Capitalism, Socialism and Democracy*", Adarsh Books, New Delhi.

6

Colonialism and Decolonization

6.1 Colonialism: Meaning and Forms

Colonization and decolonization are social processes even more than they are political processes. The phenomenon of 'overseas rule' by European Powers over the people of the backward and weak countries of Asia, Africa and Latin America came to be known as colonialism and imperialism. The colonial domination by European powers in modern times began with the discoveries of sea routes of America and India. The growth of industrialization and capitalism, in the 18th and 19th centuries led to an unprecedented development in world history, as almost all the European powers of the day vied with one another to expand outside. The Portuguese and the Spanish were the first to establish their colonies overseas. Soon they were joined by other European powers like Great Britain, France and the Netherlands (Holland). In the closing quarters of the 19th century, the imperialist powers embarked on a scramble for colonies and divided the world between them. Germany, Italy, Japan and the US also joined the fray. Colonialism reached its zenith in the closing years of the 19th century, and the first decade of the 20th century.

Most of the colonies comprised '*native-coloured*' people. The 'white' colonial masters looked down upon them as uncivilized, unruly, backward and barbaric. The relationship between the colonial masters and the native people was that of domination and subjugation. The masters rationalized that it was their obligation, the 'white man's burden', to civilize the backward masses. Considering the native population as a source of cheap labour, they exploited them by inducting them into the armed forces to fight their brethren, as well as to pursue colonial aggression in newer territories. By distinguishing the 'whites' from the 'coloured' in all spheres of socio-political life, a crude and extreme form of racism was practised by the colonial rulers.

The process of decolonization started after the Second World War in most parts of Asia, Africa and South America. The European colonial powers suffered heavily during the War. Their economies being hit hard, it became a burden for them to maintain large colonial empires. The economies and political costs of maintaining colonies were too high after the Second World War. Most colonizers lost interest and granted independence to many colonies in Asia, Africa and Latin America. In some former colonies, independence came through peaceful ways, while in some other, violence accompanied independence.

Derived from Greek, the terms "*colonization*" and "*colonialism*" broadly denotes the permanent settlement of a new territory by a group of people who have moved there from their original home: a colony. Although the two terms are frequently used interchangeably, they have distinct meanings. While foreigners frequently use colonization to refer to the process of permanent settlement of a new territory, colonialism refers to political control or rule of the people of a given territories, by a foreign state. It is, thus, possible that colonization may occur without colonialism. However, in the context of modern world, "colonization" is also often used to refer to the process of establishing the colonial rule of a state over the inhabitants of other territories, whether or not significant movements of population accompany this from the country of colonizing state to its colonial territory.

Colonialism is the practise of invading other lands and territories, for the purpose of settlement and or resource exploitation. European colonialism is characterized by genocide practices, including wars of extermination, massacres of non-combatants, biological warfare, and scorched earth policies (destroying food and shelter). Other atrocities include the torture of prisoners, rape and enslavement of indigenous population. These acts are fuelled by racist and patriarchal ideology (i.e.,

Christianity and white supremacy), greed, and a psychopathic desire to kill and inflict violence and suffering on others.

When an invading force confronts an indigenous population already occupying a territory, colonialism becomes a violent conflict between two hostile and opposing ways of life, with one attempting to impose its will on the other. This is a standard definition of war, and colonization itself can be considered a war for territory involving all the means used to carry out wars: military, political, economic, psychological, diplomatic, cultural, etc. Cecil Rhodes, a British colonial official after whom, Rhodesia (now Zimbabwe) was named, articulated the motives and goals of European colonialism in the 19th century:

"We must find new lands from which we can easily obtain raw materials and at the same time exploit the cheap slave labour that is available from the natives of the colonies. The colonies would also provide a dumping ground for the surplus goods produced in our factories".

Colonialism involves a very deep socio-economic exploitive penetration of a developed civilisation into the life of a weaker and under-developed society. Colonialism is a system of domination by an alien minority by asserting racial and cultural superiority over a materially inferior native majority. It involves a system of contact between a machine-oriented, better developed, economically powerful civilisation with a backward, under-developed and poor civilisation.

"Colonialism is the occupation of virgin territories in which conflict was incidental, or even unnecessary, and subordinate to the desire of Europeans to find a new place to live" (E.M. Winslow).

"Colonialism is natural overflow of nationality; its test is the power of the colonialists to transplant the civilisation they represent to the new natural and social environment in which they find themselves" (J.A. Hobson).

However, when this does occur, it is distinguished by the term "settler colonies". For example, in the Americas, settler

Portuguese, Spanish, French, English and other Europeans established colonies in the centuries following Columbus's fateful voyage of 1942, while a permanent settler presence was insignificant in the European colonies of Asia. Africa presents examples of both settler colonies—the French in Algeria, Portuguese in Angola and Mozambique, British in Kenya and Rhodesia (now Zimbabwe), Dutch and then British in South Africa—and other colonies where the European presence was mostly limited to the agents of political rule (civil and military officials) and economic activity (merchants, plantation managers, mining engineers), who returned "home" on retirement. However, in French colonialism, colonies were thought of as part of the mother country, meaning that colonial people were granted formal rights of citizenship.

The Marxists are probably the ones to have presented the most systematic treatment of the theory of colonialism by focusing on several general issues. *Firstly*, they try to link the direct political control of non-capitalist societies with the reproductive requirements of European and American industrial capitalist economies in the 19th Century.

Secondly, they focus on the political, economic and ideological implications of industrial capitalist entry into non-capitalist societies with a view to understanding the possibility of development of socialism in both the industrial capitalist and colonized societies. This was necessary as they considered capitalism to be a pre-requisite to socialism. And *finally*, they analyse the possible consequences of socialist developments in colonial societies for socialist transformation in colonizing countries.

Colonialism has taken many different forms and has engendered diverse effects around the world. Denis Judd argues in his book, "*Empire: The British Imperial Experience from 1765 to the Present*", 'no one can doubt that the desire for profitable trade, plunder and enrichment was the primary force that led to the establishment of the imperial structure'. Judd argues that colonialism was first and foremost part of the commercial venture of the Western nations that developed from the late seventeenth and early eighteenth centuries. The seizing of 'foreign' lands for government and settlement was in part motivated by the desire to create and control markets abroad for Western goods, as well as securing the natural resources and labour power of different lands and peoples at the lowest possible cost.

Colonialism was a lucrative commercial operation, bringing wealth and riches to Western nations through the economic exploitation of others. It was pursued for economic profit, reward and riches. Hence, colonialism and capitalism share a mutually supportive relationship with each other.

Rosa Luxemburg further developed the role of colonialism in effecting capitalist penetration in non-capitalist economies thereby transforming them in capitalist economies. She posited four capitalist mechanisms for undermining natural economies or non-capitalist modes of production.

This, she argued, could be done by introduction of a commodity economy and an internal separation of trade from agriculture, or by a forcible possession of their fertile land, raw materials and labour power. She argued that only colonialism could achieve this undermining successfully which came as a last resort when all other mechanisms like trade, investment and monetization has failed to restrict the production of the natural economy.

It was the publication of Hilferding's, "Finance Capital" in 1910 that colonialism began to be viewed more specifically as the outcome of developments in a particular phase of industrial capitalist growth. Hilferding associated colonialism with the rise to dominance of finance capital and the resultant increase in the export of capital from industrial capitalist economies in the late 19th century, leading to conflicts between industrial nation states over the annexation and consolidation of conical areas. Lenin extended this further by arguing that the export of capital to colonized areas would lead to an expansion and deepening of capitalist development.

As already noted above, Lenin was highly critical of Kautsky's theory of "ultra-imperialism" and instead focused on inter-imperialist rivalry between nation states by questioning their possibilities for cooperative exploration of colonized areas. This, coupled with Lenin's belief in Marx's nations of capitalist penetration as progressive, ultimately laid the basis for one stand of the debate on colonialism in the Third International. The views of Kautsky and Bukharin on colonialism formed other strands of the debate. They were of the view that capitalist production, rather than spreading evenly through the colonial economy, would remain confined to sectors operating in the interests of the industrial capitalist economies. However, M.N. Roy, Eugene Varga and Pronin were the ones who later on, best represented Lenin's perspective on colonialism.

6.2 Decolonization: Liberation of the Oppressed

Decolonization is a widely used concept both inside and outside academic circles, but its meaning is still ambiguous and controversial. Some commentators use 'decolonization' to mean the process by which empires disintegrate and colonies achieve independence. Scholars in developing countries now often consider decolonization as a process of struggle for ending colonial rule. From this vantage point, decolonization means liberating colonies, whereas in the West it usually means granting independence.

Decolonization signifies the surrender of external political sovereignty, largely Western European, over colonized non-European people, plus the emergence of independent territories where once the West had ruled, or the transfer of power from empire to nation-state. Decolonization means the taking of measures by indigenous people and or their white overlords intended eventually to end external control over overseas colonial territories and the attempt to replace formal political rule by some new kind of relationship.

Decolonization is taken to mean the process by which former colonies or non-self-governing territories become self-governing states. We can include the independence of the United States and Haiti two centuries ago (in 1776 and in 1804) alongside the independence of St. Lucia or the Seychelles in the past two decades. *Decolonize* means to release from being a colony; to grant independence. Moritz Julius Bon (1873-1965), coined the term 'decolonization' in the 1930s.

Decolonization is the ending of colonialism and the liberation of the colonized. This requires the dismantling of the colonial government and its entire social system upon which control and exploitation are based. Decolonization, then, is a revolutionary struggle aimed at transforming the entire social system and re-establishing the sovereignty of tribal people. In political terms, this means a radical decentralization of national power (i.e. the dismantling of the nation-state) and the establishment of local autonomy (community and region, traditionally the village and tribal nation).

Decolonization, the liberation of the oppressed and colonized people, must ultimately mean the liberation of land and territory. Just as colonialism occurs in ways unique to each situation, so too does decolonization. History has many examples of the decline and collapse of imperial systems, including those of the Romans and the Union of Soviet Socialist Republics (USSR). Colonial powers were never willing to 'decolonize' (give independence to colonies); they only retreated from colonies because they were forced to do so by the national liberation movement and other forces that were opposed to colonialism. The end of the British Empire was not determined by the will of Britain, though Britain did command a certain initiative in the course of the imperial retreat. To some extent, Britain could manage how and to whom power would be transferred. In this respect, British policy-makers showed a considerable degree of flexibility and also achieved a great deal of success. Various efforts were made to contain 'radical' nationalists, and power was transferred, wherever possible, to the more 'moderate' nationalists who showed more readiness to cooperate with the colonial power.

6.3 Neo-colonialism

Neo-colonialism means a 'new colonialism'. It involves the use of state-funded Native government, businesses and organizations to indirectly control indigenous people. In Canada, for example, the government spends billions of dollars annually to maintain a system of neo-colonialism, funding band councils, aboriginal political organizations, as well as social programs, arts and culture, etc. "Neo-colonialism involves the use of natives to control their own people. In general, it means giving some of the benefits of the dominant society to a small, privileged minority, in return for their help in making sure the majority cause trouble..; the image of successful aboriginals in government [helps] create the myth that all natives have a place in the dominant society". "The change from colonialism to neo-colonialism is a change only in how the state controls the colonized people. Colonialism is a system in which the colonized people have no control over their lives economically, socially, politically, or culturally".

The power to make decisions in these important areas of daily life are almost totally in the hands of others, either the state or corporations and businesses... the state is willing to share some of the wealth of a racist system with a few natives in return for a more effective method of controlling the majority. The most threatening and effective form of neo-colonialism devised by the state has been its efforts to intervene and control popular native organizations which had been previously independent. They began with core grants to help the associations organize; then the elected leaders of the organizations got larger and larger salaries, making them dependent on the state just as the native bureaucrats in government were. As the years went by, more money was provided to organizations—money for housing, economic development service programs etc.

"The most important effect of government funding, or state intervention, is that the state, by manipulating grants, can determine to a large extent what strategy the organizations

will use. It is no coincidence that when organizations were independent of government money in the mid-sixties, they followed a militant strategy which confronted government. Now, after twenty years of grants, they are following a strategy that requires subservience to the state" (Howard Adams, "Tortured People: The Politics of Colonization").

Many scholars like Andre Gunder Frank, Samir Amin and Wallerstein tend to believe that now-colonialism brings more miseries to the poor and peripheral states of the world. Kwame Nkrumah, who in 1957 became the leader of the newly independent Ghana, expounded the idea in his book, "Neo-colonialism: The Last Stage of Imperialism" in 1965. He stated, "the essence of neo-colonialism is that the State which is subject to it, is in theory, independent and has all the outward trappings of international sovereignty. In reality, its economic system and thus its political policy is directed from outside. Neo-colonialism is also the worst form of imperialism. For those who practice it, it means power without responsibility and for those who suffer from it, it means exploitation without redress".

6.4 Anti-colonial Struggles

The 20th century has been characterised as a century of widespread democratic upsurge. The first half of the century witnessed the overthrow of colonialism in Asia and Africa because of the liberation struggles. Anti-colonial struggles in the colonies and semi-colonies gathered momentum and strength only with the rise of nationalism from the late 19th century onwards, to the growth of which foreign rule itself had no mean contribution. It developed in response to political, economic and cultural dependency and the racial humiliation to which people had been subjected by the imperialists. The break-up of the Western colonial empires in Asia, Africa and the Pacific was primarily the result of growing nationalism and the consequent revolt against the Western domination.

Two different methods were used to achieve success of anti-colonial struggles. These were: (a) peaceful non-violent method as preached and practiced by Mahatma Gandhi, using methods such as *satyagraha*, boycott, non-cooperation with the rulers and finally peaceful disobedience of anti-people laws; and (b)armed struggles with the use of force to compel the foreign rulers to give up power, end exploitation and to withdraw themselves from the colonies.

The anti-colonial movements were of two types: (i) *the national independence movement*, and (ii) *the national liberation movement*. The *first* was primarily interested in replacing the foreign governments by national governments to build a strong state thereafter; the *second* which developed relatively late, aimed at a radical restructuring of the society (socio-economic relations), while ending the exploitative alien rule. Leftist scholars call these movements' bourgeois, professional and bureaucratic movements for political change. National independent movement took place in most of the colonies; anti-colonial struggles assumed the form of the national liberation movement is such areas as Indo-China, North Africa and Portuguese colonies of Africa.

A large number of countries, including India, followed the pattern of anti-colonial struggles known as *national independence movements*. These movements were aimed at removal of the foreign rulers, and securing political independence. It was believed that the principal concern of the leadership of freedom movements was transfer of power from the imperial masters to the local people. The aim was to replace the foreign governments by national governments and to build a strong state after independence. The critics pointed out that it simply meant change of rulers. For example, in India, Sri Lanka, Nigeria, Ghana and Kenya, the objective was to throw the British out, and secure transfer of power to the local people. The national independence movements were not immediately concerned with the restructuring of colonial societies.

National liberation movements began rather late. In very few colonies, movements that were launched and carried out for independence had twin purpose. These anti-colonial struggles were aimed at liberation of the masses from exploitation and injustice. At the same time, they wanted to defeat the foreign rulers and seek power for the people and not for the elite. This, however, is doubtful if the gains actually reached the masses. Power, when transferred, went into the hands of leadership. Vietnam can be cited as an example of the liberation movement.

The Communist Party, under the leadership of Ho Chi Minh had to wage a long struggle first against the French who wanted to regain their hold, after Japanese defeat and retain it as long as they could. Later, when the US intervened on the side of South Vietnam, where a right wing government had come to power, the Ho Chi Minh regime had to fight against the Americans and South Vietnamese. At the same time, this struggle was aimed at removal of poverty, illiteracy and exploitation. The objective of the national liberation movements (or liberation struggles), as in case of Vietnam or Congo or Angola was the ending of alien rule and radical restructuring of socio-economic system.

6.5 Three Stages of Freedom Struggles

Geoffrey Barraclough has divided the struggle for independence into three stages. Barraclough mentions three schematised stages of development: (a) proto-nationalism, (b) the rise of new leadership and (c) mass movement.

6.5.1 First Stage: It was dominated by, what he calls *proto-nationalism,* which refers to the earliest period of anti-colonial struggles. During this early phase, people in the colonies had not yet become aware of their rights and the need for independence. By and large, colonial rule was accepted by the local people. Nevertheless, social groups and political movements demanded reforms within the system of colonial rule. In India, the Indian National Congress was established in 1885, but not to oust the British rulers. For the next 20 years, the Congress remained a forum of quality debates. Its sessions were annual gatherings of western-educated well-dressed English speaking elite. The then leadership believed in the superiority of British civilisation and

Englishmen's sense of justice and fair play. The early demands of the Congress were limited to local reforms, limited share in the Councils and job opportunities for educated Indians. There was no confrontation with the colonial masters. It was the stage of submitting petitions and seeking reforms. In Indonesia, the first stage began only in 1910-11 with the beginning of religious-nationalist movement called Sarekat Islam. Similar movements began in African colonies like Algeria, Nigeria etc. only around 1920.

6.5.2 Second Stage: It is identified as *the rise of new leadership,* when nationalism began to gain ground among the middle class. During this stage, the demands made on colonial powers were substantially expanded, and independence was considered, at any rate, as a future goal. In India, this stage lasted till about the time of non-cooperation movement. The social base of the Congress had expanded, yet the struggle was far from being a mass movement. Complete independence as demanded only in 1930. Till then, the aim was dominion status. In Indonesia, Sarekat Islam committed itself to independence as early as 1917; in Tunisia and Nigeria, such turning points were reached only in 1934 and 1944, respectively.

6.5.3 Third Stage: It was a nationalist movement with a mass following or a *mass movement.* National movements became so strong by this time that, in many cases, colonial rulers had to use force (often brutal force) to retain power. In India, under Mahatma Gandhi's leadership, the movement reached the common man even in the remote villages. This process began with civil disobedience movement. The movement for *purna swaraj* was a mass struggle for independence. The British used force, arrested large number of people and often sent prominent leaders to jail. In Indonesia, a comparable movement could was by Sukarno only during the Second World War. In Nigeria, the third stage was reached only in 1951.

The three stages were not equally distinct everywhere. The process extended to longest period of time in the British colonies. In many of the French colonies, it took just 10 to 20 years. In the Belgian Congo, there were hardly any demands for independence till 1955. Many local leaders then visualised a period of 60 years or longer for independence. Still, the turn of events was so fast that the Congo was free in 1960.

All the colonies did not follow any uniform pattern in their struggle against their rulers. While some of the erstwhile colonies had to wage prolonged struggles for their independence, there was some where such struggles were waged for a shorter period. In some of the colonies, hardly any struggle was waged, and independence came in the wake of then on-going decolonization. There were two main patterns of anti-colonial struggles. In some of the colonies, the struggle was limited against their colonial masters, and not against the then existing socio-economic systems. Where struggles were merely against the rulers, and not against the system, the desire was to secure transfer of political power from the colonial masters to the people of the colonies. These struggles were described as "independence movements", which merely sought transfer of political power to the people of the countries concerned.

However, where there was a fight not only against the foreign rule, but also against the existing socio-economic system which was unjust, undemocratic and supportive of exploitation; these struggles were termed as "liberation movements" or "liberation struggles". Another important aspect of freedom struggles was the methods that were employed in different countries. While in some of the countries, like India, non-violence was insisted upon as the tool of struggle, in others nations, violent means had to be adopted to achieve the desired goal of decolonization. The struggles were, therefore, either non-violent or peaceful: or agitational in nature and using force and violence as a means for the struggle. In many countries, protest against colonial rule had existed right from the time of arrival of colonial rulers. In other countries like Ghana (Gold Coast), Nigeria, the Congo, Angola, etc., such movements began much after many of the Asian countries had already become free.

Anti-imperialist nationalism emerged historically from the

urban, coastal sector where modern, capitalist forms of knowledge, technology, capital and organization had spread more widely. Although there had been several major expressions of resistance to colonial powers organized around older, indigenous political patterns, such as the mid-19th century Taiping Rebellion or the late-19th century Boxer Uprising in China, the 1857 Rebellion in India, and the Senussi Uprising in Tunisia, the successful movements of decolonization were almost invariably led by Westernized leaders from the modernized sectors of the society.

These were the would-be administrators and entrepreneurs who felt a very concrete ceiling over their heads, and educated Chinese who bristled at the signs declaring 'Dogs and Chinese not allowed' posted in public places in the foreign settlements in Shanghai and elsewhere. These were people who experienced constant denial and humiliation because of their colour or origin, but they were also people who, like Mahatma Gandhi, clearly recognized the contradictions these actions presented to the Western doctrines of humanism and rationality. Finally, they were the people who understood the modern world well enough to know how to mobilize the resources to topple colonial domination.

6.6 Process of Decolonization

The decolonization of the European colonies in Africa and Asia was perhaps the most important historical process of the 20th century. Within less than two decades, from 1945 to the mid-1960s, several colonial empires disappeared and scores of new nations became independent. Altogether, it had taken more than three centuries to expand and consolidate these empires.

During the fifteen years or so after World War II, a wave of newly independent countries swept across Asia and Africa. Both the scope and speed of the dismantling of the European colonial empires were unforeseen. Several historical developments came together to bring about such a speedy decolonization process. The

War itself caused strains on the European colonial powers, which led them to lose grip on their overseas empires. Some of them had lost their colonies during the War and found it difficult to restore control over them afterwards, while others were so depleted economically by the War that they might viewed the maintenance of a colonial empire too great a burden to carry with. Another factor might have been the emergence of educated elite among the natives of the colonies who commanded political power locally and who sought independence for their homeland. Finally, the post-WW II restoration of freedom and self-rule in Europe certainly strengthened the pursuit of similar goals in Europe's colonies.

The decolonization process operates at four levels. *First*, an independent government with full power within the boundaries of the colony is created. The colonial power will no longer control the political structure of the colony. New elite takes over. *Second*, the provision of public goods and government services is decided and managed by the new government. The colonial power will no longer bear the cost of running the colony. *Third*, new social and economic institutions are eventually created, aiming at the establishment of political rights and at improving the levels of economic and social well-being of the population. *Fourth,* there may be a process of incorporating culturally distinct groups in the community, including non-native settlers and different native population groups. This process can be a violent one due to one group's attempt to dominate others.

There was no one process of decolonization. In some areas, it was peaceful, and orderly. In many others, independence was achieved only after a protracted revolution. A few newly independent countries acquired stable governments almost immediately; others were ruled by dictators or military juntas for decades, or endured long civil wars. Some European governments welcomed a new relationship with their former colonies; others contested decolonization militarily. The process of decolonization coincided with the new Cold War between the Soviet Union and the United States, and with the early development of the new

United Nations. Decolonization was often affected by superpower competition, and had a definite impact on the evolution of that competition.

The United Nations Special Committee on Decolonization has stated that in the process of decolonization, there is no alternative to the colonizer's allowance of self-determination but in practice, decolonization may involve either non-violent revolution or national liberation wars by the native population. It may be intramural or involve the intervention of foreign powers acting individually or through international bodies such as the United Nations. Although examples of decolonization can be found as early as the writings of Thucydides, there have been several particularly active periods of decolonization in modern times.

These are the break-up of the Spanish Empire in the 19th century; of the German, Austro-Hungarian, Ottoman, and Russian Empires following World War I; of the British, French, Dutch, and Italian colonial empires following World War II; of the Russian Empire following the Cold War and others.

The creation of so many new countries, some of which occupied strategic locations, others of which possessed significant natural resources, and most of which were desperately poor, altered the composition of the United Nations and political complexity of every region of the globe. In the mid to late 19th century, the European powers colonized much of Africa and Southeast Asia.

During the decades of imperialism, the industrializing powers of Europe viewed the African and Asian continents as reservoirs of raw materials, labour, and territory for future settlement. In most cases, however, significant development and European settlement in these colonies was sporadic. However, the colonies were exploited, sometimes brutally, for natural and labour resources, and sometimes even for military conscripts.

6.7 Decolonization in Asia

Decolonization in Asia was the process whereby formerly

colonized territories discarded their colonial controls and influences. Some of these territories assumed new forms of governance and often borrowed extensively from their colonial experience. Others retreated into the past to revive age-old forms of governance that predated colonial rule. The process of decolonization thus involved considerable change, and this change was peaceful, gradual, ugly, or violent depending on the circumstances. Colonialism got liquidated in phases and stages. It began in Asia and then moved on to Africa. The decolonization of Asia was the gradual growth of independence movements in the Asian continent, leading ultimately to the retreat of foreign powers and the creation of a number of nation-states in the region. A number of events were catalysts for this shift, most importantly, the Second World War. The first state to be decolonized was Indonesia in 1945, and the last was Macau in 1999.

Post-war decolonization began in Asia and the Middle East and then spread to other parts of the world. The late 1940s saw a number of countries emerging. These included the Philippines (1946), India and Pakistan (1947), North and South Korea (1948), Myanmar (1948), Ceylon (1948), Indonesia (1949) and Indo-China (Vietnam, Laos and Cambodia) which became independent from the French colonizers in the 1950s. Middle East experienced struggle for independence with the expulsion of the French from Syria in 1946. Iraq could also free itself from the British masters only with the ouster of King Faisal II in a nationalist revolution in 1958.

In 1947, India was set free, though into two sovereign countries, namely, India and Pakistan. With the independence of India, "the floodgates were opened for the non-white colonies", as its Gandhian mass movement had been a source of inspiration for freedom movements in all countries of Asia and Africa. Mahatma Gandhi used non-violent direct action, *satyagraha*—as a technique for struggle which won acclaim for him for the pioneering role it played in sharpening and hastening the process of dismantling the classical forms of colonialism and imperialism.

In 1946, the Philippines got independent and became a sovereign state. In Vietnam, the struggle against the Japanese provided the stage on which previous enemies could coalesce around a common cause. Thus, the Chinese nationalist wartime government collaborated with the Vietnamese communist leader, Ho Chi Minh (1890-1969), to fight the Japanese. On September 2, 1945, Ho Chi Minh pro-claimed the Democratic Republic of Vietnam (DRV) in Hanoi.

By early 1946, with the withdrawal of the Chinese occupation forces from northern Vietnam, Ho was left in undisputed control except in the south, where the French army returned in strength. It only remained to resist any further consolidation of the French, and this began with the Battle of Dien Bien Phu (1954) where the Vietnam achieved a decisive victory over the French-led army. This was followed by peace negotiations in Geneva that led to the division of Vietnam into north and south along the Seventeenth Parallel. The peace was short lived. Massive migrations took place as anti-communists fled to south to escape from the communists who now controlled the government in Hanoi. Meanwhile, American interests were further involved as the United States took on the job of fighting communism worldwide. It was only in 1975 that American troops were finally defeated and forced to leave, ignobly.

The decolonization process in Malaya (Malaysia) can be easily contrasted with the earlier period of colonial rule by the occurrence of near anarchy. As happened in other states in Southeast Asia, the weakness of British authority was revealed under the Japanese occupation in Malaya. The Malayan Communist Party (MCP), led mainly by Chinese cadres, launched a revolt in 1948 to prevent the restoration of British rule, after the Japanese surrendered.

This revolt, the so-called Emergency, lasted twelve years. It compelled the British to consider granting independence to Malaya earlier than was scheduled in order to counter the MCP propaganda that the British would only leave if forced to do so. It compelled the Malay elites to adopt multiracial political strategies to confront the communal threat of the MCP, consisting as it did mainly of Chinese followers. The outcome was the establishment of a federation of Malay States and the colonies of Penang and Melaka in 1948, with privileges entrenched for the indigenous Malays and citizenship extended to other immigrant races. The Federation of Malaya subsequently attained independence in 1957.

In the Philippines, plans for decolonization were already firmly in place by 1910. American colonial rule in the first decade of the 20th century operated on the assumption that a tutelage process was necessary to train Filipinos in the art of democratic government. The Philippines was the most important colony of the US, which had acquired it after the US-Spanish War in 1898. President Franklin D. Roosevelt, who was anti-colonial in approach, had promise independence to the Philippines as early as 1935. But events in Europe leading to the Second World War stalled the American initiative in this regard. But, the US belief in the principle of self-determination was in conflict with the continuation of the American colonial possessions and the latter had come in for criticism and charged with sticking to 'imperialism' by the Soviet Bloc. Thus, it was only in 1946, that the Philippines finally became independent.

6.8 Decolonization in Africa

After World War II, went quickly the process of decolonization in Africa. In Africa, the year 1960 saw the release of the maximum number of colonies. Most of them were French colonies and trust territories of the United Nations which had been under the French administration: Cameroon, Togo, Malagasy Republic, Congo (formerly French Congo), Dahomey, Upper Volta, Ivory Coast, Chad, Central African Republic, Gabon, Mauritania, Niger, Senegal and Mali. Independence was proclaimed by the largest country in Africa by population— Nigeria, belonging to the UK, and the largest in the territory— the

Belgian Congo. British Somaliland and Somalia Trust, operated by Italy, were merged and became the Somali Democratic Republic.

1960s changed the whole situation in the African continent. Dismantling the remaining colonial regimes was already looming. Sovereign states were declared in 1961, which included, the British ruled Sierra Leone, and Tanganyika, in 1962—Uganda, Burundi and Rwanda, in 1963—Kenya and Zanzibar, in 1964—Northern Rhodesia, which called itself the Republic of Zambia (under the name of the Zambezi River), and Nyasaland (Malawi). In the same year, Tanganyika and Zanzibar merged, creating a Republic of Tanzania. In 1965, The Gambia and in 1966, the Republic of Botswana, Bechuanaland and Basutolanda and the Kingdom of Lesotho became independent. In 1968, Mauritius, Equatorial Guinea and Swaziland and in 1973, Guinea-Bissau, also became independent. In 1975, after the revolution, countries which regained the independence of its ownership included Angola, Mozambique, Cape Verde, Comoros, Sao Tome and Principe and in 1977, the Seychelles and Somalia. In 1980, Southern Rhodesia—Republic of Zimbabwe and in 1990, the Trust Territory of South West Africa—Republic of Namibia also became free.

The only large colony that had to wait till the late 1980s to get independence was Southern Rhodesia. In 1965, the white minority government in this British colony led by Ian Smith declared the country's independence. This was apparently done to avoid power going into the hands of black majority. The Western countries had to apply strong political economic pressures on the minority government as nationalists did in Zimbabwe in 1979-80. Namibia, the former German colony in South Western Africa, was made a mandate territory under the union of South Africa in 1919. Namibians waged a bitter struggle for their independence. Finally, it achieved independence in 1990, in which the UN had played a prominent role. The proclamation of the independence of Kenya, Zimbabwe, Angola, Mozambique and Namibia, was preceded by war, insurrection and guerrilla warfare. But for most African countries, the final step of the way was passed without major bloodshed; it was the result of mass demonstrations and strikes, negotiations, and in respect of the Trust Territories—decisions of the United Nations.

6.9 Decolonization in Latin America

In Latin America, national feelings grew strong in the Spanish colonies. This happened because of the unhappy relationship between the Creoles or the American-born Spaniards and the European Spaniards. The first to champion the cause of Latin American freedom was the Venezuelan Creole, Francisco de Miranda (1750-1816). Owing to his great activity, a revolutionary congress deposed the governor and established the independence of Venezuela in 1811. The next patriot to lead Latin America to freedom was Simon Bolivar (1783-1830). He won a decisive victory against the Spaniards in 1819, and became the President of New Granada and Venezuela. He lent a helping hand to the people of Ecuador, Peru and Bolivia. The revolutionaries were successful, and the Spaniards were driven out by 1825.

He was called the Washington of South America. However the most capable leader of Latin America was San Martin (1778-1850) who played a great part in liberating Chile and Peru. Patriotic movements started in Mexico in 1810, and Mexico gained independence by 1821. A new era in the relations between the US and Latin America started during the presidency of Woodrow Wilson. In March 1913, he declared that one of the chief objectives of his administration would be to cultivate friendship and to deserve the confidence of the republics to the South. Wilson adopted the policy of "watchful waiting" and left Mexico to the solution of its own problems.

The policy of collaboration and co-operation with the Latin American states, inaugurated during Wilson's Presidency, has been continued by later administrations. President Roosevelt followed it and termed it the "Good

Neighbour" policy. In 1915, growing collaboration among the American states expressed its opinions in the meeting of a Pan-American Financial Conference at Washington and in the conclusion of an arbitration treaty by Argentina, Chile and Brazil. In 1916, commissions dealt with the problems of improved telegraph and railway communications and the elaboration of a uniform commercial law. A Pan-American Conference of 1923 made provisions for fact-finding commissions in cases of disputes. This work was elaborated at a conference in Washington in 1929, and continued in conferences in 1933, 1936 and 1938.

A declaration was made in 1938. It expressed the determination of the American states (North, South and Central) to protect them against foreign activities that might threaten them. This understanding between the American continents was exemplified when a number of Latin American countries declared war on the Axis powers, after Japan attacked the US in December 1941. Intimate and neighbourly association between the US and the Latin American countries continued. It was expressed in economic accords, providing for beneficial trade in raw materials, in the providing of financial aid and technical skill, and in the interchange of social and cultural interests and activities. The solidarity of the Pan-American nations was reaffirmed by the Western Hemisphere Defence Treaty, signed at Rio de Janeiro in 1947.

In recent years, the US has attempted to collaborate in the economic development of the countries of Latin America. The Inter-American Development Bank was established in January 1960 with a capital of US dollars 1,000 million, of which US dollars 450 million were subscribed by the US. In March 1961, President Kennedy created the Peace Corps on a temporary basis, through an executive order. Many US citizens volunteered to move to Latin American countries in order to help in their development programs. The Inter-American Social Progress Trust Fund was raised in June 1961, to carry out President Kennedy's "Alliance for Progress" program and

US dollars 600 million were provided as American aid to Latin American countries. An important development in the relationship between the US and the Latin American countries was the signing of the Panama Canal Treaty. This was signed by President Jimmy Carter in 1977. The US had gained control of the Canal Zone in 1903 and this treaty ensured that Panama could reclaim the Panama Canal on December 31, 1999.

To conclude, the end of Second World War witnessed a complete change in the international scenario. Not only did the globe witness a tussle between the capitalist world, led by the United States and communist bloc led by the Soviet Union, but also there were major upheavals in the third world. There was a continuous struggle for liberation from the colonial masters to seek political as well as economic independence from the European imperialist powers. Leaders of opposition to colonial rule before 1945 faced formidable obstacles in mobilizing support, large enough to frighten their well-armed white rulers, who could show remarkable determination and ruthlessness in putting down often ill-coordinated risings. White supremacy was to prove much more difficult to sustain in a post-1945 world dominated by superpowers America and Russia, as weakened European powers determined to recover pre-War colonial authority discovered to their cost before the Cold War intervened.

References

Ania Loomba (2005), "*Colonialism/Post-colonialism*", London; New York: Routledge.

B. Waites (1999), "*Europe and the Third World, c.1500-1998: From Colonization to Decolonization*", Basingstoke: Macmillan.

G. Thorn (2000), "*End of Empires: European Decolonisation: 1919-1980*", London: Hodder and Stoughton.

M.E. Chamberlain (1999), "*Decolonization: The Fall of the European Empires*", Malden, MA: Blackwell Publishers.

P. Duara (ed.) (2004), "*Decolonization: Perspectives from Now and Then*", London; New York: Routledge.

Partha Chatterjee (1993), "*The Nation and Its Fragments: Colonial and Post-colonial Histories*", Princeton: Princeton University Press.

Raymond E. Dumett (ed.) (1999), "*Gentlemanly Capitalism and British Imperialism: The New Debate on Empire*", Longman.

7

Constitutional Developments in Britain, Brazil, Nigeria and China

7.1 Introduction

A constitution is an act of the people if it is made by them either directly in a referendum or through a convention or constituent assembly popularly elected for this specific purpose, subject or not to formal ratification by the people in a referendum. The constitution of a State is that collection of rules and principles according to which a state is governed. In other words, the Constitution refers to the framework or the composition of a government, the structure with regards to its organs, how power is allocated and the process by which power is exercised. The criterion which served as the basis for assigning political powers reflects the ethos of a given society. Nevertheless, it is conventional for the present day constitutions to reflect the composition of government and the relationships among these institutions. Second, a constitution should provide for the distribution of governmental power over the nation's territory. Third, and more importantly, a constitution should provide a compendium of fundamental rights and duties of citizens including their rights to participate in the institutions of government.

A constitution is a mode of organizing a state and its government; a body of fundamental principles according to which a state is organized. Constitution in the wider context is the means by which people organize themselves into a political community and define the aims and objectives of its association, the condition of membership, the organs and powers necessary for the conduct of the affairs of the association and the duties and responsibilities of those organs to the individual members.

Constitutions are designed to set out the rules and regulations within which governments operate. They establish the composition, powers and functions of the institutions of the state, regulate the relations between these institutions, and enshrine the legal rights and duties of the citizenry. An important distinction can be drawn between codified and uncodified constitutions. Codified constitutions are largely written, centred around a single document, incorporating key constitutional provisions that are binding on all political institutions.

7.2 Britain

Great Britain is a constitutional monarchy. The constitution exists in no one document but is a centuries-old accumulation of statutes, judicial decisions, usage, and tradition. The development of a constitution is structured chronologically around eight "landmark" moments within British constitutional history, from the Glorious Revolution of 1688 to the Devolution Settlement of 1998. In addition to these events, it also focuses on the union between England and Scotland in 1707, the ascendancy of Robert Walpole as the Crown's first minister in 1721, the Great Reform Act of 1832, the Parliament Act of 1911, ratification of the European Convention in 1953 and the UK joining the European Community in 1972. Each of the main chapters pivots around an analysis of one of these events. In addition, other related developments are given consideration. For example, the chapter on the Great Reform Act also examines the later expansion of the franchise during the nineteenth and twentieth centuries.

Similarly, the ratification of the European Convention deals briefly with the later passage of the Human Rights Act in 1998 "incorporating" Convention rights in the UK law. This structure focuses on particular periods when constitutional issues were at the fore of British politics whilst also achieving a broadly comprehensive overview of the country's constitutional development. The British constitution is often described as an 'unwritten constitution', but it is best described as 'partly written and wholly un-codified'. The three institutional powers in the British constitution are, according to the *separation of powers* theory, the executive (Government: the administration that runs the country); the legislature (Parliament: the institution of law-making); and the judiciary (judges: the adjudicators in disputes). Of the three institutional powers, constitutional theorists have identified Parliament as being the supreme law-making body. Parliament can make, or unmake, any laws that it wants. This is the theory of parliamentary sovereignty. The constitution has evolved over time, with two main strands of historical development: *first,* the changing relationship between the monarchy, executive and the Parliament; and, *second,* the landmark reforms that have extended rights and liberties and delimited constitutional powers.

The hereditary monarch, who must belong to the Church of England according to the Act of Settlement of 1701, is almost entirely limited to exercising ceremonial functions as the head of state. Sovereignty rests in Parliament, which consists of the House of Commons, the House of Lords, and the crown. Effective power resides in the Commons, whose 646 members are elected from single-member constituencies. The executive—the cabinet of ministers headed by the prime minister, who is the head of government—is usually drawn from the party holding the most seats in the House of Commons; the monarch usually asks the leader of the majority party to be the prime minister.

Historically, the hereditary and life peers of the realm, high officials of the Church of England, and the lords of appeal (who exercise judicial functions) had the right to sit in the House of Lords, but in 1999 both houses voted to strip most hereditary peers of their right to sit and vote in the chamber. Most legislation originates in the Commons. The House of Lords may take a part in shaping legislation, but it cannot permanently block a bill passed by the Commons, and it has no authority over money bills. The crown need not assent to all legislation, but assent has not been withheld since 1707.

The British Constitution is a product of a long process of evolution. The present mechanism and functioning of government in Britain can only be understood if we analyse the process of this growth. Generally speaking, the process of development of the British Constitution can be broadly divided into six main periods, which are discussed below.

7.2.1 Anglo-Saxon Period (400-1066): The first period to which the growth of English political institutions could be traced is that of Saxon settlement. The Saxon rule continued till 1066 when William of Normandy conquered England. During this period, England was a loose aggregation of tribal Commonwealths comprising seven Kingdoms: East Anglia, Merica, Nothumberland, Kent, Sussex, Essex and Wessex. In the ninth century, Wessex established its sovereignty over all other "Kingdoms" which were absorbed into a larger territory. In the process, the institution of Kingship—a single sovereign—was born. Besides kingship, the institution of local government was another important contribution of the Anglo-Saxon period. During this period, the majority of the population lived in small villages. Each village formed a township and was a unit of local government. The local government machinery consisted of a town assembly with certain elective officers.

7.2.2 Norman Period (1066-1154): The Norman conquest of England in 1066 marked a new development in the growth of the British Constitution. The major development of the Norman period was the growth in the royal power. The king ruled with the help of the Great Council or Magnum Concilium—a body consisting of royal officers, church dignitaries and other leading men of the kingdom. To help the king carry on the government during the interval when the Great Council was not in session, another small body called Curia Regis or Little Council emerged out of the former. The British Parliament arose out of the plenary sessions of the Great Council. Likewise, the Privy Council (and the Cabinet), the Exchequer (treasury) and the High Court of Justice grew out of the Curia.

7.2.3 Angevin or Plantagenet Period (1154-1485): The political institutions established by William, were revived by Henry II who founded the Plantagenet dynasty. During the Plantagenet period, the powers of the Parliament increased. In 1341, the Parliament got King Edward I to agree to the following matters:

- The King will not levy any tax without the approval of the Parliament.
- The Parliament may appoint a Commissioner to audit the accounts.
- The Ministers will be appointed by the Parliament.
- The Ministers will resign before the commencement of the session and reply to any charge levelled against them.

The Parliament also acquired the right to dethrone a King. As a matter of fact, in 1327, Edward II was made to leave the throne. As for constitutional landmarks, the Magna Carta of 1215, signed by King John and the major feudal landowners, is still seen as a reference point for the protection of civil liberties. It required that every man accused of a crime should be given a fair trial and be judged by his peers, and that the legal system be free of bribery and corruption. These principles are of continuing relevance today. The right to a fair trial, for example, is now explicitly protected in law under the Human Rights Act, 1998, a very recent landmark in the development of the British constitution. This Act brings many of the rights and freedoms laid down in the European Convention on Human Rights into English law.

7.2.4 Tudor Period (1485-1603): The period from 1485 to 1603 is known as the Tudor period. The constitutional history of this period is the "history of consolidation of the governmental system". The Tudor monarchs concentrated wide powers in their hands and thereby strengthened the influence of Kingship. Thus, Parliament, though it survived, did not place serious obstacles in the way of royal despotism.

However, Queen Elizabeth (1558-1603) did consult the Parliament frequently and accepted its judgment on many important occasions.

7.2.5 Stuart Period (1603-1714): After the death of Elizabeth, the throne of England passed to her cousin James I (1566-1625). However, he soon came into conflict with the Parliament. This was because he believed in the divine right of Kings and laid undue stress upon the royal powers and prerogatives. During the reign of Charles I (1625-1649), the conflict between the King and the Parliament developed into a civil war. Charles I was put on trial and executed. The Kingship and the House of Lords were abolished. The Parliament formally proclaimed England a "*Commonwealth*" or Republic in 1649. A written Constitution, known as the "*Instrument of Government*", was adopted and Oliver Cromwell (1653-1658) was named Lord Protector. However, the Protector ran into trouble with the Parliament and his new Constitution failed.

After the death of Cromwell, monarchy was restored in England with the crowning of Charles II, the third Stuart. He tried to make a compromise between the royal authority and parliamentary supremacy. However, his successor, James II, soon after this ascension to the throne, quarrelled with Parliament over the right to exercise his right to suspend the operation of certain laws and tried to rule arbitrarily. Ultimately, the conflict between the King and the Parliament led to the "*Glorious Revolution*" of 1688 which saw the overthrowing of King James II (1685-1688). King William III (William of Orange) agreed to a *'bill of rights'* for the protection of individual rights and liberties and parliamentary dominance over the monarchy was declared. After 1688, Parliament continued to gain power at the monarch's expense, to the extent that the monarch is today a largely ceremonial figure with very limited powers. The events of 1688-89 established the outlines of the English Constitution. Britain became a constitutional monarchy. Parliament established its supremacy over the actual powers of the Monarchy. Till date, this basic structure of the British constitutional system remains intact.

Other notable developments in history include the Act of Settlement 1701, which provided judges with freedom from interference by the other constitutional powers; and the widening of public participation in the political process, with the extension of certain voting rights to men in the nineteenth century and to women in the first half of the twentieth century, thus creating, over time, a parliamentary democracy.

7.2.6 Hanover Period (1714-1837): The Glorious Revolution of 1688 prepared the ground for redefining the powers of the King and the Parliament. In February 1689, during the reign of the Hanover dynasty, the Parliament passed the Bill of Rights which is one of the most important documents in English constitutional history. It proclaimed the legislative supremacy of Parliament and restricted the powers of the Monarch. The Monarch could neither veto any particular law passed by Parliament nor delay its enforcement. He could no longer levy or raise any tax or make royal appointments or maintain a standing army during peacetime without the approval of the Parliament.

7.2.7 Present Constitution: The Status Quo: The United Kingdom of Great Britain and Northern Ireland consists of four countries: England, Northern Ireland, Scotland and Wales. Legislative competence for the UK resides in the Westminster Parliament, but there are three legal systems (England and Wales, Northern Ireland, and Scotland) with separate courts and legal professions.

The United Kingdom is a constitutional monarchy with a bicameral parliament composed of the Houses of Commons and Lords. Formally, executive power is vested in the Crown in the person of the Sovereign, but in reality, central government is carried out in the name of the Crown by ministers of state. The powers of the Sovereign and the Crown derive either from Acts of Parliament or are prerogative (recognized in common law). There is no formal separation of the powers of the legislature and executive and while legislative authority is vested in the Sovereign in Parliament, ministers responsible for implementing new acts are also involved in the process of legislation. Similarly, in the House of Lords, the Lords who sit as judges in the Appellate Committee can also take part in the legislative business of the upper house.

Table 7.1: Development of the British Constitution

Changing Relationship between the Monarchy, Executive and the Parliament	Landmark Reforms Extending Rights and Freedoms and Setting the Boundaries of Constitutional Powers
- Kings and Queens have absolute power up to 17th century. - English Civil War takes place, in which Parliament stands up to the monarchy. - Glorious revolution of 1688, following the civil war, gave Parliament dominance over the monarchy. - Since 1688, Parliament has gained power at the monarchy's expense. - Parliament develops procedures to keep executive governance in check.	- Magna Carta 1215: first real attempt to set out constitutional powers and give rights and freedoms to citizens. - Act of Settlement 1701: provided for judicial independence from the other constitutional powers. - Extension of voting rights (19th/20th centuries): led to parliamentary democracy. - UK joins the European Community in 1973 and therefore becomes subject to European Community law.

However, perhaps the most significant constitutional development of all has been the UK's participation as a Member State of the European Community (EC) (now European Union, or EU) since 1973. This has meant that the British constitution is subject to the exercise of powers and processes by a further set of institutions. EC law, which describes the law developed by the institutions of the European Union, is superior to English law, and there is little doubt that when the UK joined the EC, it gave away aspects of its own parliamentary sovereignty. A constitutional question that remains contentious is whether the UK can, in any circumstances, withdraw from the European Union.

It is often suggested informally, that the United Kingdom does not have a written constitution. This is not strictly true, but what it does not have is a single document setting out the legal framework and functions of the organs of government and the rules by which it should operate. Such documents are a declaration of a country's supreme law and have overriding legal force to empower a constitutional court to declare acts of the legislature illegal if they conflict with the rights embodied in such a formal constitution. In this, the UK currently differs from most other countries, for instance, the United States, Ireland, Germany, France and South Africa.

The constitution of the United Kingdom, in contrast, is a "whole system of government...(with a)...collection of rules which establish and regulate or govern the government". The system is based on a combination of "Acts of Parliament and judicial decisions...political practice…and detailed procedures established by various organs of government for carrying out their own tasks". Examples of the latter are "the law and custom of Parliament" and the "rules issued by the Prime Minister to regulate the conduct of ministers". In effect, Parliament has the right to modify the Constitution of the United Kingdom on the basis of simple majorities in the two Houses of Parliament.

The constitutional status quo in the UK has resulted in a very flexible system, in which governance depends on political and democratic principles rather than a rigid system that relies on legal rules and safeguards. This can be construed as both strength and a weakness, but for reform it has several important consequences. For example, there are no special procedures for proceeding with new constitutional arrangements, and all such acts must pass through the Westminster Parliament in the normal legislative manner. In addition, no truly federal arrangement can be established within the United Kingdom while the Westminster Parliament remains supreme: it currently retains the right to revoke power recently devolved to Northern Ireland, Scotland and Wales. There are numerous items of legislation from medieval to modern times that have affected the constitution, and a few can be singled out as particularly significant.

Magna Carta, granted by John in 1215, with the current version approved by the English Parliament granted by Edward I (1297). It established that punishment should be by judgment of one's peers or the law of the land, and that justice cannot be denied to an individual.

Table 7.2: Constitutional Reforms in Britain since the 1990s

Conservative Government (1990-1997) Publication of Ministerial Code (1992); Intelligence Services Act 1994; Promulgation of Civil Service Code (1997)
Labour Government (1997-2010) Devolution (1997 onwards); Human Rights Act, 1998; Freedom of Information Act, 2000; Constitutional Reform Act, 2005; Constitutional Reform and Governance Act, 2010
Coalition Government (2010-) Parliamentary Voting System and Constituencies Act, 2011; Fixed-term Parliaments Bill; European Union Bill; Production of Cabinet Manual

7.2.8 Constitutional and Administrative Law Reforms in Britain since 1997: The first Blair administration came into power on May 1, 1997 pledged to undertake the most radical shift in constitutional arrangements, broadly conceived, for a century. For the most part it has been as good as its word, even if its critics still clamour for more. It included a commitment to a Human Rights Act, to a Freedom of Information Act, for devolution to Wales, Scotland and Greater London, and to reform of the House of Lords. In addition, it has moved forward on devolution to the English regions, to reform of the House of Commons, to civil service reforms, to electoral and party regulation as well as a sea change in the way local government is run. Taken together, these achievements have seriously altered the constitutional map and, for the most part, the changes are irreversible, regardless of the colour of any succeeding government.

Although the Labour party has long had a predisposition towards constitutional reforms (both the Crown Proceedings Act, 1947 and Parliament Act, 1949 were products of this policy), the current major constitutional changes and proposals have their seeds in 1989 and 1993 party policy documents. Immediately on assuming office in 1997, the New Labour government established various review committees and initiated proposals covering a wide range of constitutional matters, in addition to reconsidering policies formulated for the election campaign. These included:

- Electoral reform and, in particular, the voting system for Westminster elections (Jenkins Commission, 1998).
- Electoral law and administration (Howarth Committee, 1998).
- Modernisation of the House of Commons (Select Committee, 1997-98).
- Reform of the House of Lords (Joint Committee, 2001).
- Introduction of a Bill of Rights (Consultation Paper 1996).
- Introduction of a Freedom of Information Act (Joint Consultative Committee, 1997).
- Consideration of English regional government (Labour Party Policy Paper, 1996).
- Creation of a Ministry of Justice (Labour Party Policy Document, 1995), and devolution to Scotland and Wales (White Paper, 1997).
- Plans were also announced for a revitalisation of the government's policy making capacity and capabilities (White Paper, 1999).

Many of these "bold and ambitious" initiatives resulted in a surge of important constitutional legislations early in Labour's first parliamentary session including:

- Scotland Act, 1998.
- Government of Wales Act, 1998.

- Northern Ireland Act, 1998.
- Human Rights Act, 1998.
- Regional Development Agencies Act, 1998.
- European Parliamentary Election Act, 1999.
- Bank of England Act, 1998.
- Registration of Political Parties Act, 1998.
- Greater London Authority Referendum Act, 1998.
- White Paper 1997 on freedom of information, and reform of local government (White Paper, 1999).

7.3 Brazil

With its more than 200 million inhabitants, Brazil has the largest population in Latin America and ranks fifth in the world. The majority of people live in the south-central area, which includes the industrial cities of Sao Paulo, Rio de Janeiro and Belo Horizonte. Brazil is a federal republic with 26 states and a federal district. The 1988 Constitution grants broad powers to the federal government, made up of executive, legislative, and judicial branches. The president holds office for 4 years, with the right to re-election for an additional 4-year term, and appoints the cabinet. There are 81 senators, three for each state and the Federal District, and 513 deputies. Senate terms are 8 years, staggered so that two-thirds of the upper house is up for election at one time and one-third 4 years later. Chamber terms are 4 years, with elections based on a complex system of proportional representation by states. Each state is eligible for a minimum of eight seats; the largest state delegation (Sao Paulo's) is capped at 70 seats. This system is weighted in favour of geographically large but sparsely populated states. Several political parties are represented in Congress. Since representatives to the lower house might switch parties, the proportion of congressional seats held by particular parties can change.

Brazil proceeded cautiously down the European path in the nineteenth century, tending to follow a "North European" (English-Swedish) rather than a "Latin" (French-Spanish) pattern. Under the Empire (1822-1889), the extent and significance of suffrage constituted exceedingly modest advances over the absolutistic structure of government during Brazil's subordination to Portugal (1500-1822). During the colonial period, the only elected officials in Brazil had been members of community councils and local judges, except for an extraordinary Cortes for which Brazil chose representatives at the end of the era (1821). With Brazilian independence in 1822, came new demands by the planter elite for a larger measure of representative government, and the Constitution of 1824 ("freely granted" by Emperor Pedro I) added a national parliament to the *municipio* councils.

Brazilian constitutionalism, however, was more apparent than real; although the Parliament was loosely modelled after Britain's, in fact the system more closely resembled absolutism than constitutional monarchy because of the extensive powers of the Emperor to intervene in all important matters of policy and personnel. Specific provisions of the Constitution of 1824 reveal how limited Pedro's belief in democracy really was: the Emperor himself appointed the ministers of state and presidents of the provinces; though Parliament had the power of the purse, he also could veto legislation and dissolve the Chamber of Deputies at will. In addition, the Emperor named bishops, magistrates, and ambassadors, and possessed the authority to make war and peace.

The Brazilian Constitution of February 24, 1891, the first to be promulgated after the proclamation of the Republic on November 15, 1889, remained in force for forty-three years. Dr. Getulio Vargas, during his fifteen years as President, promulgated two substitutes: the *first*, drafted by a Constituent Assembly elected in May 1933, was proclaimed on July 16 of the following year; the *second*, dated November 10, 1937, was drawn up, in complete disregard of the 1934 Constitution, by Dr. Getulio and his Ministers when he was preparing to close the Senate and Chamber of Deputies. It is a typical product of the dictatorship, repugnant to any democratic Government.

The present Constitution was drafted by the Constituent Assembly elected in December 1945, after the Dictator had been deposed, and was promulgated on September 18, 1946. The Constitution of 1891 was a concise, liberal document of ninety-one clauses, which established the form of government and the principles on which it was founded, leaving the details to be evolved by future administrations. It was based on the Constitution of the United States of North America, the States being empowered to legislate on all matters not pertaining exclusively to the federal Government. The legislative power was vested in a National Congress, composed of Senate and Chamber of Deputies. The latter was made up of one Deputy for every 70,000 inhabitants in each State and in the federal district, elected for a term of three years. The Senate was composed of three representatives from each State and the federal district, elected for nine years, one-third retiring every three years and being replaced by the elected substitute. Elections were on the basis of universal suffrage for all citizens over twenty-one, registered in accordance with the law and not disqualified for specified reasons, such as illiteracy.

In 1967, the executive power over the legislative and judiciary, yet again weakened federalism through the political and administrative centralization that was regarded as indispensable in addressing alleged threats to national security. The decentralizing tendency of the transition to democracy in Brazil was the adoption of the 1988 Constitution. After 1985, under civilian rule, democratic leaders decided that the constitution then in force (the 1967 Constitution, as amended in 1969), which had been the child of authoritarianism, should be replaced by a new, truly democratic charter. Thus, the1988 Constitution incorporated a number of provisions designed to act as safeguards against a possible return to authoritarianism.

Three of the new constitutional features must be singled out for their subsequent political and economic effects. The *first* was the reinforcement of the power of the National Congress vis-à-vis the federal executive. A *second* was the decentralization of federally collected funds to state governments (fiscal federalism). A *third* feature was the adoption of a detailed bill of rights, together with provisions that gave autonomy to the judicial branch and to public prosecutors. A more robust federalism, a reinvigorated political life in the legislature, and the so-called *judicialization of politics* were relevant consequences of these developments.

7.4 Nigeria

Nigeria is a federal republic in West Africa. With an estimated population of about 173 million people, Nigeria is the most populous country in Africa. The political system of Nigeria has undergone various changes over the last few decades. During the past few years, the country witnessed political tumult aided by military coup at different stages which destabilized the stability of the country. Historical evidences indicate that during 11th century, the vast land of Nigeria was inhabited by different tribesman and later this diversification culminated into the formation and rise of popular kingdoms. Most importantly, the north-eastern part of Nigeria was ruled over by Borno, the Hausa city-state kingdoms of Katsina, Kano, Zaria, and Gobir in the northern-central Nigeria, the Yoruba city-states/kingdoms of Ife, Oyo, and Ijebu in south-western Nigeria, the southern kingdom of Benin, and the Igbo communities of eastern Nigeria were all placed under different reigns at different times. From the second half of the 19th century to 20th century, the British took over the administrative, political and military charges of the country thereby leading to great political upheavals. Finally, after years of hard struggle, the country achieved independence in the year 1960 on October 1.

Nigeria is a federal republic with a presidential system. The constitution provides for a separation of powers among the three branches of government. General elections held in February 1999 marked the end of 15 years of military rule and the beginning of civilian rule based on a multi-party democracy. General elections were held for the second consecutive time in April 2003. In both elections, President Olusegun Obasanjo and his party, the People's Democratic Party (PDP), were victorious. Despite the consolidation of democratic rule following years of military dictatorship, some feared that in the absence of a clear successor, the incumbent president might seek to amend the constitution so that he could run for a third term in 2007.

7.4.1 Constitutional Development: Right from the colonial period, Nigerians were barely involved in the art of constitution making while the British colonial overlords employed constitution making to consolidate their imperial strategies. Post-colonial Nigerian leaders have utilized constitution drafting to ensure regime longevity. Independent Nigeria has so far experimented with five constitutions, the 1960, 1963, 1979, 1989 and 1999 Constitutions (The 1989 Constitution was not promulgated). Nigeria's current constitution, the fourth since independence, went into effect on May 29, 1999. The 1999 Constitution has given birth to the Fourth Republic, though with problems for which it faces demands for a revision or amendment. The first two of these constitutions were drawn up during civilian regimes while the last three were made or promulgated during military regimes.

The current 1999 Constitution is a product of haste because the receding military junta was in a hurry to leave the political turf. Consequently, the 1999 Constitution has all the trappings of military centralization of power resulting in de-federalization of Nigeria and the consequent clamour and agitation for the amendment of the constitution. Modelled after the US Constitution, it provides for a separation of powers among a strong executive, an elected legislature, and an independent judiciary. Critics of the Constitution complain that the federal government retains too much power at the expense of the states. Although the Constitution proclaims personal freedom and a secular state, it also permits Muslims to follow *sharia*, or Islamic law.

It is on record that until now, eight constitutions have been operated in Nigeria. It began with the Sir Frederick Lugard's Amalgamation Report of the 1914.Thereafter, there were the Sir Clifford Constitution (1922); Sir Arthur Richards Constitution (1945); Sir John Macpherson Constitution (1951), Oliver Littleton's Constitution (1954), the Independence Constitution (1960); the Republican Constitution (1963) and the 1979 Constitution (1979). There was another draft Constitution in 1989 prepared during the regime of former President Ibrahim Babangida. This was never tried until General Sanni Abacha's administration brought about the 1994-95 constitutional Conference, which laid the foundations for the 1999 Constitution.

- The Clifford Constitution, which was introduced by Sir Hugh Clifford in 1922, replaced both the Legislative Council of 1862 which was subsequently enlarged in 1914, and the Nigerian Council of 1914. Under the Constitution, a Legislative Council was for the first time established for the whole of Nigeria, which was styled as, *The Legislative Council of Nigeria*. One feature of Clifford's Constitution was that only Africans with minimum gross income of US$ 100 a year were eligible to vote and be voted for.
- When Sir Richards became the governor of the colony of Nigeria, he initiated moves to draft a new constitution. In March 1945, through a Sessional Paper Number 4, the Chief Secretary to the government, Sir General Whitely, initiated a motion in the Legislative Council which was passed unanimously in the House. This motion for a new constitution gave birth to the Richards Constitution. In this Constitution, there was one Legislature for the whole of Nigeria. It also made provisions for three delineated provinces, viz. North, West and East. There was an overwhelming African majority, but were not to be elected in the provinces and the Central Legislative House.
- In 1948, Sir Macpherson became the Governor of Nigeria and decided to fashion out a new Constitution. It represented a major advance from the pre-existing constitutional

provisions because it introduced majorities in the Central Legislature and the Regional Houses of Assembly.

- The Macpherson Constitution was set aside and replaced by the Littleton Constitution, which laid the foundation for a classical Federation for Nigeria. The component units of Nigeria were *"separate yet united"* in their sub-economies, civil service, legislature and public services.
- The constitutional evolution of Nigeria which started in concrete terms with the Clifford's constitution of 1922, climaxed with the enactment of the 1960 Independence Constitution. Its provisions were the presence of the office of Governor General who was the non-political head of State, while the prime minister was the head of government.
- In 1963, the Republican Constitution did not change this position but merely removed the constitutional umbilical cord binding Nigeria to Britain.
- Within six years of Independence, the Constitution had failed, basically due to the cracks that had started appearing within its first two years. One of the factors that led to the collapse of the first republic was the nature of political authority within the State. The President, who was constitutionally, the chief executive usually, exercised his powers on the advice of the prime minister and his cabinet members. The Westminster model could not fit into African society where "the leader wants to assert his authorities without restraint".
- One fundamental innovation in the 1979 Constitution was the primacy given to federal character principle aimed at national integration and equitable representation of all the ethnic groups.
- In 1989, an attempt was also made by General Ibrahim Babangida administration to draft a constitution for the country. Indeed, a constitution was drafted for Nigeria.
- The Constitutional conference, which produced the 1999 Constitution, was inaugurated in 1994 in the wake of the

turmoil that greeted the annulment of the June 12, 1993 Presidential election. Some members of the conference were "elected" one-third of the members of the conference. The 1999 Draft Constitution was signed into Law on May 5, 1999. In the present 1999 Constitution of the Federal Republic of Nigeria, separation of powers is a fundamental constitutional principle. Relevant sections of the Constitution place each of the basic powers of government in a separate branch. Thus, while Sections 4 and 5 deal with the legislative and executive powers respectively, Section 6 is concerned with the judicial powers.

7.5 China

China is one of the countries with the longest history in the world. The people of all nationalities in China have jointly created a splendid culture and have a glorious revolutionary tradition. Feudal China was gradually reduced after 1840 to a semi-colonial and semi-feudal country. The Chinese people waged wave upon wave of heroic struggles for national independence and liberation and for democracy and freedom. Great and earth-shaking historical changes have taken place in China in the 20th century. The Revolution of 1911, led by Dr. Sun Yat-sen, abolished the feudal monarchy and gave birth to the Republic of China. But the Chinese people had yet to fulfil their historical task of overthrowing imperialism and feudalism. After waging hard, protracted and tortuous struggles, armed and otherwise, the Chinese people of all nationalities led by the Communist Party of China with Chairman Mao Zedong as its leader ultimately, in 1949, overthrew the rule of imperialism, feudalism and bureaucrat capitalism, won the great victory of the new-democratic revolution and founded the People's Republic of China. Thereupon, the Chinese people took state power into their own hands and became masters of the country.

China is a unitary and socialist state whose constitution calls on the nation to "*concentrate on socialist modernization by following the road of building socialism with Chinese characteristics"* while adhering to the "leadership of the Chinese Communist Party (CCP) and the guidance of Marxism-Leninism, Mao Zedong Thought and Deng Xiaoping Theory" as well as "the important thought of the Three Represents", which are attributed to former CCP general secretary and president of China Jiang Zemin. The political system is led by the 86.7 million-member CCP. Political processes are guided by the CCP constitution and, increasingly, by the state constitution, both promulgated in 1982. The CCP constitution was revised in 2002, and the state constitution was amended in 1988, 1993, 1999 and 2004. Both constitutions stress the principle of democratic centralism, under which the representative organs of both party and state are elected by lower bodies, and they in turn elect their administrative arms at corresponding levels. Within representative and executive bodies, the minority must abide by decisions of the majority; lower bodies obey orders of higher-level organs. In theory, the National Party Congress is the highest organ of party power, but the real power lies in the CCP Central Committee and its even more exclusive Political Bureau.

7.5.1 Constitutional Developments: The Provisional Constitution of the Republic of China was drawn up in March 1912 and formed the basic government document of the Republic of China until 1928. It provided a Western-style parliamentary system headed by the weak president. However, the system was quickly usurped when Song Jiaoren, who as leader of the KMT (Kuomintang) was to become prime minister following the party's victory in the 1913 elections, was assassinated under the orders of President Yuan Shikai. Yuan regularly flouted the elected assembly and assumed dictatorial powers. Upon his death, China disintegrated into warlordism and the Beiyang Government operating under the Constitution remained in the hands of various military leaders.

The Kuomintang under Chiang Kai-shek established control over much of China by 1928. The Nationalist Government promulgated the Provisional Constitution of the Political Tutelage Period in 1931. Under this document, the government operated under a one-party system with supreme power held by the National Congress of the Kuomintang and effective power held by the Central Executive Committee of the Kuomintang. In Leninist fashion, it permitted a system of dual party-state committees to form the basis of government. The KMT intended this Constitution to remain in effect until the country had been pacified and the people sufficiently "educated" to participate in a democratic government.

The current Constitution traces its origins to the end of the Second Sino-Japanese War when the impending outbreak of the Chinese Civil War pressured Chiang Kai-shek into enacting a democratic Constitution that would put an end to KMT Party rule. The Chinese Communists sought a coalition, made of one-third Nationalists, one-third Communists, and one-third of members from other parties, to form a coalition government that would draft the new Constitution. However, Chiang Kai-shek refused to relinquish power and insisted on having the Nationalist Government draft the Constitution and then holding nation-wide elections in which the Communists would be permitted to participate.

Unable to resolve the impasse, the KMT-drafted Constitution was adopted by the National Assembly on December 25, 1946, promulgated by the National Government on January 1, 1947, and went into effect on December 25, 1947. The Constitution was seen as the third and final stage of Kuomintang reconstruction of China. The Communists though invited to the convention that drafted it, boycotted and declared after the ratification that not only would it not recognize the ROC constitution, but all bills passed by the Nationalist administration would be disregarded as well. Zhou Enlai challenged the legitimacy of the National Assembly in 1947 by accusing KMT of hand-picking members of the National Assembly 10 years earlier and thus could not have legal representation of the Chinese people.

7.5.2 Constitution of the Republic of China (1947): The Republic of China (ROC) Constitution was adopted on

December 25, 1946, by the National Constituent Assembly meeting, convened in Nanking. It was promulgated by the National Government on January 1, 1947, and put into effect on December 25 of the same year. In addition to the preamble, the Constitution comprises 175 Articles in 14 chapters. In essence, the Constitution embodies the ideal of "sovereignty of the people", guarantees human rights and freedoms, provides for a central government with five branches and a local self-government system, ensures a balanced division of powers between the central and local governments, and stipulates fundamental national policies.

The 1982 Constitution is essentially a Dengist constitution, reflecting Deng Xiaoping's ideas for modernising China, i.e., social stability, economic development and opening to the outside world. It is also a result of the constant, and sometimes painful, search for China's own version of socialism. It made its tentative move towards liberalisation, politically and economically, while insisting on firm control by the Party. Thus, the Preamble both upholds the so-called "Four Fundamental Principles" and emphasises the construction of socialist modernisation as a fundamental national task. Article 18 of the Constitution formally provides a constitutional basis for foreign investment and its protection in China. Article 11 of the Constitution allows the development, within the limits prescribed by law, of an individual economy as a complement to the socialist economy. Article 10, for the first time in the PRC's constitution, defines the ownership of land in China. Although hailed as "the best since the founding of the PRC", the 1982 Constitution was soon amended in April 1988, to legitimise the existence of the rapidly developing private economy as well as to provide a constitutional basis for the commercial transfer of land use rights, both of which were the results of economic reform and pre-requisites for further economic development.

- 1954 constitution was based on the constitution of the Soviet Union.

- 1975 constitution of the PRC was modelled on the ideology of the Cultural Revolution. This constitution subjected the NPC to the Communist Party and removed previous constitutional protections such as equality under the law and private property succession rights.
- 1978 constitution moved away from the ideologies of the Cultural Revolution, it did retain some remnants of it. It also retained Communist Party control over the state structure.
- 1982 constitution shifted to economic construction and modernization. This Constitution also contains more extensive rights than any of the previous constitution.
- The current constitution was adopted at the Fifth Session of the fifth National People's Congress on December 4, 1982.

Since then, the Constitution has been amended 4 times, respectively in 1998, 1993, 1999 and 2004.

Further, ideologically significant revision was necessitated by the adoption by the Party at its Fourteenth Congress of the notion of a "socialist market economy" in 1992. So not long after the Central Committee of the CPC formally submitted its "Suggestions on Amending Certain Contents of the Constitution", the NPC dutifully adopted the suggestions and translated the new Party policy into law in March 1993. As a result of the revision, the term "socialist market economy" then replaced that of "planned economy". The terms "state-run (guoying) economy" and "state-run enterprises" replaced by "state-owned (guoyou) economy" and "state-owned enterprises" respectively. Similarly, provisions on state planning were removed and in their place were put provisions that require the state to strengthen economic legislation and macroeconomic control. On the whole, the 1993 amendment provides flexibility, though not specific direction, for future development.

The Fifteenth Party Congress in 1997 laid down certain political foundations for post-Deng China, which adopted a policy to continue the reform policy launched by Deng

Xiaoping in 1979 and to incorporate a Dengist version of socialism into the Constitution. Once again, efforts took place to transform the Party policy into constitutional provisions through constitutional revision. The revision was undertaken by a Revision Group of the Central Committee of the Party, headed by Li Peng. Since its first draft, issued on December 5, 1998 for internal Party discussion, the drafting work went swiftly. By January 22, 1999, a formal proposal had already been made by the Party to the Standing Committee for consideration and adoption.

The six amendments in 1999 fall into three categories: further supplementation to the Four Fundamental Principles, a Chinese version of the "Rule of Law", and a politico-economic version of "socialism with Chinese characteristics". On the whole, the 1999 revision of the Constitution was essentially designed to carry out the conversion of the adopted ideology of the Fifteenth Party Congress of 1997 into the form of fundamental state law, that is, to convert the will of the Party into that of the state. The revision reflects the Party's determination to continue the reforms and opening-up and to administer the country according to law. Examined from a development perspective, such revision indicates the then understanding of the notion of socialism with Chinese characteristics among the Party leadership.

The First Plenary Session of the Sixteenth Party Congress (2002) began the change-over of Party leadership, which continued until the First Plenary Session of the Tenth National People's Congress in 2003. These congresses saw the partial handover of leadership power from Jiang Zemin to Hu Jintao. So, the Sixteenth Party Congress was to sum up the Party's experience (or to record its achievements) in the previous five years and to set out a policy direction for the new leadership. Not surprisingly, the policy "spirit" as adopted by the Sixteenth Party Congress would need to be incorporated into the Constitution; hence a new round of constitutional revision. As early as on March 27, 2003, a Constitutional Revision

Group headed by Wu Bangguo (the new Chairman of the Standing Committee of the NPC) and under the direct leadership of the Standing Committee of the Politburo of the Party, was established.

At the same time, the principles for the revision were also set down by the Standing Committee of the Politburo. Official consultation was swiftly conducted in the next several months within limited circles of authorities and personnel, such as of provincial leaders, leaders of the democratic parties, and selected groups of local leaders and prominent scholars. The draft suggestion on amending certain contents of the Constitution was soon taking shape by August 2003. It is at this time that the ongoing revision was first officially reported. It should be pointed out that even though this was the first formal announcement of the ongoing revision of the Constitution, there was no mention of such a Group, even though it was said that the plenary session would discuss the proposals for constitutional reform. As was the previous practice, the recommendations were dutifully and faithfully adopted by the NPC, making itself once again a rubber stamp of the Party. Sadly, this practice was patently undemocratic: If the people have no right to participate in such fundamentally important political matters, it is perhaps unrealistic, if not insulting, to tell the people that they enjoy democracy and the rule of law.

Even though the ongoing revision was not officially reported until August 2003, the Chinese media began to break the news unofficially around June 2003. It was clear that Chinese scholars were consulted at a rather early stage, and certainly no later than June 2003. Not surprisingly, academics began to express a wide range of views and opinions, suggesting far reaching revisions to the Constitution, and academic symposiums devoted to the revision were also organised, the most notable convened in Qingdao City, and in Shanghai, both in June 2003 and both of which were attended by prominent scholars consulted by the Politburo on the revision, such as Professors Jiang Ping and Wu Jinlian. However, enthusiasm among academics was quickly dampened. A secret instruction was soon issued by the Party to stop all conferences and publication of academic papers on constitutional reform, and leading economists and legal scholars actively involved in presenting their views were reported to have been harassed by the security forces. Thus, contrary to the assertion by the Chinese authorities that the revision of the Constitution was carried out on a democratic basis with wide consultations; consultations were only conducted within the strictly limited circles of the authorities and the elite.

Nevertheless, the drafting went swiftly. By mid-October 2003, the Suggestions on Amending Certain Contents of the Constitution had been adopted by the Third Session of the Central Committee of the Sixteenth Party Congress, which also decided to pass the Suggestions to the Standing Committee of the NPC to be converted into a constitutional amendment bill in accordance with the constitutional procedures. As usual, the Standing Committee of the NPC dutifully did so at its Sixth Meeting of the Tenth NPC held during December 22-27, 2003. Also on December 22, 2003, the Suggestions on Amending Certain Contents of the Constitution were, for the first time, published in full in the Chinese media. Theoretically, the Amendment Bill finally adopted by the full NPC on March 14, 2004 was no longer a Party document, but a formal legislative bill, except that the Bill was a verbatim copy of the Suggestions. As such, the revision started in late March 2003 and completed in mid-October of the same year was another world record.

Similar to the 1999 revision, the present revision was designed to incorporate policy decisions made at the Sixteenth Party Congress in 2002, including the adoption of the "Three Represents" idea, along with the "Four Fundamental Principles" and Deng Xiaoping's Theory, as guiding principles of the Party. It was meant to be a partial, not comprehensive, revision. It was expressly decided that only the matters that must be regulated by the Constitution and only the provisions that must be revised immediately would be dealt with by the revision. Other matters, though desirable for revision, would be clarified later by constitutional interpretations, rather than by the present revision. In other words, the present revision was little more than an implementation of the Party policies as adopted at the Sixteenth Party Congress in 2002. The various amendments fell into five categories: the adoption of a new guiding principle for the Constitution, an explicit recognition of human rights, further protection for private property, a more civilian-type approach to a state of emergency and some technical revisions.

References

B.O. Nwabueze (1982), "*A Constitutional History of Nigeria*", C. Hurst & Co. Publishers Ltd., UK.

Gary W. Wynia (1990), "*The Politics of Latin American Development*", Cambridge University Press, US.

Hyginus Banko Okibe (2000), "*Political Evolution and Constitutional Development in Nigeria, 1861-1999*", Marydan Publishers.

Julianon Zaiden Benin (2010), "*On the Limits of Constitutional Adjudication: Deconstructing Balancing and Judicial Activism*", London: Springer Heidelberg Dordrecht.

Kamilu Sain Fage and David Oluwatoba Alabi (2003), "*Political and Constitutional Development in Nigeria*", Northern Printers Ltd., UK.

Raoul Blindenbacher and Abigail Ostien (ed.) (2005), "*Dialogues on Distribution of Power and Responsibilities in Federal Countries*", McGill-Queen's University Press, Canada.

8

Political Economy of Britain, Brazil, Nigeria and China

8.1 Introduction

Political economy refers to the distribution of political and economic power in a given society and how that influences the directions of development and policies that bear on them. Political economy is the study of the role of economic processes in shaping society and history. Political economy (particularly when the word "radical" is added as an adjective) has come to be closely associated with the work of economists who adopted key concepts developed by Marx, in particular, his focus on class processes or relationships, but who rejected the economic determinism of orthodox versions of Marxian theory.

Thus, political economy makes extensive and intensive use of class analysis in making sense of society and history, but does so in the context of political, cultural and environmental processes, as well as other economic processes.

Political economy can be defined as the actual relationship between political and economic institutions in a particular country, as well as the policies and outcomes they create. Political economy assumed the definition of the study of economies of polities or nation states in the 18th century. Gradually, the concept of the physiocrats that land was the source of all wealth, was superimposed by the labour theory of value supported by John Locke, Adam Smith and Karl Marx. Notably, political economy incorporates liberal, realist, Marxian and constructivist theories from political science. Starting from the 19th century, "economics" or the study of the economy replicated the term "political economy". The latest version of the term i.e. International Political Economy (IPE), among other things, studies the effect of domestic monetary and fiscal policies on international trade and finance in relation to a specific country.

8.2 Britain

UK is one of the world's most globalised countries. London is the world's largest financial centre alongside New York and has the largest city GDP in Europe. Free trade had been the pillar of British political economy since the repeal of the Com Laws in 1846 and withstood the international drift towards neo-mercantilism in the late 19th century. Joseph Chamberlain's tariff reform crusade in 1903 put the future of free trade once again at the centre of British politics. In the 18th century, the UK was the first country in the world to industrialise, and during the 19th century, possessed a dominant role in the global economy. From the late 19th century, the Second Industrial Revolution in the United States and the German Empire presented an increasing challenge to Britain's role as leader of the global economy.

In the 1945 general election, just after the War's end, the Labour Party was elected, introducing sweeping reforms in the British economy. Taxes were increased, industries were nationalised, and a welfare state with national health, pensions, and social security was created. The coming years saw some of the most rapid growth Britain had ever experienced, recovering from the devastation of the Second World War and then expanding rapidly past the previous size of the economy. By 1959, tax cuts had helped boost living standards and allow for a stronger economy and low unemployment rates.

By the end of the 1960s, this growth began to slow and unemployment was rising again. During the 1970s, Britain suffered a long running period of relative economic malaise, dogged by severe inflation, strikes and union power as well as inflation, with neither the Conservative government of 1970-1974 (led by Edward Heath) nor the Labour government which succeeded it (led by Harold Wilson and from 1976 James

Callaghan) being able to halt the country's economic decline. Unemployment exceeded 1,000,000 by 1972 and had risen even higher by the time the end of the decade was in sight. This led to the election of Margaret Thatcher, who cut back on the government's role in the economy and weakened the power of the trade unions.

Margaret Thatcher blamed the weakened economy on the socialist policies set in place by the government after World War II. Her policies were further influenced by a distinct movement left by the Labour Party that gave a great deal of power to labour unions. In response, she privatized business and industry, cut back on social welfare programs, strengthened national defence, got tough with the labour unions, and returned to market force controls on the economy. She was a controversial prime minister for eleven years. Her supporters believed her to be the capable and firm "Iron Lady", but her critics felt that her policies made economic problems worse and that her personality further divided the country. Thatcher resigned office in 1990 when other Conservative Party leaders challenged her leadership.

After the jolts of the economic crisis of the 1970s and Margaret Thatcher's firm redirection of the political system to the right, moderation again became characteristic of political change in Britain. Thatcher's hand-picked successor, John Major, at first followed her policies, but later moderating them by abolishing Thatcher's poll tax, reconciling with the European Union, and slowing social cutbacks and privatization. The Conservative Party retained the majority in the 1993 parliamentary elections, but only by a very slim margin. Then, in 1997, Labour's gradual return in the centre was rewarded with the election of Tony Blair, who promised to create a "New Labour" Party and rule in a "third way" a centrist alternative to the old Labour Party on the left and the Conservative Party on the right.

The problem was that the labour movement was floundering in the ideological vacuum left by New Labour party. It has neither the alliances across civil society nor the political agency to secure a new radical electoral agenda. It lacked a story that defined what it stood for. Market fundamentalism—with its belief in self-regulating markets and a minimal state, and its narrow view of human beings as rational economic actors—may be fantasy. But it remained the only story of economic life on offer. The task for Labour now was to offer voters a different story; to outline a vision for the economy different from what was on offer just before the crash. The answer it comes up with will determine its future. The answer was not self-evident. Labour had not only lost an election; it had also lost people's trust. Between 1997 and 2010, it lost 1.6 million lower-income voters and 2.8 million middle-income voters—mostly people who had gained very little from Labour's economic boom.

In government, Labour bowed to the interests of the City. It failed to protect the security of its citizens because it did not regulate the dangerous activity of the financial markets. It allowed the housing bubble to grow and personal debt to balloon—as a means of covering up for the huge gulf that was growing between the small wealthy elite and the rest. The British had wealth and record growth—but it was unsustainable and mostly benefited the rich. Too many people had to borrow to keep up their standard of living. Society looked prosperous but below the surface a lot of people were frantically paddling to stay afloat. Many were at risk of sinking. The UK was in recession for the first time since 1991, official government figures had confirmed. The latter decades of the 20th century had seen an increase in service-providers and a drop in industry, combined with privatisation of some sections of the economy. This change led some to describe this as a 'Third Industrial Revolution', though this term was not widely used.

The world changed on the day that Lehman Brothers went bust. Thirty years of neo-liberalism came to an end in the month of mayhem that followed in the world's financial markets. Things will never be the same again, after the collective and decisive action taken by finance ministries and central banks from the G20 countries to prevent the Great

Recession in the winter of 2008 becoming a second Great Depression. During August 2008, the IMF warned that the UK economic outlook had worsened due to a twin shock: financial turmoil as well as rising commodity prices.

Gross domestic product fell by 1.5 percent in the last three months of 2008 after a 0.6 percent drop in the previous quarter. That means that the widely accepted definition of a recession—two consecutive quarters of negative economic growth—had been met. It represented the biggest quarter-on-quarter decline since 1980 and a 1.8 percent slide on the same quarter a year ago. The worse-than-expected contraction sent sterling to a 24-year low against the dollar, with one pound buying US$ 1.355. Meanwhile, the FTSE 100 index fell almost 2 percent, below 4,000 points.

Growth since then has been patchy, held back by weak credit growth, a contraction in real incomes, and the poor economic outlook in the U.K.'s major trading partners. The U.K. economy contracted on a quarterly basis in the final quarter of 2010 and the final quarter of 2011. In response to the financial crisis, the British Government implemented a wide-ranging stability and recovery plan that included a fiscal stimulus package, bank recapitalization, and credit stimulus schemes. Extraordinary monetary policy measures, including very low interest rates (0.5 percent) and a quantitative easing program (£ 325 billion), remain in place. Despite this, domestic demand remained weak and unemployment was yet to return to pre-recession levels, standing at 8.4 percent in November 2011. The Conservative-Liberal Democrat coalition government that took power in May 2010 initiated a planned 5-year austerity program, which aimed to lower the U.K.'s budget deficit from over 11 percent of GDP in 2010 to near 1 percent by 2015. Poorer than expected growth meant that the coalition's budget deficit plans would only be met in 2016-17.

8.3 Brazil

From the 1930s to the mid-1970s, Brazil was one of the

fastest growing economies in the world. Since then, average growth rates have been below par and highly volatile as the country successively failed to regain the previous level of performance. Economic globalization was largely a result of the decline of the world economic conditions which prevailed during the Cold War era. During this era, efforts were made to maintain peace, as well as to liberalize trade through GATT negotiations, though with limited results, and to sustain a regime of virtually fixed exchange rates worldwide, buttressed by financial assistance provided by the International Monetary Fund (IMF) to governments facing balance-of-payments difficulties. Many countries in the world had adjusted to these new world economic conditions. In Brazil, however, transitions were slow, and matters came to a breakpoint with the onset of three-digit inflation in the 1980s. Indeed, while most Latin American countries had adopted pro-market reforms by the early 1990s, the sluggishness of the Brazilian reaction to globalization has been largely attributed to the "stickiness" of existing state structures and the historically embedded ideas and practices prevalent in the policy-making process.

The year 1930 was indeed a landmark in Brazilian history, for it brought a radical shift from local-oligarchic to national-populist politics when President Getulio Vargas came to power. It was under Vargas and subsequent governments that the so-called "developmentalist model" of policy-making was instituted in Brazil. This model lasted for many decades and facilitated economic growth led by industrial production boosted by import substitution. With some simplifications, the duration of this "model" can be divided into five broad periods:

- The period of transition from decentralized oligarchy to political centralization (1930-37);
- The period of civil dictatorship (1937-45);
- The "populist-democratic" period (1946-64);
- The period of military dictatorship (1964-85); and

- The period of transitional reforms (1986 to the present).

With respect to economic policy orientations, the "developmentalist model" was characterized by:

1. The active role of the state in the promotion of economic growth through rapid industrialization.
2. A protectionist trade policy.
3. The creation of regulatory and financial (official credit) state structures,
4. The direct participation of the state in production through the creation of public sector enterprises.

Another institutional feature also developed and grew in importance after the 1960s. This was the political use by the federal executive of macroeconomic management and its distributive impacts. This can be called the "political use of economic policy", which in the Brazilian case took the form of "economic populism". The "political use of economic policy" is in a sense the result of the policy-induced social experience of variations in economic production and consumption, which may be combined with the plebiscitarian legitimation of the power of the president.

During the military regime (1964-84), economic populism employed three major policy mechanisms: monetary correction from 1964, small exchange-rate devaluations from 1967, and tax exemptions. These were "automatic devices" in economic policy-making that were able to avert political crises during the period of military dictatorship by suppressing the direct adversarial procedures typical of political competition.

The comeback of democracy in 1985 could have been just another 'turn of the wheel', another moment in a cyclical pattern in which civilian and military governments alternated in power while essentially keeping the same policy-making model (the 'developmentalist model'). A second experience of 'democratic populism' in line with the 'developmentalist model' could have been yet another turn in the cycle of Brazilian politics. The difference came as a result of the combination of:

1. Institutional reforms introduced in the process of rebuilding

the Brazilian democratic regime, especially a revitalized federalism which reinstituted adversarial procedures as part of the decision-making process, thus rendering "economic populism" less manageable;

2. The emergence of a richer "interest pluralism" in Brazilian society, given the massive growth of the urban population during the decades of rapid industrialization; and
3. The shift from "economic populism" to "economic pragmatism" under Cardoso's Plano Real, with the brief, but decisive interregnum of Fernando Collor de Mello's "plebiscitarian liberalism".

In 1989, Fernando Collor de Mello (1990-92) was chosen as the second civilian president (and the first chosen by direct popular vote) since the transition to democracy in 1985. Collor established a much more ambitious privatization program, which was intended to "reduce public deficit, increase the efficiency of the state, and to promote the democratization of capital, as well as the modernization and competitiveness of the economy". The trade liberalization reforms were adopted without internal political negotiations with the Brazilian Congress or interest groups, and also without external political negotiation in multilateral bodies that could have provided needed economic opportunities for Brazilian interests. Collor's strategy was seen as a radical move that instituted broad liberalization but without gaining a corresponding tangible advantage from foreign competitors, including the US.

On October 3, 1994 Fernando Henrique Cardoso was elected President with 54 percent of the votes. Cardoso took office January 1, 1995, and pursued a program of ambitious economic reforms. He was re-elected in 1998 for a second 4-year term. LuizInacio Lula da Silva, commonly known as Lula, was elected president in 2002, after his fourth campaign for the office. He was re-elected in 2006 for a second 4-year term. President Lula, a former union leader, was Brazil's first working-class president.

In office, he took a prudent fiscal path; warning that social reforms would take years and that Brazil had no alternative but to maintain tight fiscal austerity policies. The Brazilian economy's solid performance during the 2008 financial crisis and its strong and early recovery, including 2010 growth of 7.5 percent, contributed to the country's transition from a regional to a global power. Brazil is the world's seventh-largest and is expected to rise to fifth within the next several years. During the administration of former President Lula, surging exports, economic growth, and social programs helped lift tens of millions of Brazilians out of poverty.

In October 2010, Brazil held its sixth consecutive presidential and general elections since the reinstatement of democracy in 1985. Dilma Vana Rousseff, the Workers' Party (PT) candidate, won a runoff election against the Brazilian Social Democratic Party candidate, becoming the first woman president of Brazil.

Rousseff took office on January 1, 2011 and has prioritized growth with equity policies to eradicate poverty and fiscal austerity. President Dilma Rousseff has indicated her intention to continue the former president's economic policies, including sound fiscal management, inflation control, and a floating exchange rate.

Low unemployment and strong domestic demand pushed 12-month inflation to 7.3 percent through the first three quarters of 2011, above the upper limit of the government's target of 2.5-6.5 percent. Brazil is generally open to and encourages foreign investment. It is the largest recipient of foreign direct investment (FDI) in Latin America, and the United States is traditionally the top foreign investor in Brazil. Since domestic savings are not sufficient to sustain long-term high growth rates, Brazil must continue to attract FDI, especially as the government plans to invest billions of dollars in off-shore oil, nuclear power, and other infrastructure sectors over the next few years.

Brazil is the world's seventh-largest economy, and its population of almost 200 million is heavily concentrated on the

Atlantic coast. President Dilma Rousseff, former President LuizInacio "Lula" da Silva's hand-picked successor, became Brazil's first female president in 2011 and until mid-2013 enjoyed a high popularity rating. Increases in public transportation fares in 2013 provided an excuse for hard-left militants to vandalize property and block roads, but the events also heightened popular grievances against the corrupt political system and slowing economic growth.

Brazil has benefited from surging prices for commodity exports. The middle class is growing, and millions have been lifted out of poverty, but heavy government intervention in the economy continues to cause the misallocation of capital, limit mobility, and fuel a sense of injustice. Ensuring security and adequate infrastructure for the 2016 Rio Olympic games will challenge the government's administrative capacity. Agricultural subsidies doubled from 2011 to 2013 and totalled about US$ 10 billion. In 2013, subsidies for electricity were also increased.

8.4 Nigeria

As an undeveloped nation-state, factors of the political economy are many, complex and inter-related. There include four major ones, namely: primacy of the state over and above society, economy and even the policy; underdevelopment and dependence upon the external global economy; state monopoly of primary public utilities and economic activity sectors; and the nature and character of social classes. At Independence in 1960, the country's political economy was already laid out with the state as the primary and dominant factor in the social relations of production. Itself a product of colonization and colonialism, the state was, and still largely is, the main instrument or institutional factor for development of the economy, society and political system. As a federal state system, the post-colonial economy revolves almost completely around the state especially in the struggles to transcend underdevelopment and simultaneously achieve social justice and equity for the people. The regime understood both the difficulties and the dynamics of the Nigerian post-colonialist state; and it was guided in the direction of breaking the umbilical cord which tied the state to its pre-colonial and colonial roots.

The practices of Nigerian federalism, aided by prolonged military rule, added further significance to the primacy and dominance of the state over the political economy. As the country increasingly became over-centralized and over-concentrated in the accumulation and distribution of power, it inexorably drew upon itself intense struggle that provided the environment as well as the content for political instability, the fears as well as the facts of marginalisation, ethnicity and manipulation of religion and primordial ingredients in the politics and governance of the country.

Nigeria's political economy is that of under-development and dependence of productive forces upon the external global system. Nigerian's economy is underdeveloped in the sense that the factors of production and productive forces were not, and are still not, fully transformed by science and technology vis-à-vis their abundance and potentials for the lives of the large majority of the people. This underdevelopment equally afflicts the issue of distributive justice in terms of the spread of available goods and services to the various communities and people across the country. Similarly, the economy was, and still is, heavily dependent upon the productive forces of the world capitalist system.

The commanding heights of economic activities in Nigeria are generally induced and articulated largely from outside the country. This is so in spite of the abundance of foreign exchange earnings, which the export of crude oil and recently gas has made available to the state. There is an uneven development pattern as well as an unjust and inequitable relation among the social classes. The ownership and control of capital for development are conditioned by foreign interest and foreign domination. In the same way, the benefits of available development are skewed in favour of urban settlements and against the large majority of the rural population. Access to power, wealth and status and the exercise of these resources are dominated and monopolised by the interests related to the state. This is the fact about the abject powerlessness of the large majority of the Nigerian people.

Nigerian political economy derives directly from the preceding two factors, namely, the regulation of social and economic activities by the state. Fiscal and monetary policies, the provision of public utilities such as communication and telecommunication, electricity and water, major transport facilities by road and air are among other state monopolies. Consequently, market forces were thereby constricted. While it is understandably plausible for the state to monopolise these services at a time when the domestic market was small, Nigeria's political economy demands that such monopolies should be dismantled in order for the country to play an appropriate role in the global economy.

The oil revenues and the ensuing resource curse have also profoundly affected on the political economy of Nigeria, both in economic and political terms. The Nigerian oil income has led to deteriorating social services, increased poverty, military coups and maladministration, and weak institutions. Although a wide range of economic and political reforms have been formulated and implemented, most of them with popular support and some with donor support, the deep structural problems of the resource curse have hindered their efficient implementation and produced few tangible outcomes.

Nigeria has been ruled by military regimes for almost 30 of its 55 years of Independence, with several coups and counter-coups. The putative democracy at Independence in 1960 lasted only until 1966 when the first military coup took place. The military retained power from 1966 until 1979, but this was not a period of stability or peace. The Biafra secessionist war lasted from 1967 to 1970 and claimed more than one million lives through violence, starvation, and disease. This war of secession was led by the Igbo (of south-eastern Nigeria, including the Delta) due to economic, ethnic, cultural and religious tensions. While not at the root of the attempted secession, the prospect of oil wealth (or the prospect of losing it, as seen from the federal government viewpoint) exacerbated the conflict. After the civil war ended in 1970, Nigeria's ruling military continued to be afflicted by violent power struggles. The country saw one head of state ousted in a coup and another murdered in an attempted coup before the discredited military returned power to civilian hands in 1979.

The civilian government of the Second Republic from 1979 to 1985 was, however, but a tragic interlude. This civilian regime of Shehu Shagari launched huge industrial and infrastructure projects that quickly proved to be unsustainable and economically irrational ('white elephants'). This was a civilian government with rapidly declining economic discipline, reckless spending (civilian rulers and politicians doling out contracts and favours to siphon off profits and to build political alliances), and growing foreign debts. From 1985 until 1993, the military dictator General Ibrahim Babangida governed Nigeria, but also this period proved disastrous as Babangida only further entrenched the patterns of corruption and human rights abuse. Babangida was widely accused of institutionalising corruption as a tool of political control and as much as US$ 12.2 billion in oil revenues simply 'disappeared'.

Nigeria is heavily affected by the so-called 'resource curse': despite an estimated US$ 400 billion in oil income since independence in 1960, the country has experienced five military coups, one civil war, a very poor economic development, and it has a population more impoverished now than it was 50 years ago. Primarily, petroleum accounts for 40 percent of GDP, 95 percent of foreign exchange earnings, and about 65 percent of government revenues. There are also signs that the economic growth in Nigeria is moving beyond petroleum exports (and the oil-dependent state administration) into manufacturing and industrial production, trade, and services. It is estimated that the so-called middle class constitutes roughly 30 percent of the population in Lagos, and that the proportion is increasing.

The high levels of poverty have not been tackled, however. Despite various reform efforts, it is unlikely that Nigeria will achieve any of the Millennium Development Goals (MDGs) by 2015. In political terms, the dominance of oil and gas in the Nigerian economy has led to a narrow revenue base that has lent itself to rent-seeking and 'elite capture', and it has developed a ruling elite in control of the state apparatus ('political class' in Nigerian parlance). The lack of a diversified economy has stunted the development of a private sector based 'national bourgeoisie' or middle class, and thus the development of independent civic institutions. Nigeria has been ruled by military regimes for almost 30 of its 55 years of independence, with several coups and counter-coups. The Biafra secessionist war lasted from 1967 to 1970 and claimed more than one million lives through violence, starvation and disease.

The first major contradiction of the current attempt at democratization is that the program is being implemented within the context of a neo-colonial dependent economy. The rhetoric of self-reliance notwithstanding, the economic programs of the Babangida regime, particularly the Structural Adjustment Program, are deepening Nigeria's entrenchment within the global capitalist system. Despite the domination of the Nigerian economy by multinational corporations, new incentives are being provided to lure more foreign investments into Nigeria. A number of incentives have been provided to Nigerians who wish to export non-oil raw materials. External loans have been used as instruments to consolidate Nigeria's integration into the global capitalist system. Although billions of dollars of foreign loans have been repaid, the external indebtedness of Nigeria jumped from US$ 15 billion in 1985 to US$ 31 billion in 1989.

Much of Nigeria's economic diplomacy now revolves

around the search for new loans or requesting creditors to reschedule old loans. For instance, in December 1986, the Babangida regime rescheduled the repayment of US$ 6.5 billion debt with the Paris Club. This agreement will, according to the Analyst, generate payments from Nigeria in the period up to May 15, 1997, of more than US$ 10 billion. The bulk of these payments was scheduled to begin on January 1, 1990 and became particularly heavy as from November 15, 1992. Under the terms of this and other rescheduled loans, the incoming civilian regime was required to devote an increasing percentage of foreign exchange earnings to service the debts.

Only in 1999, did Nigeria return to civilian rule. Elections installed retired General Obasanjo as the first president of Nigeria's Fourth Republic in 1999, and Nigeria has since held two presidential and parliamentary elections. The quality of the elections has deteriorated over the years, however, to the extent that the elected government is hardly legitimate (in terms of 'expressing the popular will').

Nigeria is deeply divided by regional, religious, ethnic, economic and political rifts. Besides, the military coups, the dictatorships, the chaotic civil administrations, corruption, and the constant pushing and pulling from oil and big money have weakened Nigerians' sense of law, trust in each other, and trust in government. The Niger Delta has been the main area of petroleum extraction for more than half a century, now producing about 90 percent of the country's oil. At the same time, the Niger Delta is densely populated and a nightmare in terms of civil strife, pollution and ecologic degradation, abductions, and production stoppages by local protesters and criminal gangs.

The economic conditions of Nigeria have advanced over the last few years as a result of the rapid phase of industrialization. The economy of Nigeria also improved tremendously with foreign investment aided by high quality research and development. Nigeria was under the British colonial rule for a considerable period of time. During this phase, major raw materials and minerals were exported to foreign countries along with food grains which in due course of time spearheaded the rise of slavery and exploitation of labour class by the Europeans. After the achievement of Independence in Nigeria, efforts were made to revive the economic growth of the country through a set of economic reforms. It is important to note that before the discovery of oil in Nigeria, the country survived mainly on its agricultural production. The GDP growth rate has been 7 percent in the past few years.

During 2003-07, Nigeria attempted to implement an economic reforms program called the National Economic Empowerment Development Strategy (NEEDS). The purpose of NEEDS was to raise the country's standard of living through a variety of reforms, including macroeconomic stability, deregulation, liberalization, privatization, transparency and accountability. NEEDS addresses basic deficiencies, such as the lack of freshwater for household use and irrigation, unreliable power supplies, decaying infrastructure, impediments to private enterprise and corruption. The government hoped that NEEDS would create 7 million new jobs, diversify the economy, boost non-energy exports, increase industrial capacity utilization and improve agricultural productivity. A related initiative on the state level reforms was the State Economic Empowerment Development Strategy (SEEDS).

A longer-term economic development program was the United Nations (UN)-sponsored National Millennium Goals for Nigeria. Under the program, which covers the years from 2000 to 2015, Nigeria is committed to achieve a wide range of ambitious objectives involving poverty reduction, education, gender equality, health, the environment and international development cooperation. In an update released in 2004, the UN found that Nigeria was making progress toward achieving several goals but was falling short on others. Specifically, Nigeria had advanced efforts to provide universal primary education, protect the environment, and develop a global development partnership.

Oil-rich Nigeria has been hobbled by political instability, corruption, inadequate infrastructure, and poor macroeconomic management but in 2008 it began pursuing economic reforms. Nigeria's former military rulers failed to diversify the economy away from its overdependence on the capital-intensive oil sector, which provides 95 percent of foreign exchange earnings and about 80 percent of budgetary revenues. Following the signing of an IMF stand-by agreement in August 2000, Nigeria received a debt-restructuring deal from the Paris Club and a US$ 1 billion credit from the IMF, both contingents on economic reforms. Nigeria pulled out of its IMF program in April 2002, after failing to meet spending and exchange rate targets, making it ineligible for additional debt forgiveness from the Paris Club.

In November 2005, Abuja won Paris Club approval for a debt-relief deal that eliminated US$ 18 billion of debt in exchange for US$ 12 billion in payments—a total package worth US$ 30 billion of Nigeria's total US$ 37 billion external debt. Since 2008, the government began to show the political will to implement the market-oriented reforms urged by the IMF, such as modernizing the banking system, curbing inflation by blocking excessive wage demands, and resolving regional disputes over the distribution of earnings from the oil industry. GDP rose strongly in 2007-10 because of increased oil exports and high global crude prices in 2010. President Jonathan pledged to continue the economic reforms of his predecessor with emphasis on infrastructure improvements. Infrastructure has been the main impediment to growth and in August 2010 Jonathan unveiled a power sector blueprint that included privatization of the state-run electricity generation and distribution facilities. The government also worked towards developing stronger public-private partnerships for road development. Nigeria's financial sector was hurt by the global financial and economic crises and the Central Bank governor took measures to strengthen that sector. Nigeria's political future is, of course, inextricably tied to its economy.

Nigeria since Independence had tried several economic development models including central planning. However, the federalism practiced in Nigeria did not engender the required plan discipline even under the military with its regimental tendencies. After the First, Second, Third, Fourth, Fifth and Sixth economic development plans, planning was abandoned. Outside influence and interests dictated practically the content and direction of development programmes in quantitative terms and set targets. The structural adjustment programme (SAP) which was prescribed for the country by the IMF/ World Bank in the 1980s set the tone for the economy and to some extent, the political direction.

This was a part of the conditionalities for financial support from those foreign institutions. The debtor must obey while the creditor dictates terms. Naira was devalued. The nation was weighed down by heavy external financial indebtedness. The outcome of the SAP was a brief growth in the economy. Foreign debt mounted, but the country won debt forgiveness during the tenure of Chief Olusegun Obasanjo as civilian President. However, in a sad turn of events, the Administration of Dr. Goodluck Ebele Jonathan since May 6, 2010 when the National Assembly proclaimed him president with full constitutional powers, the country returned to borrowing and the debt mountain gradually ballooned. The foreign reserve and money from excess crude sales had depleted to uncomfortable levels.

The 2011 budget, tagged budget of '*fiscal consolidation*' was designed to break from the past, attract investment, and facilitate private sector growth, boost employment especially among the youth, ensure wealth creation and other socio-economic developmental goals under the Vision 2020 framework. These worthy goals were spelt out against serious concerns about unemployment, rise in recurrent expenditure, quality and efficiency of spending, the need for and urgency to establish Sovereign Wealth Fund (SWF), huge infrastructural deficit and revenue leakage. President Jonathan assured that the Nigerian economy remains 'resilient' but requires hard choice, difficult decision, determination and discipline to achieve the developmental goals and complete the journey of national transformation, to be channelled into capital development.

Vision 2020 was prepared as a '*politically-neutral*' document and was expected to be one which successive governments in the country would respect and implement with equal zeal and in a sustained manner. To further make assurance doubly sure, legislation with sanctions were enacted to 'compel all tiers of government to have a multi-year development plan programmes and projects right through the cycle'. This was to be complemented with an 'institutionalised monitoring and evaluation' mechanism. Among the punitive actions to be taken was to prohibit erring entities 'from access to the Federation Account and other consolidated revenues'. The third success factor taken into account was 'collective goodwill of our people'. The other essential back up was 'economic diplomacy' declared as the new 'central theme of Nigeria's foreign policy'.

8.5 China

When the Peoples Republic of China was established in 1949, almost 90 percent of China's population lived in rural areas and agriculture accounted for 65 percent of national income. The communist regime under Mao proceeded to create a diversified industrial structure through a system of central planning modelled on the Soviet system as well as a uniquely Chinese system of collectivized agriculture (the commune system), and laid the groundwork for the exceptionally rapid economic growth that was to characterize the reform period, which began at the end of 1978. Even so, much of the period between 1949 and 1978 was marked by dramatic conflict over economic and social policy, and by massive social upheavals. Of particular, importance for the socialist project, rural and urban incomes were stagnant during the last two decades of this period. During the reform era that began at the end of 1978, economic growth in China has averaged more than 9 percent, and per capita growth in gross domestic product (GDP) has been about 8 percent; such dramatic, sustained growth in a large country is unprecedented in human history.

Today, we know China as the new form of communism which came about after the death of Mao Zedong in 1976 and the further solidification of Deng Xiaoping as paramount leader of the Chinese communist party. Deng Xiaoping, was a veteran of the revolution and had held various high ranking positions before being sent to exile by Mao, who saw him as a 'capitalist roader'. He was recalled by Mao in 1973 to take eventual charge of the army, as he was the only high-ranking communist Mao WHO could turn to in order to stabilize the army.

Following Mao's death, Deng rejected the 'ultra-leftism' that characterized the decade of the Cultural revolution (1966-1976), referring to this period as being *"virtually at a standstill or in a lingering state"* and in December 1978, at the famous Third Plenum of the Eleventh Party Congress, the Communist party of China (CPC) committed itself to modernization, broad-based economic development and the rule of law. From this point, China's development has been characterized by the so called '*gradualist reform*' model by form of which the Chinese government gradually opens up whilst at the same time solving the various problems through reforms. This model of development has radically transformed China into a prosperous country with an economy which in 2007 was calculated to be more than 9 times larger than it was in 1978, thus placing it in fourth place, after Germany, Japan and the United states.

Deng's economic reforms started in the countryside, with farmers being given the right to sell their crops on the free market as well as individuals being encouraged to set up enterprises, special economic zones were also created on China's southern coast, which, along with highly preferential tax rates attracted foreign direct investment. This, along with the opening up of Shanghai in the 1990s laid down the first phase of economic growth which began with manufacturing and industry. Companies from Hong Kong and Taiwan flocked to China, attracted by a seemingly unending supply of low-wage workers. Furthermore, the Chinese government has indeed been very successful in building a modern, efficient infrastructure comprising of ultra-modern ports and roads, along with cheap container ship transport and low factory building costs; which has made Chinese products up to 70 percent cheaper.

China's open door policy (*duiwaikaifeng*) is largely the adoption of a liberal economic framework, driven by the demands of a centralised state, whose economic agencies are at the forefront of a process of development that is couched within the rhetoric of "socialism with Chinese characteristics'.' China's economic growth model shares the goals of a classical East Asian developmental state, but at the policy level is severely constrained by the paradoxical task of dismantling the old communist economic system while maintaining the Communist Party's absolute monopoly on political power.

Beginning in 1978, China gradually abandoned most elements of the Soviet-style planned economy it had set up in the 1950s and 1960s. China deliberately avoided privatization and focused on deregulating prices and creating competitive markets. The state sector still controls around 40 percent of business-sector output and state firms dominate many key industries, including aviation, shipping, steel, oil, chemicals, telecom, coal, metals and power generation. China has a huge number of private companies but they are mostly tiny; there are no large private business groups able to exercise political influence at the national level. Meanwhile, the party-state, which has shown a surprising degree of resilience, has done an impressive job of restructuring and rationalizing the largest state enterprises, evidently with the view of keeping these business groups firmly in state hands, but at greatly increased levels of profitability and global competitiveness.

A vital component in China's policy to open its economy and integrate it into the world economy was the decentralisation of the foreign trade apparatus. From a highly centralised system of foreign trade agencies governing international economic relationships, China has managed to introduce a flexible structure that promotes, nurtures and facilitates economic policy-making that is not entirely dependent upon state diktats.

Even in the aftermath of Asian financial crisis and slow down of the global economy, China's trade expansion still recorded an outstandingly high growth for both imports and exports, which has led to a steady rise in China's share in world trade. After prolonged negotiation, China eventually joined the World Trade Organization (WTO). The bilateral and multilateral agreements that China entered for this membership committed China for wide-range liberalization of its trade and investment policy. On the other hand, for the first time, China is also taking a lead in pushing for trade liberalization in the Asia by launching a free trade area project with ASEAN states. All these moves indicate that China is not only becoming a part of the globalization process, but also a vital driving force of the globalization process.

In 1990, six special economic zones were established including Shanghai Pudong zone specifically designed for attracting foreign capital. The government supported agriculture through creation of contract responsibilities. In this special arrangement, farmers could sell their commodities abroad with an aim to finance China's modernization agenda. Between late 1980s and early 1990s, the focus was on creating a pricing system using dual tracking system and increasing the role of state in resource allocation. The government diversified the market economy of private enterprises and foreign capital by reducing state monopoly. The market economy was left to invisible hands to influence economic pattern in driving the economy.

By late 1990s, the government focused on reforming

unprofitable state enterprises and banking system insolvency. State-owned enterprises and banks underwent a rapid transformation promoting effectiveness and efficiency. In the beginning of 21st century under Hu Jintao, focus was on domestic economic development to ensure a harmonious society.

Sacks and Woo (2003) accentuate that China is now in the midst of three historic economic transformations and transition from a planned economy to a market economy, economic development from a largely subsistence peasant economy to an industrialized economy with a modern service sector, and economic globalization from autarky to an important node within the global production network.

The economic reform of China began in 1979 under Deng Xiaoping. Deng pursued an "Open Door Policy" from Mao's "Isolation Policy" employing a hybrid model of socialist free market. The reform focused on international trade and privatization of all state-owned enterprises.

35 years after inaugurating reforms, China shows few signs of adopting political changes, liberalization or democratization, corresponding to its economic growth.

China often referred to as a nation whose businesses are governed by a capitalist structure, is dominated by state-owned enterprises (SOEs) that produces roughly 60 percent of China's GDP. China's industries can be sorted into three tiers that make up China's economic structure.

The first tier, which consists of the large SOEs or other central-government controlled firms, primarily exists in sectors that have some degree of natural monopoly or market power. The first tier also includes industries that are vital to national security, which include the aluminium, auto manufacturing, aviation transport and manufacturing, construction, banks, electric power, petrochemicals, rail, steel and telecommunications. In 2010, three Chinese companies were on Fortune's Global Top Ten, while only one was listed in 2009 and none any year prior.

8.5.1 China's Economic System:

- China implements socialist market economy.

- The basis of the system is socialist public economy with the public ownership remaining dominant.
- Individual, private and other non-public sectors of the economy exist and are major components of the socialist market economy.
- The state encourages, supports and guides the development of the non-public sectors of the economy, and exercises supervision and control over the non-public sectors of the economy in accordance with the law.
- Socialist public property is inviolable.
- The state protects socialist public property. Appropriation or damaging of state or collective property by any organization or individual by whatever means is prohibited.

Control of tier-one industries is consolidated in the State-owned Assets Supervision and Administration Commission (SASAC). As of 2012, 117 firms were controlled by the SASAC as compared to 153 in 2007. This is the case because the larger firms in the SASAC absorbed the small, less viable ones. While ownership of parts of tier one firms is private, the government remains in control.

Because of this system, firms can raise private capital while remaining in government control, without becoming overly tied to market priorities and time lines, or the state risking asset looting as was seen in Russia. Managers of the larger firms in this tier are appointed directly by the Chinese Communist Party (CCP) and actually have ministry-level standing, while the remaining managers are appointed by SASAC. The responsibility of SASAC is to manage these firms in the public interest, which can even consist of managing competition between firms.

The second tier of industrial firms in China consists of medium-sized firms that exist in competitive markets. They can originate from the state sector or management buyouts, foreign investment, or domestic start-ups. This sector consists of the most dynamic group of firms, but can sometimes cause confusion as industries, such as the auto industry, can overlap across tiers one and two. Firms in this sector range from telecommunications and networking equipment manufacturers, microwave production firms, piano producers, and "white-goods" producers. All firms in this sector are global economic players and have achieved quite a degree of success and growth.

The major production facilities in China are all relatively new and are all well capitalized. This allows China's firms to utilize leading equipment and methods as opposed to holding on to old production methods because of sunk costs. Such reticence to let go off old investments plagued the US steel industry and led to its subsequent descent. The comparable newness of Chinese firms makes it difficult for the companies of other countries to adapt to Chinese competition. This is reflected in China's "*Go Out*" leadership challenge that encourages Chinese firms to attack companies overseas in their own markets as a way of defending themselves from foreign competition. Thus far, China has identified 22 firms that they intend to make global competitors.

Tier-three consists of mostly town/village enterprises (TVEs) that have been privatized, which are small-scale sector firms. Most of these firms are relatively low-tech, with little government intervention. Despite the size of the individual firms, when examining the industry they make up, you can see the power of their collective nature. For example, roughly 700 companies located in Wanzhou represent the source of 70 percent of the world market for lighters. By clustering these industries, high levels of competitive efficiency are achieved and innovation must be fast enough in order to compete.

Foreign direct investment (FDI) equates to about 4 percent (US$ 60 billion) of China's GDP over recent years, versus 0.5 percent in Japan and Korea.

8.5.2 Reforms: There are four main types of reforms that stimulated China's economic success. The *first* is the privatization of state-owned enterprise managed by the Bureau of Managing Council. In this new arrangement, workers do not own shares but only receive salary based on performance. The Bureau employs mostly Chinese western-graduate nationals and home-grown nationals to manage the enterprises with an objective to give confidence to their own nationals.

Second, the stock companies were converted from state control to private control. In this arrangement, enterprises earn some shares whilst the rest go to state. Managers are also legally allowed to hold some shares.

Third, the government promoted a market-oriented private businesses protected by the government. All banks provide low interest loans to variety of businesses to facilitate economic modernization. *Final* and last is the conversion of foreign fund enterprises (joint ventures and wholly foreign-owned enterprise).

The Chinese economic reforms constitute some distinct characteristics which play an important role in driving the political economy.

- State-led policies.
- Decentralization of state powers to different individuals, groups, and business in decision-making and management of the market economy.
- A socialist free market.
- Development of special economic zones.
- Diversification of state banks to meet private business needs at low interest rates.
- Employ highly educated nationals.
- Combination of Chinese characteristics and modern management skills.
- Encourage modern management and technological innovation.
- Non-state led enterprise reform.
- International trade focusing on agricultural areas as the economic base.
- Convert state-owned entities into private business or enterprises.

According to one OECD survey, China's growth

represents one of the most sustained and rapid economic transformations seen in the world economy in the last 50 years". It goes on to note that China could be the largest exporter in the world by the start of the next decade. Other changes to economic policy include:

- Abolition of price regulation.
- Changes to company law allowing private ownership of limited liability companies.
- Permitting foreign direct investment.
- Abolition of the state export trading monopoly.
- Abolition in 2005 of rules preventing the private sector being involved in various sectors of the economy such as infrastructure, public utilities and financial services.

The reforms have been successful for over 3 decades. The outcome from three processes of economic transformation was astounding proving a sustainable average annual GDP growth rate of 8 percent from 1979-2012. Industrialization, open organization and internationalization extremely drive the shift towards market economy. The reforms overwhelmingly attracted foreign investment, for instance, in 2004, 45 percent export was produced by foreign funds and enterprises. China was ranked as the third biggest trading country after US and EU. Interestingly, free market under invisible hand had played an important role in the economy. In 2001, the central command was replaced by market and economic forces with entry of China in the WTO. Decisions were decentralized. Chinese management of business was also successful with a combination of Chinese culture and modern management skills. Chinese were more eager to learn by experience and apply management innovation and technological innovation.

China's economic reforms can drive Vision 2050 by:

1. Diversifying the market economy into special economic zones:

- Agriculture as the backbone of international trade in some highlands and coastal regions;
- Encourage more banking system through the country, more

ICT Business, competition in state-owned enterprises and stock markets.

2. State playing an important role in creating a conducive environment for economic take-off through sound economic policies.
3. Combine indigenous knowledge with modern innovative management skills and technological skills.
4. People being eager to learn and hardworking, government efforts should promote 'work to live' rather than 'live to work'.

China's export-oriented strategy of development has been spectacularly successful thus far—it has meant that China has had to strengthen and create diplomatic and economic ties with other countries in order to secure the necessary raw materials to keep production at current levels. Indeed, all over the world, one can find how Chinese firms are investing in various projects. This investment has been spread all around the world; however Africa has been amongst the biggest recipients of Chinese investment in the world due to the continent's vast richness in natural resources. In late 2007, the Congolese government announced that Chinese state-owned firms would build or refurbish various railways, roads and mines around the country at a cost of US$ 12 billion. This would all be done in exchange for the rights to mine copper ore of an equivalent value. China's vast investment in Africa does not stop there, among many projects all around the continent; China is rebuilding the railroad network in Nigeria and a new one in Gabon. In Rwanda, it paved more than 80 percent of the main roads. In more than a dozen countries, Chinese firms are exploring for oil and gas and rebuilding electricity grids and telephone networks.

In economic terms, China's burgeoning consumption over the years has helped push the price all sorts of fuels metals and grains to new peaks. Even the price of shipping raw materials reached a record high. The recent economic downturn has not had an effect on commodity prices either, as imports for liquidated natural gas (LNG), coal and copper imports rose sharply since the beginning of 2008. China has a population of approximately 1.35 billion people which amounts to a fifth of the World population; it now consumes a third of its steel and over a quarter of its aluminium.

It becomes clear that China's role in the global economy is no longer limited to production, as was the intention of reforms. A sustained commitment to ensuring that foreign investments lead to the transfer of technology and the acquisition of skills amongst Chinese, would ensure China meeting one of the key points of the four modernizations as Chinese leaders have long been aware of. Japan, Taiwan and Korea soon moved away from becoming manufacturing hubs to providing high value-added goods to the world. Furthermore, China is clearly using its great purchasing power to create the necessary links needed in order to keep production levels high and it is also acquiring the necessary knowledge from companies abroad. China's place in the global economy does seem to have been solidified over the last 30 years. It is now a major player in the international field, making alliances and investing beyond its borders and actively contributing to the international community.

References

Charles P. Kindleberger (2000), "*Comparative Political Economy: A Retrospective*", Massachusetts Institute of Technology, US.

David Zweig and Zhimin Chen (2007), "*China's Reforms and International Political Economy*", Routledge, New York.

Godson Dinneya (2006), "*Political Economy of Democratization in Nigeria*", Concept of Publications Limited, UK.

Ibi Ajayi (2003), "*Nigeria and the Political Economy of Development: The Dreams, the Myth, and the Reality*", Nigerian Economic Society, Ibadan.

Joseph Fewsmith (2010), "*China Today, China Tomorrow: Domestic Politics, Economy, and Society*", Rowman and Littlefield Publishers Inc., UK.

Lael Brainard and Leonardo Martines-Diaz (eds.), "*Brazil as an Economic Superpower?: Understanding Brazil's Changing Role in the Global Economy*", The Brookings Institution, Washington D.C.

Mark Blyth (2009), "*Routledge Handbook of International Political Economy (IPE)*", Routledge, New York.

Shaun Gerard Breslin (2013), "*China and the Global Political Economy*", Palgrave Macmillan, UK.

Uwe Becker (2014), "*The BRICS and Emerging Economies in Comparative Perspective: Political Economy, Liberalization and Institutional Change*", Routledge, Canada.

9

Executive Powers in Britain, Brazil, Nigeria and China

9.1 Introduction

Executive is usually described as the government. It is the wheel of the ship of the state. The executive branch of government provides national leadership these days. In the words of *Laski,* "It is the central governing, directing and initiating element in the nation's life". As the modern state marches on the road of welfare of the masses it has to assume more and more functions and this results in the growing importance of the executive. Lord Hewart has called it, "The New Despotism".

The executive may be broadly divided into two categories such as the parliamentary and the presidential executive. Parliamentary government evolved in Great Britain during the course of several centuries. It was the consequence of a continuous struggle between the hereditary absolute monarch and the parliament. The parliamentary government provides for a nominal executive besides the real one. The nominal executive head exercises only ceremonial powers and acts as the constitutional head of the state. But in sharp contrast to this, in the presidential system, the president is both nominal and real executive head of the state. He is the head of the state as well as the government. Executive in all states is responsible for the overall direction, supervision and control of the administrative machinery. Political executive does not enforce law directly. It controls the civil service or the permanent executive who enforces the law in accordance with the policy laid down by the political executive.

In most of the states, the executive has supreme control over the armed forces of the state. In India and the US, the chiefs of the army, navy and air force are appointed by the president. The vital task of war and peace is in effect vested in the executive. Executive in most of the states also performs certain types of judicial functions. Right to grant pardon, reprieve, remission, etc., are some of the quasi-judicial powers enjoyed by the executive.

9.2 Britain

United Kingdom is a constitutional monarchy—succession to the British throne is hereditary. Under the British Constitution, sweeping executive powers, known as the royal prerogative, are nominally vested in the Sovereign. In exercising these powers, however, the Sovereign normally refers to the advice of the prime minister or other ministers. This principle, which can be traced back to the Restoration, was most famously articulated by the Victorian writer Walter Bagehot as, "the Queen reigns, but she does not rule".

United Kingdom is a parliamentary monarchy—that is, the head of state is a monarch with limited powers. Britain's democratic government is based on a constitution composed of various historical documents, laws and formal customs adopted over the years. Parliament, the legislature, consists of the House of Lords, the House of Commons, and the monarch, also called the crown. The House of Commons is far more influential than the House of Lords, which in effect make the British system unicameral, meaning the legislature has one chamber. The chief executive is the prime minister, who is a member of the House of Commons. The executive branch also includes Her Majesty's Government, commonly referred to simply as "the government". The government is composed of ministers in the Cabinet, most of whom are members of the House of Commons; government departments, each of which is responsible to a minister; local authorities; and public corporations. Because the House of Commons is involved in both the legislative and executive branches of the British government, there is no separation of powers between the executive and legislature as there is in the United States.

9.2.1 King or Queen and the Crown: The title 'the Crown' is given to the monarch or sovereign of the country, that is, the Royal Head of State. The British monarch is also the Head of the Church of England and Head of State for assenting countries within the Commonwealth (an association of former colonial nations). In its practical operation, the Crown represents the monarch and, more significantly, the Government of the day—the executive—that has responsibility for governing the country, and can call upon *'royal prerogative'* powers that have been established during the historical development of the common law. The Crown has legal significance in two main respects:

- Through exercise of the royal prerogative.
- Through Crown immunity.

9.2.2 Prerogative Powers of the 'Queen in Parliament':

- The monarch has the prerogative power to open new parliamentary sessions and to dissolve Parliament for the purposes of a general election. The former power is illustrated by the Queen's (or King's) speech during the state opening of Parliament, a ceremonial occasion in which the monarch reads a speech prepared by the Government outlining its proposals for new laws. In July 2007, Prime Minister Gordon Brown broke with tradition by pre-empting the Queen's Speech and announcing a draft legislative programme which would, he reasoned, allow more time for consultation.
- The monarch has the prerogative to give the 'royal assent' to legislation, thus formally making bills (draft legislation) into operative acts of the Parliament. However, this is a formality rather than a power (the last time power was exercised by the monarch in such circumstances was as long ago as in 1707). It used to be the case, historically, that the monarch signed all the bills, but today, assent can be given by the signing of general documents to announce the giving of assent to the two Houses of Parliament. It is

unrealistic to assume that the monarch reads the bills that have been given assent, though detailed briefings would have to be provided.

- The monarch has prerogative powers to appoint and dismiss the prime minister of the country; this is a matter of political convention rather than informed choice. Here, the monarch merely follows the choice of the political party with a majority in the House of Commons and appoints the leader of that party as prime minister after a general election victory. Moreover, the monarch will accept the resignation of a prime minister who loses a '*vote of no confidence*' in Parliament, or who leads a party to defeat at the general election.

9.2.3 Crown Immunity from Legal Action: Part of the character of the Crown is that it is an entity with powers and rights as distinct from the citizens of the State. For this reason, the Crown enjoys legal immunity in certain respects because of its status. The origins of Crown immunity lie in the maxim that 'the King can do no wrong'. It is still the case that the monarch cannot be sued in a personal capacity, though servants of the Crown—such as Government departments and other executive bodies and institutions—can be subject to civil legal action in the areas of contract and tort (Crown Proceedings Act, 1947). With regard to criminal law, the constitutional position is very controversial since the royal prerogative suggests that the Crown is immune from criminal prosecution.

There is a fear that such a power allows the security services, in the name of the Crown, to obtain intelligence and maintain security through criminal activities, such as burglary and unlawful surveillance. However, this area is subject to the developing legal framework of human rights law, following the passing of the Human Rights Act, 1998—even though some of the rights are limited to take into account the need for 'national security'. The issue of Crown immunity remains highly sensitive and controversial, as shown by media coverage of the unsuccessful attempts by lawyers for Mohammed Al-Fayed, in 2007, to require the Queen (and the Duke of Edinburgh) to give evidence at the inquest into the deaths of Diana, Princess of Wales and Dodi Al-Fayed.

The precise extent of the royal prerogative has never formally been delineated, but in 2004, Her Majesty's Government published some of the powers, in order to be more transparent.

9.2.4 Domestic Powers:

- Power to dismiss and appoint a prime minister.
- Power to dismiss and appoint other ministers.
- Power to summon, prorogue and dissolve Parliament.
- Power to grant or refuse Royal Assent to bills (making them valid and law).
- Power to commission officers in the Armed Forces.
- Power to command the Armed Forces of the United Kingdom.
- Power to appoint members to the Queen's Council.
- Power to issue and withdraw passports.
- Power to grant Prerogative of mercy (though Capital Punishment is abolished, this power is still used to remedy errors in sentence calculation).
- Power to grant honours.
- Power to create corporations via Royal Charter.
- Power to appoint bishops and archbishops of the Church of England.

9.2.5 Foreign Powers:

- Power to ratify and make treaties.
- Power to declare war and peace.
- Power to deploy the Armed Forces overseas.
- Power to recognize states.
- Power to credit and receive diplomats.

The most important prerogatives still personally exercised by the Sovereign are the choice of whom to appoint prime minister, and whether to grant dissolution of Parliament on the request of the prime minister. The most recent occasion the monarch has had to exercise these powers were in February 1974, when Prime Minister Edward Heath resigned after failing to secure an overall majority in Parliament. Queen Elizabeth II appointed Harold Wilson, leader of the Labour Party, as Prime Minister, exercising her prerogative after extensive consultation with the Privy Council. The Labour Party had the largest number of seats in the House of Commons, but not an overall majority. The 2010 general election also resulted in a hung parliament. After several days of negotiations, between the parties, Queen Elizabeth II invited David Cameron to form a government on the advice of the outgoing Prime Minister Gordon Brown.

The Sovereign normally grants any request of the prime minister for dissolution of Parliament. However, several authorities agree that a prime minister who is granted dissolution must win at least one vote of confidence from the newly elected Commons before he or she has the right to request any further dissolution. This would mean that, for example, a sitting prime minister who suffered defeat in a general election, and was then defeated in the first confidence motion he or she faced in the new Commons, would not be granted a dissolution. No refusal of a requested dissolution has happened since the beginning of the twentieth century.

9.2.6 Executive Powers of the British Government: The chief executive of the government is the prime minister. He or she is the leader of the party that holds the most seats in the House of Commons. The monarch goes through the ceremony of selecting as prime minister the person from the House of Commons who is head of the majority party. The prime minister presides over the Cabinet and selects the other cabinet members, who join him or her to form the government that is part of the functioning executive. Acting through the cabinet and in the name of the monarch, the prime minister exercises all of the theoretical powers of the crown, including making appointments. In the past, prime ministers also came from the

House of Lords. Today, in the unlikely circumstance that a peer (a member of the House of Lords) is sought as a prime minister by one of the parties, he or she must first resign from the House of Lords and gain election to the House of Commons.

9.2.7 Executive Power: The Prime Minister: When legislation comes before the House of Commons, the prime minister can usually count on the support of a majority of the votes because his or her party has a majority of the seats, and party discipline tends to be strong in Britain. In some circumstances, prime ministers must depend on a coalition of strong parties. This was the case during both World Wars and during the worst of the Great Depression in the 1930s. At times, a prime minister comes from a party that does not quite have a majority of seats in the House of Commons. In such a case, that party must rely on an alliance with smaller parties, the smaller parties voting with the party in power on necessary legislation. A government formed from a party without a majority in Parliament is called a minority government. Between 1974 and 1979, for example, a minority Labour Party government was able to stay in power because the Liberal Party generally voted with it.

The prime minister, the head of government and the chairman of the cabinet, is part of the legislature and the executive in the United Kingdom. The prime minister's power is said to vary according to personality and personal circumstances. As head of the Government, the prime minister is ultimately responsible for the policies and decisions of Government, oversees the civil service and government agencies, appoints members of the cabinet, and is the principal government member in the House of Commons. The power of the prime minister largely derides from the royal prerogative, where what the monarch said was law. The prime minister is said to be 'primus-inter-pares', first among equals, which is meant to describe the prime minister's position in contrast to the other ministers of state. The prime minister decides the policy of the cabinet and thus the government, the party and the country. The prime minister can appoint anyone to his cabinet, if one of his cabinet minister disagrees with the policy he wants to push through, that minister is expected to resign.

9.3 Brazil

The Brazilian Constitution of 1988 gave relatively strong powers to the president. The head of the Federal Executive Power is the President of the Republic who is also head of state and head of government. As this is an unusual assignment, the Executive helps to control the Judiciary by appointing the ministers of the Supreme Court of Brazil (STF) and other High Courts, and also the Legislative Power, in the preparation of laws, and either assent or veto thereof. The President of the Republic is also responsible for appointing ministers to the Brazilian Court of Audit.

The President of the Republic is elected by direct suffrage for a period of four years, and could not be re-elected for the term immediately following. He could be impeached by the Supreme Federal Court after the Senate or Chamber of Deputies had upheld an accusation against him of official misconduct or common crime. According to Article 76, the Executive Power is exercised by the President of the Republic, assisted by the Ministers of State. According to Article 77, the election of the President and Vice-President of the Republic shall take place simultaneously, on the first Sunday of October, in the first round, and on the last Sunday of October, in the second round, as the case may be, of the year preceding the one in which the current presidential term of office ends.

As a republic with a presidential Executive, Brazil grants significant powers to the President. He or she effectively controls the Executive branch, represents the country abroad, and appoints the Cabinet and, with the approval of the Senate, the judges for the Supreme Federal Tribunal. The president is also the Commander-in-Chief of the armed forces. Presidents in Brazil also have significant law-making powers, exercised either by proposing laws to the National Congress, or else by using provisional measures, an instrument with the force of law that the President can enact in cases of urgency and necessity, except to make changes to some areas of law (provisional measures cannot be used to change criminal law, electoral law, tax law, among other cases). A provisional measure comes into effect immediately, before Congress votes on it, and remains in force for up to 60 days unless Congress votes to rescind it. This 60 day period can be extended once, up to a maximum of 120 days. If Congress, on the other hand, votes to approve the provisional measure, it becomes an actual law, with changes decided by the Legislative Branch. The provisional measure expires at the end of the 60 day period (or 120 day, in case of extension), or sooner, if rejected by one of the Houses of Congress.

9.3.1 Powers of the President in Brazil:

Article 84 of the current Constitution determines that the President has the power to:

- Appoint and dismiss the ministers of state.
- Exercise, with the assistance of the ministers of state, the higher management of the federal administration.
- Start the legislative procedure, in the manner and in the cases set forth in the Constitution.
- Sanction, promulgate and order the publication of laws, as well as to issue decrees and regulations for the true enforcement thereof.
- Veto bills, wholly or in part.
- Provide, by means of decree, on organization and structure of federal administration, in the cases where there is neither increase of expenses nor creation or extinction of public agencies; and extinction of offices or positions, when vacant.
- Maintain relations with foreign States and to accredit their diplomatic representatives.
- Conclude international treaties, conventions and acts, subject to the ratification of the National Congress.

- Decree the state of defence and the state of siege, in accordance with the constitutional procedures that shall precede and authorize those emergency decrees.
- Decree and enforce federal intervention, in accordance with the constitutional procedures that shall precede and authorize such exceptional action.
- Upon the opening of the legislative session, send a government message and plan to the National Congress, describing the state of the nation and requesting the actions he deems necessary.
- Grant pardons and reduce sentences, after hearing the entities instituted by law, if necessary.
- Exercise the supreme command of the Armed Forces, appoint the commanders of Navy, Army and Air Force, promote general officers and to appoint them to the offices held exclusively by them.
- Appoint, after approval by the Senate, the Justices of the Supreme Federal Court and those of the superior courts, the Governors of the territories, the Attorney General of the Republic, the President and the directors of the Central Bank and other civil servants, when established by law.
- Appoint, with due regard for the provisions of Article 73, the Justices of the Federal Court of Accounts.
- Appoint judges in the events established by the Constitution and the Advocate General of the Union.
- Appoint members of the Council of the Republic, in accordance with Article 89, VII.
- Summon and preside over the Council of the Republic and the National Defence Council.
- Declare war, in the event of foreign aggression, authorized by the National Congress or confirmed by it, whenever it occurs between legislative sessions and, under the same conditions, to decree full or partial national mobilization.
- Make peace, authorized or confirmed by the National Congress.
- Award decorations and honorary distinctions.

- Permit, in the cases set forth by supplementary law, foreign forces to pass through the national territory, or to remain temporarily therein.
- Submit to the National Congress the pluriannual plan, the bill of budgetary directives and the budget proposals set forth in the Constitution.
- Render, each year, accounts to the National Congress concerning the previous fiscal year, within sixty days of the opening of the legislative session.
- Fill and abolish federal government positions, as set forth by law.
- Issue provisional measures, with force of law, according to Article 62.
- Perform other duties set forth in the Constitution.

9.4 Nigeria

In Nigeria, executive power is vested in the president, who is simultaneously chief of state and head of the government. The president is eligible for two four-year terms. The president's Federal Executive Council, or cabinet, includes representatives from all 36 states. The National Assembly, consisting of a 109-member Senate and a 360-member House of Representatives, constitutes the country's legislative branch. Three senators represent each of Nigeria's 36 states, and one additional senator represents the capital city of Abuja. Seats in the House of Representatives are allocated according to population. Therefore, the number of House members from each state differs. Members of the National Assembly are elected to a maximum of two four-year terms. The judicial branch comprises the Supreme Court, the Court of Appeal, the Federal High Court, and, on the state level, high courts, *sharia* courts, and customary courts. The president appoints members of the Supreme Court subject to confirmation by the Senate.

Under Section 130 of the 1999 Constitution, the President is described as the "*Head of State, the chief executive of the federation and commander-in-Chief of the Armed forces*". In addition to the monstrous and alarming executive powers bestowed on the President, the President is empowered with legislative judicial powers to alter, amend, repeal, or modify any existing law so as to bring the law into conformity with the provisions of the Constitution. Section 5 of 1999 Constitution confers on the president, the federal executive powers and this could be exercised by him either directly or indirectly or through the Vice-President and Ministers of the Government of the Federation or officers in the public service of the Federations. Although the President may due to practical necessities, delegate executive powers to such officials, he is not under any obligation to do so, unless the law otherwise requires. The executive power at the state level is vested in the Governor of the state concerned, while the local government chairman, captains the ship of his domain. As the case is with the Federal executive power, state Governors and local government chairmen are at liberty to delegate some of these powers to their subordinates.

To be elected as President, the candidate has to have a majority of the votes in the election, and no less than one-quarter of votes cast in at least two-thirds of the states. In situations where the former criterion is not met, there shall be held a new election with two candidates. If there are more than two candidates in the first election, the candidate who has the highest number of votes and the candidate with the majority of votes in the highest number of states shall continue to the second round of the election. To be elected, the candidate still needs to fulfil the above mentioned criteria in the second election, if not there will be a third election. The President is elected for four years, and can only serve two periods. The vice-president is nominated by the President to run as a candidate with the President. The Ministers of the Government should be nominated by the president, and confirmed by the Senate.

President is also the Head of the Executive arm in the tripartite. The office of the President is, undoubtedly, a concentration of considerable powers and a repository of vast responsibilities. As Head of the State, the President is the ceremonial head of the Nigerian government. As the chief executive, he/she bears ultimate responsibility for the smooth and effective running of the government on a day-to-day basis and must accept the ultimate blame for any failures or shortcomings that may occur therein. As Commander-in-Chief of the Armed Forces, he/she is responsible for how those forces are organised, trained and equipped and is accountable for how they are deployed to ward off external aggression and guarantee internal security. As the position is paramount in the making of foreign policy, he/she is also the country's chief diplomat.

Furthermore, although not explicitly specified in the Constitution, the President must share responsibility with the National Assembly in the making of laws for good governance of the Federation and the public looks up to him as the leading formulator and expounder of public opinion in the country. In the same vein, the public looks up to him/her as the overall manager of the nation's economy, in which capacity he may claim credit in times of prosperity but must surely suffer unsparing criticism for any failures of economic performance.

The President is not a member of the National Assembly (the legislature). But he may attend any session of the Assembly either to deliver an address on major national issues, including fiscal measures, or to make such statement on the policy of government as he considers being of crucial national importance. The office of the President is an elective one and no President is allowed to hold office for more than two terms of four years each. The vice-president assists the President. The vice-president is nominated by the presidential mandate as his running mate for election to the office of President. This nominated presidential associate, or running mate, automatically becomes the vice-president if the President is elected. The vice-president's tenure of office is concurrent with that of the President. He assumes the office of President if that office becomes vacant before the expiration of their term, by reason of death or resignation or the removal of the

President from office on the terms provided for in the Constitution.

The President is empowered by the Constitution to appoint Ministers after due screening and confirmation of the list of nominees by the Senate, and to assign to them responsibilities for any business of the Government of the Federation, including the administration of any department of that government. The Constitution enjoins the President to appoint his ministers from all the 36 States of the Federation. No Minister appointed to the Federal Executive Council or Cabinet from a legislative post is allowed to serve concurrently as a member of the National Assembly. Where a member of the National Assembly is appointed a Minister, he or she is deemed to have resigned his membership of any of the Assemblies on his taking the oath of office as a Minster.

The President and his ministers form the Federal Executive Council, with the President as the Chairman. This body initiates the policies and programmes of the Federal Government and ensures that they are properly implemented after they may have been passed into law by the legislature. All executive powers of the federation, subject to the provisions of the 1999 Constitution, are vested in the President. In addition, Section 153(1) provides for the establishment of 14 "*federal executive bodies*", like the Code of Conduct Bureau, the Council of State and the Federal Character Commission, to name a few. Section 5(2) of the Constitution vests executive powers of a state in the Governor of that state.

Section 315 of 1999 Constitution gives the executive the power to modify an existing law as may be necessary to bring it into conformity with the Constitution.

The executive is also empowered to make regulations relating to citizenship. It does appear here that he is exercising original legislative power, since the regulations derive their authority and force directly from the Constitution. The executive in practice also exercises certain powers over the judiciary. The Judges are appointee(s) of the executive. Also where the court passes judgment, especially in criminal cases, the executive can use its prerogative of mercy power to pardon a convict or mitigate the sentence. The executive has the power by which it can terminate criminal proceedings any time before the judgment of the courts. The executive also has the power to remove Judges.

Unlike in Great Britain, where the Prime Minister is the leader of the party that has the majority in the Parliament, and has a parliamentary status, President in Nigeria is elected in a general election on the basis of Universal Adult Suffrage and for the time in power as the head of the Executive and Commander-in-Chief, has no parliamentary status. The Judiciary headed by the Chief Justice of the Federation is an independent body charged primarily with the responsibility of interpreting law and does not have its membership drawn from legislative or executive branches and as such cannot exercise legislative or executive powers unless the powers are delegated. Separation of power is an integral part of the Nigerian governmental process based on her adoption of the US modelled presidential system of government since 1979.

The President has the powers entrusted by the Constitution and legislation, including those necessary to perform the functions of the head of the state and head of the national executive. The President is responsible for:

- Assenting to and signing bills.
- Referring a bill back to the National Assembly for reconsideration of the bill's constitutionality.
- Referring a bill to the Constitutional Court for a decision on the bill's constitutionality.
- Summoning the National Assembly, or Parliament to an extraordinary sitting to conduct special business.
- Making any appointments that the Constitution or legislation requires the President to make, other than as head of the national executive.
- Appointing commissions of inquiry.
- Calling a national referendum in terms of an Act of

Parliament.

- Receiving and recognising foreign diplomatic and consular representatives.
- Appointing ambassadors, plenipotentiaries, and diplomatic and consular representatives.
- Pardoning or reprieving offenders and remitting any fines, penalties or forfeitures.
- Conferring honours.

9.5 China

The head of state in China is the president. The presidency is an independent State apparatus and an important component of the State organs. Citizens of the PRC (People's Republic of China) who have the right to vote and stand for election and have reached the age of 45 are eligible for election as president of the PRC. The president of the PRC is nominated by the Presidium of the National People's Congress (NPC) and elected by the NPC by voting, based on a single candidate. The NPC has the power to remove from office, the president of the PRC. The president of the PRC is elected for a term of five years and shall serve no more than two consecutive terms. In the event that the office of the president of the PRC falls vacant, the vice-president succeeds to the office of the president. In the event that the office of the vice-president of the PRC falls vacant, the NPC shall elect a new vice-president to fill the vacancy. In the event that the offices of both the president and the vice-president of the PRC fall vacant, the NPC shall elect a new president and a new vice-president. Prior to such election, the chairman of the NPC Standing Committee shall temporarily act as the president of the PRC.

The president "engages in activities involving State affairs and receives foreign diplomatic representatives". In pursuance of the decisions of the NPC Standing Committee, the president appoints and recalls plenipotentiary representatives abroad, and ratifies and abrogates treaties and important agreements concluded with foreign states. The vice-president assists the president in his work, "*may exercise such parts of the functions and powers of the President as the President may entrust to him*".

The functions and powers of the President can be summarized as follows:

1. The power of promulgating laws. Laws adopted by NPC or its Standing Committee shall go into effect only after being promulgated by the President, which is the last act in the legislative processes in the People's Republic of China.
2. Statutes adopted by the NPC and its Standing Committee go into official effect upon promulgation by the President of the PRC (People's Republic of China). The president of the PRC has no power to veto the statutes and shall promulgate any statute adopted by the NPC and its Standing Committee. No statute shall become effective without the promulgation of the president of the PRC.
3. The power of issuing orders. The appointment and removal of the premier of the State Council, the issue of the order of special amnesty, the proclamation of martial law, a state of war and general mobilization can only be made or announced by the President. Since 1959, the President has issued the order of special amnesty on six occasions.
4. The president of the PRC, in pursuance of the decisions of the NPC and its Standing Committee, appoints or removes the premier, vice-premiers, state councillors, ministers in charge of ministries or commissions, the auditor general and the secretary general of the State Council; confers State medals and titles of honour; issues orders of special pardons; proclaims martial law; proclaims a state of war; and issues mobilization orders.
5. The power of making appointment or removals, i.e., the power to appoint or remove officials constituting the State Council.
6. The power of conferring titles, i.e., the power to confer state honour.

7. Receive the credentials offered by foreign diplomatic representatives on behalf of the PRC.
8. Appoint or recall plenipotentiary representatives abroad in pursuance of the decisions of the NPC Standing Committee.
9. Ratify or abrogate treaties and important agreements concluded with foreign states in pursuance with the decisions of the NPC Standing Committee. The president of the PRC shall promulgate the treaties and agreements concluded by the State Council or its relevant departments with foreign countries, which have been ratified or abrogated by the NPC or its Standing Committee.

The President is both the head of state and the commander-in-chief of the armed forces. The president has authority over five administrative branches (Yuan): executive, legislative, control, judicial, and examination.

The Executive Yuan comprises the premier, vice-premier, and the cabinet members who are responsible for policy and administration. The President appoints the Premier, who is officially the president of the Executive Yuan.

The executive branch of the People's Republic of China includes the central and local executive organs. The central executive organ refers to the Central Government, known as the State Council.

Local executive organs are local people's governments at four levels: the provinces (autonomous regions and centrally administered municipalities), cities and prefectures, counties and townships.

The government is led by the State Council, the equivalent of a cabinet. There also are four vice-premiers and five state councillors (one of whom is the secretary general of the State Council). One of the vice-premiers and two of the state councillors double as ministers with such key portfolios as national defence, public security, and public health. In addition, the People's Bank of China (China's central bank) and the National Audit Office are part of the State Council system. The five-year terms of office run concurrently with those of the National People's Congress (NPC) and are limited to no more than two consecutive terms.

Executive meetings of the State Council are attended by the premier, vice-premiers, state councillors, and secretary general of the State Council. The State Council reports on its work to the NPC and, when the NPC is not in session, to its Standing Committee.

9.5.1 Legal Status and Functions of the State Council:

The State Council is the highest state executive organ. The Constitution prescribes the following extensive functions of the State Council, including:

1. To adopt administrative measures, enact administrative rules and regulations and issue decisions and orders in accordance with the Constitution and law.
2. To submit proposals to the National People's Congress or its Standing Committee.
3. To stipulate the tasks and responsibilities of various ministries and commissions, exercise unified leadership over the work of the ministries and commissions and direct all other administrative work of a national character that does not fall within the jurisdiction of any specific ministries or commissions.
4. To exercise unified leadership over the work of local executive organs of the state at various levels throughout the country, and to formulate the detailed division of functions and powers between the Central Government and local governments of provinces, autonomous regions, and municipalities directly under the Central Government.
5. To draw up and implement the plan for national economic and social development and the state budget.
6. To direct and administer economic affairs and urban and rural development.
7. To direct and administer the affairs in respect of education, science, culture, public health, physical culture and family planning.

8. To direct and administer civil affairs, public security, judicial administration, supervision and other related matters.
9. To conduct foreign affairs and conclude treaties and agreements with foreign countries.
10. To direct and administer the build-up of national defence.
11. To direct and administer ethnic affairs and safeguard the equal rights of the ethnic minorities and the right to autonomy of ethnic autonomous areas.
12. To protect the legitimate rights and interests of Chinese citizens residing abroad and of returned overseas Chinese and their family members.
13. To alter or annul inappropriate orders, directives and regulations issued by the ministries or commissions.
14. To alter or annul inappropriate decisions and orders issued by local executive organs at various levels.
15. To approve the geographic division of provinces, autonomous regions and municipalities directly under the Central Government, and to approve the establishment and geographic division of autonomous prefectures, counties, autonomous counties and cities.
16. To decide on the enforcement of martial law in parts of provinces, autonomous regions, and municipalities directly under the Central Government.
17. To review and decide on the size of administrative organs and, in accordance with the law, appoint or remove administrative officials, train them, evaluate their performance and reward or punish them.
18. To exercise such other functions and powers as the National People's Congress or its Standing Committee may assign to it.

References

Abu Bakarr Bah (2005), "*Breakdown and Reconstitution: Democracy, the Nation-state, and Ethnicity in Nigeria*", Lexington Books, US.

Akhtar Majeed, Ronald L. Watts and Douglas Brown (2006), "*Distribution of Powers and Responsibilities in Federal Countries*", McGill-Queen's University Press, Canada.

David Curtis Wright (2001), "*The History of China*", Greenwood Press, US.

F.O. Nyemutu Roberts (2002), "*Models of Executive Power and Nigeria's Neo-presidentialism: Implications for Governance and Development*", Nigerian Institute of Social and Economic Research, Nigeria.

Great Britain: Ministry of Justice (2007), "*The Governance of Britain: War Powers and Treaties Limiting Executive Powers*", Constitutional Paper CP 26/07, Published on October 25, 2007.

Guoli Liu (2011), "*Politics and Government in China*", ABC-CLIO, LLC, US.

Hui-yun Zhuang (2010), "*Idealism and the Abuse of Powers: Lessons from China's Cultural Revolution*", Ashgate Publishing Limited, US.

Jody C. Baumgartner and Naoko Kada (2003), "*Checking Executive Power: Presidential Impeachment in Comparative Perspective*", Praeger Publishers, US.

Kalu N. Kalu (2009), "*State Power, Autarchy and Political Conquest in Nigerian Federalism*", Lexington Books, United Kingdom.

Mark Kesselman, Joel Krieger and William Joseph (2013), "*Introduction to Comparative Politics*", sixth edition, Wadsworth, US.

Patrick Diamond (2014), "*Governing Britain: Power, Politics and the Prime Minister*", I.B. Tauris & Co. Ltd., New York.

10

Judiciary in Britain, Brazil, Nigeria and China

10.1 Introduction

The judiciary is the branch of government that deals with interpretation of a nation's laws, resolution of legal conflicts, and judgments for violations of the law. The judiciary, also known as the judicial system, is composed of judges and courts. The judicial system is deliberately kept separate from the nation's legislative body, such as the parliament or the congress, which creates or abolishes the nation's laws as part of the political process. Attorneys are specialists who study the law in order to help clients navigate the judicial system.

Legal systems of various kinds have existed since the dawn of civilization. Precedents of the modern judicial system include ancient Greek and Roman laws and the law speakers of medieval Scandinavia. English common law established by the Magna Carta is the most direct ancestor of many current legal systems. France's Napoleonic Code was also influential in replacing local customs with a set system of laws and courts. By the 18th century, many countries around the world had developed some form of judiciary.

In many nations, the law is established by a constitution or similar document created when the nation was founded. The legislative body then creates further laws that are intended to carry the spirit of the constitution into specific situations. It is the responsibility of the judiciary to determine if these new laws are, in fact, true to the intent of the constitution. For this reason, judges must be extremely well versed with the laws of the nation. Most begin their careers as attorneys before moving on to the judicial bench.

The judiciary is best known for its administration of criminal court cases. Anyone caught violating a law must eventually face a judge, who will determine whether the violation occurred, the severity of the offence and the penalty. Judges are aided in this process by their understanding of the law, their own interpretation of its meaning, and in some cases by a jury or a panel of fellow judges. The majority of court cases, however, involve civil law, such as trademark or copyright violations, bankruptcy, or individual lawsuits. In the United States, 80 percent of court cases involve civil law, while only 20 percent are criminal cases.

10.2 Britain

English ideas about justice have shaped those of many other modern democracies. For example, the concept of trial by jury goes back to the time of Henry II in the 13th century. Britain has had a judicial branch for centuries, but ironically, the modern judiciary has much more limited powers than those in the United States, France and Germany. In Britain, the principle of parliamentary sovereignty (parliament's decisions are final) has limited the development of judicial review (the courts' ability to determine actions, laws and other court decisions unconstitutional). British courts can only determine whether government decisions violate the common law or previous acts of the Parliament. Even then, the courts tend to rule narrowly because they refer to the authority of the Parliament. By tradition, the courts may not impose their rulings on Parliament, the prime minister or the cabinet.

There are three separate judicial systems in the United Kingdom: that of England and Wales, that of Scotland, and that of Northern Ireland. Under the Constitutional Reform Act, 2005, the final court of appeal for all cases, other than Scottish criminal cases, is the newly created Supreme Court of the United Kingdom: for Scottish criminal cases, the final court of appeal remains with the High Court of Judiciary.

This has come about partly as a result of the integration of European legislation into British law and the need to decide in the face of challenges whether UK legislators and public administrators were acting in consonance with EU requirements. The other reason for the increasing power of the courts is the result of the use of precedent, i.e. previous legal decisions, to decide cases.

10.2.1 Levels of the English Court System: It must be pointed out that Scotland and Northern Ireland have their own, highly distinct judicial systems.

A. District Judge (Magistrates' Courts): It deals with nine out of ten cases and which are locally-based. At one time, they were called 'police courts' but they were removed from the control of the police in the 1960s. These courts are overseen by unpaid and part-time magistrates drawn from the local community. District judges (magistrates' courts) hear criminal cases, youth cases and also some civil proceedings in magistrates' courts. They can be authorised to hear cases in the family proceedings courts. Some are authorised to deal with extradition proceedings and terrorist cases. They are also authorised to sit as prison adjudicators. District judges (magistrates' courts) usually hear cases alone. By virtue of their office they are "justices of the peace".

District judges (magistrates' courts) are appointed by the Queen, on the recommendation of the Lord Chancellor, following a fair and open competition administered by the Judicial Appointment Commission. The statutory qualification is a seven-year right of audience—the right of a lawyer to appear and speak as an advocate for a party in a case in the court—in relation to all proceedings in any part of the Supreme Court, or all proceedings in county courts or magistrates' courts.

B. County Courts: It deals with basic civil cases. Types of civil case dealt within the county courts include:

- Businesses trying to recover money they are owed.
- Individuals seeking compensation for injuries.
- Landowners seeking orders that will prevent trespass.

All county courts can deal with contract and tort (civil wrong) cases and recovery of land actions. Some county

Courts can also deal with bankruptcy and insolvency matters, as well as cases relating to wills and trusts (equity and contested probate actions) where the value of the trust, fund or estate does not exceed £ 30,000, matters under the Race Relations Act, 1976, and actions which all parties agree to have heard in a county court (e.g. defamation cases). Most county courts are assigned at least one circuit judge and one district judge.

In England and Wales since 2014, there is a single civil court named the County Court, with unlimited financial jurisdiction. Before 2014, there were numerous county courts, each with jurisdiction across England and Wales, but each with a defined county court district (which bore no relation to a county: the name "county court" is used for purely historical reasons).

C. Crown Court: It deals with any criminal case not dealt by the magistrates' courts. A magistrate's court may remit a case to the Crown Court if it believes it is sufficiently serious as the sentencing powers of magistrates are severely limited. The most famous criminal court in the England, and quite possibly the most famous court in the world, 'The Old Bailey' in London is a Crown Court. It deals with serious criminal cases which include:

- Cases sent for trial by magistrates' courts because the offences are 'indictable only' (i.e. those which can only be heard by the Crown Court).
- 'Either way' offences (which can be heard in a magistrates' court, but can also be sent to the Crown Court if the defendant chooses a jury trial).
- Defendants convicted in magistrates' courts, but sent to the Crown Court for sentencing due to the seriousness of the offence.
- Appeals against decisions of magistrates' courts.

There are three different types of Crown Court centres, based on the type of work they deal with. These are:

- *First-tier centres*—visited by High Court Judges for

Crown Court criminal and High Court civil work.

- *Second-tier centres*—visited by High Court Judges for Crown Court criminal work only.
- *Third-tier centres*—not normally visited by High Court Judges and handle only Crown Court criminal work only.

D. High Court: This has three 'divisions'. These are:

1. Family Division which deals with non-criminal cases to do with domestic law;
2. Chancery Division which deals with business and property law; and
3. Queen's Bench Division which deals with other civil law cases including those of libel, slander and breach of contract.

High Court judges are appointed by the Queen on the recommendation of the Lord Chancellor, after a fair and open competition administered by the Judicial Appointments Commission.

High Court judges must have had a right of audience—the right of a lawyer to appear and speak as an advocate in a court case—for all proceedings in the High Court for at least seven years, or have been a circuit judge for at least two years.

E. Court of Appeal: Court of Appeal, in England and Wales, part of the Supreme Court of Judicature and the highest court below the House of Lords. Its courtrooms are in London in the Royal Courts of Justice.

The Court of Appeal consists of a number of lord justices who are legally eligible to hear appeals, the lord chief justice, the master of the rolls, and several other *ex-officio* members who serve on a part-time basis. Three members of the court typically decide a case, though some decisions may be rendered by only two justices.

The Court of Appeal comprises of two divisions: the civil division and the criminal division. The civil division, which is presided over by the master of the rolls, hears appeals from the High Court, the county courts, and several other smaller tribunals. In civil appeals, the Court of Appeal proceeds by a method called "rehearing". Under this method, the court typically does not recall witnesses or hear evidence but reviews the case from the record made at trial and from the judge's notes. The criminal division, presided over by the lord chief justice, decides appeals from the Crown Court and from courts-martial. Within the criminal division, courts are constituted by the Lord Chief Justice and Lord Justices, with frequent assistance from High Court judges. The criminal division also acts as an advisory body on points of law for the attorney general.

F. House of Lords or the Supreme Court: The Supreme Court of the United Kingdom was established by Part 3 of the Constitutional Reform Act, 2005 and came into being on October 1, 2009. It replaces the House of Lords in its judicial capacity and has assumed the jurisdiction of the House of Lords under the Appellate Jurisdiction Acts, 1876 and 1888. The Supreme Court also has jurisdiction in relation to devolution matters under the Scotland Act, 1998, the Northern Ireland Act, 1998 and the Government of Wales Act, 2006; this was transferred to the Supreme Court from the Judicial Committee of the Privy Council. The Supreme Court, as well as being the final court of appeal, plays an important role in the development of United Kingdom law. As an appeal court, the Supreme Court cannot consider a case unless a relevant order has been made in a lower court. The Supreme Court is the final court of appeal for all United Kingdom civil cases, and criminal cases from England, Wales and Northern Ireland and hears appeals on arguable points of law of general public importance, concentrates on cases of the greatest public and constitutional importance and maintains and develops the role of the highest court in the United Kingdom as a leader in the common law world.

The Supreme Court hears appeals from the following courts in each jurisdiction:

England and Wales

- The Court of Appeal, Civil Division.

- The Court of Appeal, Criminal Division.
- (In some limited cases)—the High Court.

Scotland

- The Court of Session.

Northern Ireland

- The Court of Appeal in Northern Ireland.
- (In some limited cases)—the High Court.

G. European Courts: While few cases reach these courts, the European Court of Human Rights takes precedence over the decisions of the UK courts and the European Court of Justice is able to declare British laws as incompatible with treaties agreed as part of the development of the European Union. British courts do make distinctions between original and appellate jurisdiction. District courts hear cases that may be appealed to the High Courts, which may in turn be appealed to the highest court in the land—the law lords.

They are actually members of the House of Lords who are designated as a "Supreme Court" to settle disputes from lower courts. Of course, the law lords do not have the powers of judicial review, hence their authority is limited. The role of the law lords would change as a result of the Constitutional Reform Act of 2005 that provides for a Supreme Court of the United Kingdom to take over the existing role of the law lords.

By and large, judges have the reputation of being independent, impartial, and neutral. Few have been MPs, and almost none are active in party politics. Judges are appointed on "good behaviour", but they are expected to retire when they reach the age of 75. Most judges are educated at public schools and at Oxford and Cambridge, and their positions are prestigious.

Despite the limited policy-making power of the judiciary, Britain's membership in the European Union has given judges a new responsibility that promises to become even more important in the future. Since Britain is now bound by EU treaties and laws, it is the judges' responsibility to interpret them and determine whether or not EU laws conflict with parliamentary statutes. Since the British tend to be sceptical about their EU membership, the way that possible conflicts between supranational and national laws are settled by British judges could impact the policy-making process considerably.

10.3 Brazil

As one of the three powers of governance in the Constitution, the judiciary has a vital role in upholding the civil liberties of the Brazilian people and enabling them to hold their executive to account. Brazil is a civil law country and its legal system, which has its origin in Roman law, was implemented by the Portuguese during the colonization period. The system is based on codes and legislation enacted primarily by the federal legislature power, and also by the legislatures from the states and municipalities. Brazil is a federative republic formed by the indissoluble union of the states, municipalities, and the Federal District. The legislative, executive, and judicial branches compose the Brazilian government. The judiciary consists of the Federal Supreme Court; National Council of Justice; Superior Tribunal of Justice; Federal Justice; Labour Justice; Electoral Justice; Military Justice; and State Justice.

The 1988 Constitution contains 43 separate articles on the role of Brazil's judiciary and the structure and powers of the courts and public prosecutors. After the experience of the military dictatorship, its drafters were concerned to entrench judicial independence and the ability of the courts to hold the government to account through judicial review.

However, the weakness of the executive at the time of the Constitution's drafting allowed judges to maximise their influence and minimise their accountability in what Macaulay describes as 'a classic case of producer capture'. She notes that the Brazilian judiciary now enjoys more political and operational independence than any other country in Latin America, but the resultant 'hyper-autonomy and insulation' has created more problems than it solved.

Brazil has five parallel court systems each of which

supports lower courts, state or regional appellate courts and supreme courts. These are: the ordinary civil and criminal courts organised at state-level; federal courts, which deal with matters of federal or constitutional relevance; and a specialised justice system which consists of electoral courts, labour courts and military courts.

Each of Brazil's states organizes their own judicial systems although these must adhere to the same laws and basic constitutional principles. The Brazilian legal system relies heavily on constitutional guarantees, which means that a large number of cases are appealed all the way to the STF.

While direct challenges to the constitutionality of laws can only be made in the STF, any judge can rule on the constitutionality of a law as a matter incidental to any type of court case under consideration, and this may then be appealed all the way up to the STF.

Every judge in lower-level courts is free to interpret the law regardless of previous rulings by higher level courts. Lower courts routinely overturn or stall legislative decisions and are free to set new precedents on civil and criminal issues and also constitutional questions.

This diffusion of the power of judicial review combined with the complicated and overlapping structure of the Brazilian judiciary has made law and policy-making by central government difficult as the executive has to defend itself against multiple levels of judicial challenges every time it promulgates a new law.

This has massively increased the number of cases that the judiciary deals with and often produces conflicting and ambiguous decisions.

10.3.1 Levels of the Court System:

A. Supreme Federal Court (Supremo Tribunal Federal —STF): The Federal Supreme Court is the highest court in Brazil and is entrusted with the responsibility of safeguarding the Constitution, as well as functioning as a court of review. The Federal Supreme Court also has original jurisdiction to try and decide direct actions of unconstitutionality of a federal or state law or normative act, or declaratory actions of constitutionality of a federal law or normative act, which somewhat resemble the issuance of advisory opinions—a situation not allowed in the Supreme Court of the United States. It also deals with complaints against higher authorities, such as the President or members of Congress and resolves differences between the central government and states. The STF comprises 11 judges nominated by the President of the Republic with the approval of the Senate.

Brazil does not follow the doctrine of *stare decisis* and, only after the amendment of the Brazilian Constitution in 2004, did the Supreme Court start issuing, in special situations, binding decisions. The Brazilian Supreme Federal Court is composed of eleven Justices, chosen among native Brazilian citizens, who are more than thirty-five and less than sixty-five years old and have notable legal knowledge and soundness of character (Articles 12, and 3, IV, and Article 101, both from the Federal Constitution) and are appointed by the President, after the nomination has been approved by the absolute majority of the Federal Senate.

Article 102, I, "f", of the Constitution, grants the Supreme Federal Court, the original competence to judge "the disputes and conflicts between the Union and the States, the Union and the Federal District, or between one another, including their respective indirect administration bodies". Furthermore, in relation to the impeachment process of the President of the Republic, it is the competence of the Supreme Federal Court's Chief Justice to preside over the trial session at the Federal Senate (Constitution, Article 52, sole paragraph). As it is known, the republican form of government subjects all the civil servants to the precept of responsibility, which is inherent in the concept of democracy.

B. Superior Tribunal of Justice (Superior Tribunal de Justiça—STJ): Created by the Constitution of 1988, the Superior Tribunal of Justice is responsible for standardizing the interpretation of federal law in Brazil, following constitutional principles and the guarantee and defence of the rule of law. The STJ is the last instance in the Brazilian legal system for consideration of infra-constitutional issues not directly related to the Constitution.

The Superior Tribunal of Justice consists of 33 judges, chosen from among Brazilians over thirty-five and less than sixty-six years of age and appointed by the President of the Republic, after their nomination has been approved by an absolute majority of the Federal Senate. Article 105 of the Constitution establishes the STJ's competence and regulates which cases starts at the STJ (initial process) and on which cases the STJ acts only as a reviewing Court, including the judgment of special appeals. The STJ has also attribution to judge crimes committed by the governors of Brazilian states or the Federal District, crimes committed by judges from courts of justices, by counsellors from courts of auditors, members of each one of the 5 regional federal courts and members of the electoral and labour courts.

The Court also decides *habeas corpus* involving these authorities or state ministers, likewise decides the appeals of *habeas corpus* granted or denied by federal or regional courts of the states, and the cases decided in those instances when there is federal law involved. In 2005, as a part of the judicial reform, the STJ began to have jurisdiction to review the grant of letters rotatory and the homologation of foreign judgments. Until then, such requests used to be considered at the Supreme Federal Court (STF).

C. Federal Justice (Justiça Federal): The Federal Justice is composed of Federal Regional Tribunals and Federal Courts.

(a) Federal Regional Tribunals: Federal Regional Tribunals have original jurisdiction to hear:

- Cases against federal judges, including military judges and labour law judges whenever they are involved in common crimes and crimes of responsibility; and the members of the Public Prosecutor's Office with the exception of the competency of the Electoral Justice;

- Criminal reviews and annulment actions of federal court decisions;
- Writs of mandamus and habeas data against an act of the Federal Regional Tribunal or federal judge;
- *Habeas corpus*, when the constraining authority is a federal judge; and
- Conflicts of jurisdiction between federal judges subordinated to the Federal Regional Tribunal.

Federal Regional Tribunals act as courts of review in cases decided by federal judges and in cases decided by state judges exercising federal authority in the area of their jurisdiction. Federal Regional Tribunals consists of a minimum of 7 Judges appointed by the President of the Republic from among Brazilians over thirty-five and less than sixty-five years of age. 1/5th must be attorneys with more than ten years of professional experience and members of the Federal Prosecutor's Office with more than ten years in the position. 4/5th of federal judges should be more than five years in the position.

(b) Federal Courts: Federal courts have jurisdiction to try cases in which the Federal Government, its agencies, foundations, and federal public companies are listed as plaintiffs or defendants and in all other matters listed in Article 109 of the Constitution. The Brazilian system of judicial review combines features from both abstract review and concrete review systems. As in the American concrete review system, Brazilian judges are conferred ample powers to analyse the constitutionality of governmental acts, allowing any judge or court to declare that a law or regulatory act is unconstitutional and, just as in the European abstract system, the Brazilian Constitutional model concentrates at the Supreme Court, the competence to prosecute and adjudicate independent actions concerning the constitutionality "in abstract" of a law.

In this way, the Brazilian system of Judicial Review displays original and diverse procedural instruments for both verifying the constitutionality of legislation and protecting fundamental rights. These include the *habeas corpus*, habeas data, and writ of mandamus, injunctive writ, public civil action and popular action. This diversity, so typical of the diffuse model, is complemented by a variety of instruments enabling the Supreme Court to exercise abstract review such as direct unconstitutionality suits, declaratory actions of constitutionality, direct unconstitutionality suits due to omission and claims for non-compliance of a fundamental precept.

Although all judges have the power to declare that a law or regulatory act is unconstitutional within the judgment of a concrete case, it is important to notice that there are procedural constitutional instruments (named "extraordinary appeals") aimed at ensuring verification by the Brazilian Supreme of any possible violation to the Constitution as a result of judicial decisions issued by a Court or single judge.

Another innovation, also brought by the Judiciary Reform of 2004, that, likewise, should help to strengthen the authority of the Supreme Court of Brazil, is its new power to issue the so-called "*binding precedents*", which render obligatory, as a rule, a certain decision from the Court, similarly to the institute of *"stare decisis"* in the American law.

According to the Constitution, the "binding precedent" must be approved by a two-thirds majority of the votes at the Supreme Court (eight votes); it must deal with constitutional matters that have been the object of repeated decisions by the Court; and it has the goal of overcoming a current controversy over the validity, interpretation and efficacy of specific norms that may generate legal insecurity and a significant multiplication of court cases. It encompasses, therefore, current questions on the interpretation of constitutional norms or of these in light of infra-constitutional norms. The approval, as well as the review and the annulment of a binding precedent, may be proposed by anyone who has the legitimacy to file a direct unconstitutionality action.

10.4 Nigeria

Nigeria operates a federal political structure under the Constitution of the Federal Republic of Nigeria, 1999. The Federation consists of 36 States and a Federal Capital Territory. This Constitution vests the legislative, executive and judicial powers of the Federal Republic of Nigeria in the National Assembly, the Executive and the courts established there under respectively. The development of the Nigerian Judicial system has been greatly influenced by its colonial past as a part of the British Commonwealth. The common law of England, the doctrines of equity as well as statutes of general application in force in England as at January 1, 1900, form an integral part of the laws in addition to certain English statutes that have been received as laws by local legislation. Other sources of Nigerian law include local legislation (State and Federal), Nigerian case law as well as customary law. The principles of judicial precedent and hierarchy of courts is also a fundamental part of the legal system with the Supreme Court of Nigeria at the apex of the court system.

Nigeria's judicial system is based on a combination of statutory (legislative) law, English common law, customary law, and, in the north, Islamic law (*sharia*). Nigeria's federal and state courts apply statutory and English common law, whereas local courts recognize the legitimacy of customary and Islamic law. Bribes paid to influence judges and delays in bringing cases to trial sometimes impair the fair and efficient administration of justice. These deficiencies partially explain the popularity of Islamic law in the 12 northern states. *Sharia* is criticized for the imposition of draconian penalties, although no death penalties have been carried out in recent years. Testimony from women and non-Muslims also carries less weight in Islamic courts.

At the federal level, the judicial branch consists of the Supreme Court, Court of Appeal, and Federal High Court. At the state level, there is the State High Court, and, at the local level, there are the *sharia* courts and customary courts.

- The judicial powers of the Federation shall be vested in the courts to which this section relates—being courts established for the Federation.
- The judicial powers of a State shall be vested in the courts to which this section relates, being courts established, subject as provided by this Constitution, for a State.
- The courts to which this section relates, established by this Constitution for the Federation and for the States, specified in sub-section (5)(a) to (1) of this Section, shall be the only superior courts of record in Nigeria; and save as otherwise prescribed by the National Assembly or by the House of Assembly of a State, each court shall have all the powers of a superior court of record.

While the Legislature is responsible for making laws and the Executive is charged with the implementation of such law, the Judiciary is responsible for the interpretation of the law in accordance with the provisions of the Constitution. In line with the doctrine of separation of powers, which is a cardinal feature of a democratic system, the Nigerian Constitution guarantees the independence of the Judiciary. The Constitution provides for Federal and State Courts, as well as Election Tribunals. At the apex of the Judiciary is the Supreme Court.

The other Federal Courts are:

- Court of Appeal.
- Federal High Court.
- High Court of the Federal Capital Territory, Abuja.
- *Sharia* Court of Appeal of the Federal Capital Territory, Abuja.
- Customary Court of Appeal of the Federal Capital Territory.

The State Courts are:

- High Court.
- *Sharia* Court of Appeal.
- Customary Court of Appeal.

The Election Tribunals are:

- National Assembly Election Tribunal.

- Govern ship and Legislative Houses Election Tribunals.

In addition to the Courts and Tribunals established by the Constitution, there are other court and tribunals created by Federal or State laws. These include: Magistrate Courts, Area Courts, *Sharia* Courts and Customary Courts.

The 1999 Constitution makes provisions for the establishment and constitution of the following courts:

10.4.1 The Supreme Court of Nigeria: This is the apex court in the hierarchy of courts in Nigeria and is situated in the Federal Capital Territory, Abuja. The Chief Justice of the Federation heads the Judiciary of Nigeria and presides over the Court. The Supreme Court of Nigeria shall consist of:

- The Chief Justice of Nigeria; and
- Such number of Justices of the Supreme Court, not exceeding twenty-one, as may be prescribed by an Act of the National Assembly.

1. The appointment of a person to the office of *Chief Justice* of Nigeria shall be made by the President on the recommendation of the National Judicial Council subject to confirmation of such appointment by the Senate.
2. The appointment of a person to the office of a *Justice* of the Supreme Court shall be made by the President on the recommendation of the National Judicial Council subject to confirmation of such appointment by the senate.

The court has limited but exclusive original jurisdiction in any dispute between the Federation and a State or between States if and in so far as that dispute involves any question (whether of law or fact) on which the existence of a legal right depends. Its appellate jurisdiction is to determine appeals from the Court of Appeal and this is also to the exclusion of any other court. The court consists of the Chief Justice of Nigeria and such number of justices not exceeding twenty-one as may be prescribed by the National Assembly. Ordinarily, the Court is duly constituted if it consists of not less than five Justices of the Court, except where it is exercising its original jurisdiction or a matter involves a question as to the interpretation or application of the constitution or whether any provision relating to the Fundamental Rights provisions of the Constitution has been, is being or is likely to be contravened. In this regard, the Court is duly constituted if it consists of seven Justices of the Court.

The decision of the Supreme Court on any matter is final and is not subject to an appeal to any other body or person. This is however without prejudice to the power of the President or Governor of a State's exercise of Prerogative of Mercy in appropriate cases. The decisions of the Court are binding on all other courts in Nigeria.

10.4.2 The Court of Appeal: This is next in the hierarchy of courts in Nigeria and its decisions are binding on all other lower courts. The Court of Appeal shall consist of:

- A President of the Court of Appeal; and
- Such number of Justices of the Court of Appeal, not less than forty-nine of which not less than three shall be learned in Islamic personal law, and not less than three shall be learned in customary law, as may be prescribed by an Act of the National Assembly.

The court has original and exclusive jurisdiction over questions as to whether a person has been validly elected to the office of president or vice-president of the Federation or whether the term of office of such person has ceased or whether the office has become vacant. It also has appellate jurisdiction to hear appeals from decisions of the High Courts of the States and the Federal Capital Territory, Federal High Court, the *Sharia* Courts of Appeal of the States or of the Federal Capital Territory, Customary Courts of Appeal of the States or of the Federal Capital Territory as well as from decisions of a court martial or other tribunals as specified by an Act of the National Assembly. The court is duly constituted by not less than three Justices for the purpose of exercising any of its stated jurisdictions. For administrative convenience, the court is divided into judicial divisions which sit in various parts of the country namely, Abuja, Lagos, Enugu, Kaduna, Ibadan, Benin, Jos, Calabar, Ilorin and Port Harcourt.

10.4.3 The Federal High Court: The Federal High Court shall consist of:

- A Chief Judge of the Federal High Court; and
- Such number of Judges of the Federal High Court as may be prescribed by the Act of the National Assembly.

The court has limited but exclusive jurisdiction in civil and criminal causes or matters as set out in the Constitution. It however has no appellate jurisdiction. In exercising its jurisdiction, the Court is duly constituted by one Judge of the Court. Like the Court of Appeal, the Federal High Court is divided into judicial divisions for administrative convenience but has a wider geographical spread as these divisions are currently situated in over seventeen states of the Federation with plans to establish a Division of the Court in all the States of the Federation.

10.4.4 The High Court: There is a High Court in each State of the Federation and the Federal Capital Territory. Each Court is made up of a Chief Judge and such other number of judges as the State House of Assembly or the National Assembly (in the case of the High Court of the Federal Capital Territory) may prescribe. The High Courts of the various States have general original jurisdiction over civil and criminal matters except matters in respect of which any other court has been vested with exclusive jurisdiction, making them the courts with the widest jurisdiction under the Constitution. The court is duly constituted by one judge. Each High Court is divided into judicial divisions for administrative convenience.

10.4.5 The *Sharia* Court of Appeal: There is a *Sharia* Court of Appeal for the Federal Capital Territory and any State that requires it. This Court has appellate and supervisory jurisdiction in civil proceedings involving questions of Islamic personal law, which the Court is competent to decide in accordance with the Constitution. The Court comprises of a Grand *Khadi* and other *Khadis* as the National Assembly or the State Houses of Assembly (as the case may be) may prescribe. All appeals involving Islamic personal law go to the

Sharia Courts of Appeal. Since 1999-2000, in the twelve sharia states, the inferior courts in which Islamic law is applied have been reorganised once again: the Area Courts have been abolished and replaced by *Sharia* Courts, charged to apply the full range of Islamic law, civil and criminal, to Muslims. Appeals from the *Sharia* Courts in all types of cases have been directed to the *Sharia* Courts of Appeal.

10.4.6 The Customary Court of Appeal: The jurisdiction of the Customary Court of Appeal has been spelt out in Section 247(1) of the Constitution. It provides, *"A Customary Court of Appeal of a State shall exercise appellate and supervisory jurisdiction in civil proceedings involving questions of customary law"*. There is a Customary Court of Appeal for the Federal Capital Territory and any State that requires it. This Court has appellate and supervisory jurisdiction in civil proceedings involving questions of customary law and is comprised of a President and such number of Judges as the National Assembly or the State Houses of Assembly (as the case may be) may prescribe.

A Customary Court of Appeal has no original jurisdiction. Its jurisdiction is only appellate. Its appellate jurisdiction does not extend to appeals from Magistrates Courts. The appeals must come from no other courts than Customary or Area Courts. Not every appeal from Customary Courts can be entertained by it. The appeal must emanate from a claim based on customary law. Not only that, if the claim is based on customary law, the appeal arising there from rests on questions of customary law otherwise the jurisdiction of the Customary Court of Appeal is ousted.

In addition to these courts created by the Constitution, there also exist Magistrate Courts, District Courts, Area Courts and Customary Courts established in various states by state laws. These courts are of limited jurisdiction as specified in their enabling laws and appeals from them lie to the High Court, *Sharia* Court of Appeal or Customary Court of Appeal as the case may be.

10.5 China

China's judicial system only refers to people's court system. According to Criminal Procedure Law of PRC, during the criminal proceeding, *people's court, people's procuratorates and public security* organ shall perform their task respectively as well as cooperate. In this meaning, people's procuratorates and public security organ both execute judicial power, although their judicial function are limited in a very relatively narrow scope. Thus, broadly speaking, China's judicial system institutionally comprises of three parts: people's court system, the people's procuratorates system and the public security system. Corresponding to this, judicial structure in the Chinese broad sense does not only refer to courts, but also to procuratorates and public security organs.

The security organ is one branch in the administrative system; the other two branches are created by the people's congress and, in the legal sense, are on an equal footing with the administrative branch. The presidents of courts and the procurator-generals of procuratorates are selected and appointed by the people's congresses on the same levels. The judges and procurators are selected and appointed by the standing committees of the respective people's congresses, and assistant judges and assistant procurators are appointed by the respective courts and procuratorates.

China's highest court is the Supreme People's Court. There also are people's courts at provincial, local, municipal, and lower levels, as well as military courts and other special people's courts. Constitutionally, the court system exercises judicial power independently and is technically free of interference from administrative organs, public organizations, and individuals. The Supreme People's Court supervises the administration of justice by local courts and special courts, and courts at higher levels supervise the administration of courts at lower levels.

At each level, the courts are "responsible to the organs of state power which created them". Judges are limited to two consecutive terms running concurrently with the National People's Congress or local people's congresses. Citizens have a constitutional guarantee of the right to use their own spoken and written language in court proceedings. Courts and procuratorates are told by the Constitution that they "*should provide translations for any party to the court proceedings who is not familiar with the spoken or written languages in common use in the locality*". The procuratorates are "state organs for legal supervision" and operate at the same levels as the people's courts.

China has a four-level court system. At the top is the Supreme People's Court in Beijing. Lower courts are the higher people's courts in provinces, autonomous regions and special municipalities; intermediate people's courts at the prefecture level and also in parts of provinces, autonomous regions, and special municipalities; and basic people's courts in counties, towns, and municipal districts. Special courts handle matters affecting the military, railroad transportation, water transportation and forestry. The court system is paralleled by a hierarchy of prosecuting organs called people's procuratorates; at the apex stands the Supreme People's Procuratorate.

10.5.1 People's Courts: The people's courts are judicial organs exercising judicial power on behalf of the states. According to the Constitution and the Organic Law of the People's Courts of 1979 as amended in 1983, China practices a system of courts characterized by "four levels and two instances of trials". The judicial authority of the PRC is exercised by the following people's courts: local people's courts at various levels; military courts and other special people's courts and the Supreme People's Courts. The local people's courts are divided into basic people's courts, intermediate people's courts and higher people's courts.

10.5.2 Supreme People's Court (SPC): The Supreme People's Court is the highest trial organ in the country and exercises its adjudicative right independently. It is also the highest supervisory organ over the trial practices of local people's courts and special people's courts at various levels. The NPC is entitled to appoint or remove president, vice-presidents and members of the Trial Committee of the SPC.

The functions and responsibilities of the SPC are:

- To try the following cases: cases of first instance over which it has jurisdiction according to law and regulations and cases of first instance it deems that it should try, cases of appeal and protests against the judgments and orders of High People's Courts and special people's courts and cases of protests filed by the Supreme People's Procuratorate in accordance with the procedures of trial supervision.
- To review and approve death sentence. The SPC shall review and approve death sentences rendered against offenders involved in the cases of manslaughter, rape, robbery, bombing and other crimes that severely endanger public security and social order.
- To supervise the trial work of local people's courts and special people's courts at various levels.
- To try the case by itself or remand the case to original court for retrial which has already been legally enforced, when discovering real mistakes in the verdict of local people's courts.
- To review and approve the verdict of crimes which is not specially stipulated in the criminal law and shall be tried by means of analogy.
- To interpret the application of law in trial process.

10.5.3 The Higher People's Courts: The Higher People's Courts are courts of provinces, autonomous regions and municipalities directly under the Central Government. The internal structure is almost the same as that of the Supreme People's Court according to the definition of the organic law.

A higher people's court deals with cases of the first instance assigned by laws and decrees, cases of the first instance transferred from people's courts at the next lower level, cases of appeals and of protests lodged against judgments and orders of people's courts at the next lower level, and cases of protests lodged by people's procuratorates.

10.5.4 The Intermediate People's Courts: They are the courts established in capitals or prefectures in the provincial level. The scope of jurisdiction by an intermediate people's court covers cases of first instance assigned by laws and decrees, cases of first instance transferred from the basic people's courts, and appealed and protested cases from the lower court.

10.5.5 The Grass-roots (Basic) People's Courts: The Grass-roots People's courts, as the lowest level, are normally located at the county, municipal districts and autonomous counties. A grass root people's court may set up a number of people's tribunal according to the conditions of the locality, population and cases involved. A people's tribunal is a component of the basic people's court, and its judgments and orders are considered as judgments and orders of the basic people's court with the same legal effects. In practice, a tribunal of this nature is often set up in big town or townships where there is a concentrated population. As defined in the organic law, the basic people's court adjudicates all criminal and civil cases of the first instance except where the law provides otherwise. Besides trying cases, a basic people's court is also responsible for settling civil disputes, handling minor criminal cases that do not require formal handling, and directing the work of the people's mediation committees.

10.5.6 The Special Courts: The special courts include military courts, railway courts and maritime courts. The military court that is established within the PLA is in charge of hearing criminal cases involving servicemen. This is a relatively closed system. The railway and transport court deals with criminal cases and economic disputes relating to railways and transportation.

10.5.7 The Supreme People's Procuratorates: The Constitution defines it as "the highest procuratorial body". The procurator-general of the Supreme People's procuratorates shall be elected and removed by the NPC. The deputy procurator-general, member of the procuratorial committee and procurators of the Supreme People's procuratorates shall be appointed and removed by the Standing Committee of the NPC upon the recommendation of the procurator-general. The Supreme People's Procuratorates is responsible to the NPC and its Standing Committee. The Supreme People's Procuratorates may establish a number of procuratorial departments and other professional departments as needed.

10.5.8 The Local People's Procuratorates: The local people's procuratorates apply the system of dual leadership and the principle of democratic centralism. The chief procurators of people's procuratorates of provinces, autonomous regions and municipalities directly under the Central Government and their branches shall be elected and removed by correspondent people's congress; the deputy chief procurators, members of procuratorial committees and procurators shall be appointed and removed by the standing committees of the people's congresses upon the recommendation of the chief procurators.

Nevertheless, the appointment and removal of the chief procurators of the local people's procuratorates must be reported to the procurator-general of the people's procuratorate at the next higher level, who should then submit the matter to the corresponding standing committee of the people's congress for approval.

The chief procurators, deputy chief procurators, members of procuratorial committees and procurators of people's procuratorates set up, in industrial and mining areas, agricultural reclamation areas and forest zones, by people's procuratorates at the provincial or counties level shall be appointed and removed by the standing committee of the people's congress at the corresponding level, upon the recommendation of the chief procurators of the dispatching people's procuratorates.

10.5.9 Public Security Organs: Public security branches

lead and direct the people's police, as functional departments of the people's governments. They are responsible for maintaining social and public order and State security, and also for conducting investigations, arrest and preliminary hearings in criminal cases. According to the Constitution, leaders of public security are appointed by the people's congresses or by their standing committees when the congresses are not in session, at the corresponding level.

References

Colin Turpin and Adam Tomkins (2011), "*British Government and the Constitution: Text and Materials*", Cambridge University Press, UK.

Donald C. Clarke (2008), "*China Legal System: New Development, New Challenges*", Cambridge University Press, UK.

Duncan Watts (2012), "*British Government and Politics: A Comparative Guide*", Edinburgh University Press Ltd., UK.

Fiona Macaulay (2003), "*Democratisation and the Judiciary*", in Maria Dialva Kinzo and James Dunkerley, "Brazil since 1985: Economy, Polity and Society", Institute of Latin American Studies.

Jag Griffith (1977), "*The Politics of the Judiciary*", Manchester University Press, UK.

James F. Hoge and James Hoge Jr. (2010), "*China on the World Stage*", Council on Foreign Relations, US.

John H. Merryman and David S. Clark (1978), "*Comparative Law: Western European and Latin American Legal Systems*", The Bobbs-Merril Co. Inc.

Martin M. Shapiro (1981), "*Courts: A Comparative and Political Analysis*", The University of Chicago Press Ltd., London.

Olivia F. Robinson et al. (1987), "*An Introduction to European Legal History*", 2nd edition, Little Brown & Company, Boston.

Bibliography

Bibliography

A. Hoogvelt (2002), "*History of Capitalism Expansion*", in Globalization and Third World Politics, Palgrave, London.

Abu Bakarr Bah (2005), "*Breakdown and Reconstitution: Democracy, the Nation-state, and Ethnicity in Nigeria*", Lexington Books, US.

Akhtar Majeed, Ronald L. Watts and Douglas Brown (2006), "*Distribution of Powers and Responsibilities in Federal Countries*", McGill-Queen's University Press, Canada.

Ania Loomba (2005), "*Colonialism/Post-colonialism*", London; New York: Routledge.

B. Waites (1999), "*Europe and the Third World, c.1500-1998: From Colonization to Decolonization*", Basingstoke: Macmillan.

B.O. Nwabueze (1982), "*A Constitutional History of Nigeria*", C. Hurst & Co. (Publishers) Ltd., UK.

Bhiku Parekh (ed.) (1976), "*The Concept of Socialism*", Ambika Publications, (New Delhi.

Charles Hauss (2006), "*Comparative Politics: Domestic Responses to Global Challenges*", Thomson Wadsworth Higher Education, US.

Charles P. Kindleberger (2000), "*Comparative Political Economy: A Retrospective*", Massachusetts Institute of Technology, US.

Colin Turpin and Adam Tomkins (2011), "*British Government and the Constitution: Text and Materials*", Cambridge University Press, UK.

D. Deol (1976), "*Liberalism and Marxism: An Introduction to the Study of Contemporary Politics*", Sterling Publishers Pvt. Ltd., New Delhi.

David Curtis Wright (2001), "*The History of China*", Greenwood Press, US.

David Schweichart (2011), "*After Capitalism*", Rowman & Littlefield Publishers, UK.

David Zweig and Zhimin Chen (2007), "*China's Reforms and International Political Economy*", Routledge, New York.

Donald C. Clarke (2008), "*China Legal System: New Development, New Challenges*", Cambridge University Press, UK.

Duncan Watts (2012), "*British Government and Politics: A Comparative Guide*", Edinburgh University Press Ltd., UK.

F.O. Nyemutu Roberts (2002), "*Models of Executive Power and*

Nigeria's Neo-presidentialism: Implications for Governance and Development", Nigerian Institute of Social and Economic Research, Nigeria.

Fiona Macaulay (2003), "*Democratisation and the Judiciary*", in Maria Dialva Kinzo and James Dunkerley, 'Brazil since 1985: Economy, Polity and Society', Institute of Latin American Studies.

G. Thorn (2000), "*End of Empires: European Decolonisation, 1919-80*", London: Hodder and Stoughton.

Gabriel A. Almond, G. Bingham Powell, Kaare Strom Jr. and Russell J. Dalton (2009), "*Comparative Politics Today*", Pearson Education, India.

Gary W. Wynia (1990), "*The Politics of Latin American Development*", Cambridge University Press, US.

Godson Dinneya (2006), "*Political Economy of Democratization in Nigeria*", Concept of Publications Limited, UK.

Great Britain: Ministry of Justice (2007), "*The Governance of Britain: War Powers and Treaties Limiting Executive Powers*", Constitutional Paper CP 26/07, published on October 25, 2007.

Guoli Liu (2011), "*Politics and Government in China*" ABC-CLIO, LLC, USA.

Hee Min Kim (1997) "*Rational Choice Theory and Third World Politics: The 1990 Party Merger in Korea*", Comparative Politics 30(1): 83-100.

Hui-yun Zhuang (2010), "*Idealism and the Abuse of Powers: Lessons from China's Cultural Revolution*", Ashgate Publishing Limited, US.

Hyginus Banko Okibe (2000), "*Political Evolution and Constitutional Development in Nigeria, 1861-1999*", Marydan Publishers.

Ibi Ajayi (2003), "*Nigeria and the Political Economy of Development: The Dreams, the Myth and the Reality*", Nigerian Economic Society, Ibadan.

J. Howard, Esther Wiarda and M. Skelley (2007), "*Comparative Politics: Approaches and Issues*", Rowman and Littlefield Publishers, Inc., US.

Jag Griffith (1977), "*The Politics of the Judiciary*", Manchester University Press, UK.

Jagdish Bhagwati (2004), "*In Defence of Globalisation*", Oxford University Press, New Delhi.

James F. Hoge and James Hoge Jr. (2010), "*China on the World Stage*", Council on Foreign Relations, US.

Jeffrey Kopstein and Mark Irving Lichbach (2005), "*Comparative Politics: Interests, Identities and Institutions in a Changing World*", Cambridge University Press, US.

Jody C. Baumgartner and Naoko Kada (2003), "*Checking Executive Power: Presidential Impeachment in Comparative Perspective*", Praeger Publishers, US.

John H. Merryman and David S. Clark (1978), "*Comparative Law: Western European and Latin American Legal Systems*", The Bobbs-Merril Co., Inc.

John McCormick (2010), "*Comparative Politics in Transition*", Woodsworth, US.

Joseph A. Schumpeter (2011), "*Capitalism, Socialism and Democracy*", Adarsh Books, New Delhi.

Joseph Fewsmith (2010),"*China Today, China Tomorrow: Domestic Politics, Economy, and Society*", Rowman and Littlefield Publishers, Inc.,US.

Julianon Zaiden Benin (2010), "*On the Limits of Constitutional Adjudication: Deconstructing Balancing and Judicial Activism*", London: Springer Heidelberg Dordrecht.

Kalu N. Kalu (2009), "*State Power, Autarchy, and Political Conquest in Nigerian Federalism*", Lexington Books, UK.

Kamilu Sain Fage and David Oluwatoba Alabi (2003), "*Political and Constitutional Development in Nigeria*", Northern Printers Ltd., UK.

Lael Brainard and Leonardo Martines-Diaz (ed.), "*Brazil As an Economic Superpower?: Understanding Brazil's Changing Role in the Global Economy*", The Brookings Institution, Washington D.C.

M.E. Chamberlain (1999), "*Decolonization: The Fall of the European Empires*", Malden, MA: Blackwell Publishers.

Mark Irving Lichbach and Alan S. Zuckerman (2002), "*Comparative Politics: Rationality, Culture and Structure*", Cambridge University Press, UK.

Mark Kesselman, Joel Krieger and William Joseph (2013), "*Introduction to Comparative Politics*", 6th edition, Wadsworth, US.

Martin M. Shapiro (1981), "*Courts: A Comparative and Political Analysis*", The University of Chicago Press Ltd., London.

Matt Buttsworth (2011), "*Beyond Eurocentrism: Rethinking the Commercial, Scientific and Industrial Revolution*", Matt Buttsworth, Australia.

Nicloa Yeates (2001), "*Globalisation and Social Policy*", Sage Publications, New Delhi.

Olivia F. Robinson et al. (1987), "*An Introduction to European Legal History*", *2nd* edition, Little Brown & Company, Boston.

P. Duara (ed.) (2004), "*Decolonization: Perspectives from Now and Then*", London; New York: Routledge.

Partha Chatterjee (1993), "*The Nation and Its Fragments: Colonial and Post-colonial Histories*", Princeton: Princeton University Press.

Patrick Diamond (2014), "*Governing Britain: Power, Politics and the Prime Minister*", I.B. Tauris & Co. Ltd., New York.

Rajani Kannepalli Kanth (2009), "*The Challenge of Eurocentrism: Global Perspectives, Policy, and Prospects*", Palgrave Macmillan, New York.

Raoul Blindenbacher and Abigail Ostien (ed.) (2005), "*Dialogues on Distribution of Power and Responsibilities in Federal Countries*", McGill-Queen's University Press, Canada.

Raymond E. Dumett (ed.) (1999), "*Gentlemanly Capitalism and British Imperialism: The New Debate on Empire*", Longman.

Samir Amin (2009), "*Eurocentrism*", Monthly Review Press, New York.

Shaun Gerard Breslin (2013), "*China and the Global Political Economy*", Palgrave Macmillan, UK.

Todd Landman (2008), "*Issues and Methods in Comparative Politics: An Introduction*", Routledge, New York.

Uwe Becker (2014), "*The BRICS and Emerging Economies in Comparative Perspective: Political Economy, Liberalization and Institutional Change*", Routledge, Canada.

V.I. Lenin (1982), "*Imperialism: The Highest Stage of Capitalism*", Progress Publishers, Moscow.

Index

Index